Crime–Terror N(

This book examines the crime–terror nexus in South Asia, focusing in particular on the activities of non-state actors that operate out of Pakistan and challenging the conventional wisdom that the Pakistan Taliban (TTP) and Al-Qaeda are Pakistan's most serious security threats.

Much research has focused on the policies of India and Pakistan towards Kashmir. But surprisingly little attention has been paid to several notable Pakistan-based non-state actors who are increasingly operating on their own, and who have the potential to greatly inhibit, if not derail, the peace process there. These groups blur the line between terrorism and organized crime with serious implications for policy in the region. India and Pakistan can engage in confidence-building measures, but if criminal actors such as Lashkar-i-Taiba (LeT) and D-Company cannot effectively be controlled, a lack of trust between both sides will remain.

Although the role of regular military forces is not to be discounted, many of the non-state actors in Indian-Held Kashmir such as LeT are not confined by the same restraints as state forces, thus allowing them engage in more violent actions without fear of reprisal. In order for lawmakers, security personnel and others to develop sound, comprehensive policies, these forces and their potential to undermine political initiatives must be fully appreciated. This book explores the dynamics of the relationship between Pakistan, D-Company and LeT and how it affects strategic thought, decision-making and security interests in the region, and explains the triangular relationships between states, terrorist groups and organized criminal syndicates in general, and in India and Pakistan in particular.

This book will be of much interest to students of South Asian politics, terrorism, organized crime, war and conflict studies and security studies in general.

Ryan Clarke is at the East Asian Institute, National University of Singapore and has a PhD in Politics and International Relations from Cambridge University.

Asian Security Studies
Series Editors: Sumit Ganguly, *Indiana University, Bloomington* and Andrew Scobell, *US Army War College*

Few regions of the world are fraught with as many security questions as Asia. Within this region it is possible to study great power rivalries, irredentist conflicts, nuclear and ballistic missile proliferation, secessionist movements, ethnoreligious conflicts and inter-state wars. This book series publishes the best possible scholarship on the security issues affecting the region, and includes detailed empirical studies, theoretically oriented case studies and policy-relevant analyses as well as more general works.

China and International Institutions
Alternate paths to global power
Marc Lanteigne

China's Rising Sea Power
The PLA Navy's Submarine Challenge
Peter Howarth

If China Attacks Taiwan
Military strategy, politics and economics
Edited by Steve Tsang

Chinese Civil-Military Relations
The transformation of the People's Liberation Army
Edited by Nan Li

The Chinese Army Today
Tradition and transformation for the 21st century
Dennis J. Blasko

Taiwan's Security
History and prospects
Bernard D. Cole

Religion and Conflict in South and Southeast Asia
Disrupting violence
Edited by Linell E. Cady and Sheldon W. Simon

Political Islam and Violence in Indonesia
Zachary Abuza

US-Indian Strategic Cooperation into the 21st Century
More than words
Edited by Sumit Ganguly, Brian Shoup and Andrew Scobell

India, Pakistan and the Secret Jihad
The covert war in Kashmir, 1947–2004
Praveen Swami

China's Strategic Culture and Foreign Policy Decision-Making
Confucianism, leadership and war
Huiyun Feng

Chinese Military Strategy in the Third Indochina War
The last Maoist war
Edward C. O'Dowd

Asia Pacific Security
US, Australia and Japan and the New Security Triangle
Edited by William T. Tow, Mark J. Thomson,
Yoshinobu Yamamoto and Satu P. Limaye

China, the United States, and Southeast Asia
Contending perspectives on politics, security, and economics
Edited by Evelyn Goh and Sheldon W. Simon

Conflict and Cooperation in Multi-Ethnic States
Institutional incentives, myths, and counter-balancing
Brian Shoup

China's War on Terrorism
Counter-insurgency, politics and internal security
Martin I. Wayne

US Taiwan Policy
Constructing the triangle
Øystein Tunsjø

Conflict Management, Security and Intervention in East Asia
Third-party mediation in regional conflict
Edited by Jacob Bercovitch, Kwei-Bo Huang, and Chung-Chian Teng

South Asia's Cold War
Nuclear weapons and conflict in comparative perspective
Rajesh M. Basrur

The Rise of China and International Security
America and Asia respond
Edited by Kevin J. Cooney and Yoichiro Sato

Nuclear Proliferation in South Asia
Crisis behaviour and the bomb
Edited by Sumit Ganguly and S. Paul Kapur

Nuclear Weapons and Conflict Transformation
The case of India-Pakistan
Saira Khan

Managing the China Challenge
Global perspectives
Edited by Quansheng Zhao and Guoli Liu

India and Counterinsurgency
Lessons learned
Edited by Sumit Ganguly and David P. Fidler

Cooperative Security in the Asia-Pacific
The ASEAN Regional Forum
Edited by Jürgen Haacke and Noel M. Morada

US–China–EU Relations
Managing the new world order
Edited by Robert S. Ross, Øystein Tunsjø and Zhang Tuosheng

China, Europe and International Security
Interests, roles and prospects
Edited by Frans-Paul van der Putten and Chu Shulong

Crime–Terror Nexus in South Asia
States, security and non-state actors
Ryan Clarke

Crime–Terror Nexus in South Asia

States, security and non-state actors

Ryan Clarke

Routledge
Taylor & Francis Group
LONDON AND NEW YORK

First published 2012
by Routledge
711 Third Avenue, New York, NY 10017

Simultaneously published in the UK
by Routledge
2 Park Square, Milton Park, Abingdon, Oxon OX14 4RN

Routledge is an imprint of the Taylor & Francis Group, an informa business

First issued in paperback 2013

British Library Cataloguing in Publication Data
A catalogue record for this book is available from the British Library

Library of Congress Cataloging-in-Publication Data
Clarke, Ryan.
Crime-terror nexus in South Asia : states, security, and non-state actors/ Ryan Clarke.
p. cm.
1. Terrorism—Pakistan. 2. Terrorism—South Asia. 3. Crime—Pakistan. 4. Crime—South Asia. 5. Security, International—South Asia. 6. National security—South Asia. 7. Non-state actors (International relations) I. Title.
HV6433.P18C53 2011
363.3250954—dc22
2010042302

ISBN: 978–0–415–61031–5 (hbk)
ISBN: 978–0–415–72403–6 (bk)
ISBN: 978–0–203–81894–7 (ebk)

Typeset in Sabon
by Swales & Willis, Exeter, Devon

Contents

Introduction

Much research has focused on the official government policies of India and Pakistan towards Kashmir. Many choose to focus on the political process, prospects for a peaceful resolution, diplomatic hurdles, or the impact that the stalemate has on the economies of the parties involved. Surprisingly little attention in the West has been paid to several notable Pakistan-based non-state actors who are increasingly operating on their own and who have the potential to greatly inhibit, if not derail, the peace process between India and Pakistan. These groups are also blurring the line between terrorism and organized crime with serious implications for policy. Up until now, this dynamic has almost been completely ignored thus causing a crucial gap in knowledge that this book seeks to fill. Meetings can take place, documents can be signed, statements can be made, and both India and Pakistan can engage in confidence building measures, but if actors such as Lashkar-i-Taiba (LeT) and D-Company cannot effectively be controlled, a lack of trust between both sides will remain. If New Delhi feels that Islamabad is not in complete control of its territory, India will be very reluctant to make concessions, especially on Kashmir. In order to ensure that peace and cooperative agreements are worthwhile and lasting, these types of groups must be contained.

This book will focus on Dawood Ibrahim and D-Company for a variety of reasons. For one, D-Company is the largest organized criminal syndicate in Asia. Its network spans the globe and has operations in India, Pakistan, Afghanistan, Thailand, Saudi Arabia, United Arab Emirates and South Africa, amongst others. Second, D-Company controls much of the smuggling activity at key ports such as Mumbai, Karachi and Dubai. Further, D-Company is unique in that it is one of the only criminal syndicates to only include members from a particular religious background (Islam), to have its most senior leadership based overseas (primarily in Karachi), to consist of members ready and willing to attack their own country (India), and to have blurred the line between an organized criminal group and a terrorist network. In addition to narcotics and weapons trafficking, extortion, racketeering, money laundering and contract killings, D-Company is accused of permitting Al-Qaeda and Pakistan's Inter-Services Intelligence (ISI) to use its smuggling routes. D-Company has been also been accused of allowing the ISI to utilize Ibrahim's network in Mumbai to engage in intelligence gathering missions within India and to carry out attacks. It is widely known that D-Company was intricately involved in the 1993 Mumbai bombings and that members were flown to Pakistan prior to the attacks to receive training.

The decision was made to focus on the activities of LeT over other Kashmir-centred militant groups such as Jaish-e-Mohammed (JeM) and Hizbul Mujahedeen (HM) because LeT is often referred to as the largest group operating within Indian territory and has the strongest links with D-Company, a relationship facilitated and nurtured by the ISI. Further, LeT has openly stated that it has the intention to cause the collapse of the entire Indian state. Also, LeT has secured its own sources of funding and weaponry and is no longer dependent on Islamabad. It has even developed its own agenda, forged links with the Tehrik-i-Taliban Pakistan (TTP) and Al-Qaeda, and has begun to attack the secular regime in Islamabad. Lastly, LeT militants are believed to have carried out the audacious November 2008 attacks that, aside from representing a major jump in the capabilities of South Asian terrorist groups, also could have pulled India and Pakistan into a war.

This book challenges the conventional wisdom that TTP and Al-Qaeda are Pakistan's most serious security challenges. LeT has benefited from decades of state patronage and military training, enjoys strong relationships with criminal syndicates and other terrorist groups (Pakistani and otherwise), and, critically, enjoys a favourable perception and legitimacy amongst everyday Pakistanis due to its carefully crafted image of being on the frontline against a hostile India. Neither Al-Qaeda nor the TTP have the level of domestic sympathy that approximates LeT.

This book focuses on a dynamic of the Kashmir impasse that receives an inadequate amount of attention. Although the roles of regular military forces are not to be discounted, many of the non-state actors in Indian-Held Kashmir (IHK), such as LeT, are also very powerful but are not confined by the same restraints as state forces, thus allowing them engage in more violent actions without as much fear of reprisal. LeT is unlikely to be affected by economic sanctions or arms embargoes and neither is D-Company. In order for lawmakers, security personnel and others to develop sound, comprehensive policies, this underworld relationship and its potential to undermine political initiatives must be fully appreciated. Although opinions vary when trying to determine the status of Kashmir, most are in agreement that the illicit activities undertaken by groups such as LeT and D-Company are undesirable. It is in the interest of both India and Pakistan to reign in these hybrid crime–terror groups and the common goal of dismantling them could potentially serve as a very powerful confidence building measure and stabilizing factor that could help to thaw relations.

In the West, despite often having the use of violence at their core, organized crime and terrorism are viewed as fundamentally different phenomena that are driven by their own distinct motivations and therefore must be viewed as being on opposite ends of the spectrum. When it comes to crime, especially organized crime, the profit motive is viewed as the key motivation and a preference for the status quo and a stable, predictable operating environment is witnessed. However, terrorism is believed to be a by-product of extremist ideology that can be motivated by religion, ethno-nationalism, socio-political considerations, or opposition to a particular action or policy (otherwise known as 'single-issue terrorism') and seeks to violently overthrow the existing order with which they have an issue. This book will challenge that notion and explore the dynamics of the relationship between Pakistan, D-Company and LeT and how it affects strategic thought, decision-making and overall interests. However, other auxiliary questions will also be explored:

- Does LeT intend to extend its operations in a sustainable manner outside of Kashmir and throughout the whole of India? If so, does it seek an already-established local partner or does it seek to form its own subsidiary? How will LeT mobilize the necessary resources within India itself?
- After considering their support base, logistical network and demonstrated capabilities, which terrorist or insurgent group poses the greatest long-term threat to Pakistan, India and the rest of South Asia and beyond?

Many analysts are tempted to try to predict too much of the future and, as a result, they give only superficial attention to a wide range of issues while failing to dedicate ample focus on a selected group of questions. However, this book will remain focused and firmly within this framework. This work aims to contribute to a greater understanding of the triangular relationships between states, terrorist groups and organized criminal syndicates in general and in India and Pakistan in particular.

Why do states support terrorism?

In a landmark article in *Terrorism and Political Violence* in 1989, Edward Mickolus constructed several general degrees of government support and attitudes towards terrorists. In rough order of culpability, they are:

- intimidated governments
- ideologically supportive regimes
- generally facilitative supporters
- direct support in incidents by governments
- official participation.[1]

During the time that this article was written, Pakistan appeared to have been in the 'generally facilitative stage'. Mickolus notes that this stage usually involves governments permitting terrorist groups to establish safe houses and train on local soil, general government training of umbrella guerrilla bands which have terrorist appendages, large financial contributions to these bands, and arms provisions to or lax supervision of third party arms transfers to terrorist group/s.[2] While Pakistan played a major role in the initial stages of the uprising in IHK, it started off as an indigenous phenomenon thus preventing Islamabad from controlling it directly. Rather, Pakistan's civilian leaders were either unwilling or unable to prevent its military and intelligence establishment from providing arms, training and other logistical assistance to terrorist groups based in both India and Pakistan. Further complicating the matter was the fact that many of these groups were claiming to assist Pakistan in achieving a core foreign policy goal that has remained constant since independence: to remove the whole of Kashmir from the Indian Union.

Daniel Byman has built upon this analysis in the contemporary period and claims that states that support terrorism and insurgent groups are now primarily motivated by geopolitics rather than ideology, ethnic affinity or religious sentiment. Though these less-strategic rationales at times played some role in the decision of states to support irregulars, these are less frequent motivations compared to increasing regional influence, destabilizing regional rivals, or otherwise ensuring that a regime has a prominent voice in local affairs.[3] This holds true for Pakistan in that although Islamabad claims to be safeguarding the rights of its Muslim brethren in Kashmir, its interests are more motivated by larger concerns and Islamabad views the Kashmir dispute through the lens of greater Indo-Pak relations. Pakistan's continued support for terrorist outfits such as LeT serve a number of strategic objectives. First, it has proved to be a low-cost and, until recently, a relatively low-risk method to tie down a disproportionate amount of Indian troops and make sure that the Kashmir issue remains in the spotlight. Second, by ensuring that the Indian portion of Kashmir remains an insurgency, Pakistan and its proxies have so far frustrated Indian efforts to fully incorporate Kashmir into the country. This has prevented India from deploying troops into other needy areas, namely its Maoist-hit central and eastern provinces as well as the northeast. Further, it communicates to New Delhi that, even if embroiled in a domestic crisis, Pakistan is still a force to be reckoned with. New Delhi appears to have arrived at the conclusion that it is unable to impose a military solution on the Kashmir dispute or to rely on the use of force to coerce Pakistan, something that surprises many analysts given India's clear conventional superiority. Ironically, it is Pakistan's backing of irregulars, who are often unquantified variables in a conflict scenario, that has played a major role in causing New Delhi to re-evaluate its past approaches towards Pakistan. In addition, Islamabad has been able to influence previous elections in IHK and still exerts influence over several IHK-based separatist leaders.

State support is still an important source of strength for many insurgencies in the post-Cold War world. Outside government assistance helps insurgents improve their military power, recruiting base, diplomatic leverage and other ingredients to success. Most state support tends to be provided by local governments that border the country in which a group is fighting.[4] Newer state sponsors of terrorism can be extremely difficult to deal with as they often have a more complicated relationship with terrorist groups. In many cases, the government in question does not actively train or arm a terrorist group, but rather lets it act with relative impunity – an approach that allows the government to claim either ignorance or incapacity. Strategic rationales are the driving factor behind their actions and have several dimensions:

1. Making enemies bleed: supporting terrorists, particularly terrorists tied to insurgent movements, can tie down large numbers of troops and security forces of an adversary and weaken the adversary's control over key parts of its territory. Pakistan's support for various groups fighting in Kashmir epitomizes this approach. Although Pakistan's ultimate aims for Kashmir are irredentist, in the short term its leaders are content to keep Indian forces occupied and prevent Kashmir's integration into the rest of India.
2. Subservient (or at least friendly) neighbours: states are particularly concerned about their neighbours, and support for terrorists offers a form of influence. Pakistan has long supported the Taliban as well as other groups to maintain its influence in Afghanistan. Iran has ties to a range of militants in Iraq – including many that at times have openly criticized Tehran – effectively giving it a veto power over decisions in parts of the country. Syria has used Hizballah and other actors to intimidate the anti-Syrian 'March 14' movement in Lebanon.
3. Diplomatic strength: states back terrorists as a form of diplomatic leverage in negotiations. Syria for many years used Hizballah as such a pawn in its talks over the Golan Heights. Some observers believe Iran sought to trade the senior Al-Qaeda members that it is holding for US concessions on the Mujahedin-e Khalq (MEK), an Iranian group opposed to the Islamic Republic and which the US forces have interned in Iraq.
4. Power projection: support for terrorists gives weak states with global ambitions influence outside their neighbourhood. Iran's ties to various Palestinian groups and Hizballah gives Tehran tremendous influence in the Israeli–Palestinian theatre and Lebanon: influence Iran would lack if it only relied on its weak military and economic power.
5. Local power: at times a group that uses terrorism also functions as a militia, giving it tremendous influence in part of a country. Syria's cooperation with Hizballah today is driven in part by the 'street power' offered by this strongest of all Lebanese organizations, both in Beirut and southern Lebanon. Similarly, Iran backs several factions that use terrorism, partly because they also are politically and militarily strong in key parts of Iraq close to the Iranian border.
6. Deterrence: finally, supporting terrorists gives weak states a means of striking back against a militarily superior foe. Iran uses both its overseas

> network and its proxy killing machine in Iraq to deter the United States from increasing pressure over Tehran's nuclear program and other US–Iranian disputes.[5]

Byman notes that one of the most important shifts in state sponsorship in recent years is the decline in the number of regimes with a revolutionary agenda. This shift has tremendous implications for counter-terrorism in that regimes that are motivated by strategy are far more sensitive to diplomatic and economic costs as well as the risk of regime change.[6]

State support for terrorism can take multiple forms, one of which is passive sponsorship and occurs when a government knowingly allows a terrorist group to raise money, enjoy a sanctuary, recruit or otherwise flourish, but does not directly aid the group itself. Passive support may prove to be the more intractable problem and has the following characteristics:

- The regime in question does not provide assistance but knowingly allows other actors in the country to aid a terrorist group.
- The regime has the capacity to stop this assistance or has chosen not to develop this capacity.
- Passive support is often given by political parties, wealthy merchants or other actors in society that have no formal affiliation with government.[7]

In the case of Kashmir-centred terrorist groups, Pakistan has become a passive sponsor. While disagreeing with the brazen attacks by groups such as LeT that directly target civilians in areas outside of Kashmir, successive Pakistani governments have either been unwilling or unable to meaningfully curtail their activities. Though these groups have been formally proscribed, many still continue to exist under different names and continue to enjoy indirect assistance from a variety of sources in Pakistan. When faced with pressure and accusations that Pakistan lacks the political will to crack down on terrorist groups operating on its territory, Islamabad often claims that it is actually a lack of capacity that prevents it from doing so.

States give passive support to terrorists due to factors such as domestic sympathy, a low level or perceived threat to themselves, and strategic opportunities.[8] All of these factors are present in Pakistan, especially domestic sympathy. Kashmir-based militants are often referred to as 'freedom fighters' or 'mujahedeen' that are fighting for a just cause in their effort to free the Kashmiri people from perceived Indian oppression. Even many of Pakistan's leading thinkers refuse to accept the terrorism label that is placed on these groups by the West, India and others. Needless to say, any sustained attempts to dismantle groups such as LeT have proved to be most unpopular and extremely dangerous for those involved in the implementation of the crackdown. Further, it is still widely accepted in Pakistani society that as most of the cadres of the Kashmiri groups are Pakistani and officially fighting against India, they pose no threat to the state and that the recent terrorism in the country is the result of US influence in the region. Given this reality, it should not be surprising that few anticipated LeT posing a serious threat to the security of Pakistan itself and also helps to explain why Islamabad has largely been reactive to recent developments.

These miscalculations are hardly unique to Pakistan. Terms such as 'proxy' and 'client' are often used to describe the power dynamic between Hizballah and its allies Iran and Syria. The vital resources of these states and their critical political sponsorship largely placed Hizballah in the position that it is in today. However, this image of Hizballah as a client of Iran and Syria has become obsolete due to the power base that the Shia group has nurtured and expanded in Lebanon and the growing political capital that it has acquired in the Middle East thanks to the perception of its military victories, namely in the war against Israel in the summer of 2006. By holding its ground against Israel, Hizballah demonstrated its capacity to shake the Lebanese and regional political landscape and resisted Israel without substantive Syrian support. By partnering with Hizballah, Damascus sought to defy isolation and reclaim its role as a pivotal power in the region and to revitalize the Asad regime. However, Hizballah has now acquired a degree of autonomy and flexibility in recent years vis-à-vis Syria and Damascus no longer determines Hizballah's activities, something that used to guarantee the predictability and restraint that prevented all-out war. Hizballah has emerged as a more independent actor and is now able to operate in Lebanon and the wider Middle East on its own terms and has enough confidence and prestige to become more than simply a pawn for Syria to manipulate. As such, El-Hokayem feels that 'for strategic and ideological motives, Syria is more pro-Hizballah than Hizballah is pro-Syria'.[9]

The relationship between Tehran and Hizballah is also vulnerable, though to what extent is debatable. No two actors have identical objectives and Hizballah, with its extensive presence in southern Lebanon as well as Beirut, now has its own constituencies to account for and must always be mindful of Arab nationalism and the apprehensiveness regarding Iran's rising profile in the region. In the future it is not unrealistic to suggest that Hizballah may deem it to be in its own interest to regenerate its image, distance itself from state sponsors and emerge as an entirely independent, self-sufficient entity that portrays itself as the Arab world's most effective response to Israel. This is much more likely if Hizballah's leadership assess that aggressive Iranian moves are damaging the group's local interests and support base in Lebanon.

Today Israel is the biggest target of Iranian-backed terrorism, with Tehran supporting several Palestinian groups as well as Lebanese Hizballah. These groups' attacks against Israel serve three purposes: they support Iranian leaders' opposition to the existence of the Jewish state, they give Iran prestige in the Muslim world and, by keeping violence alive, they undermine the peace process, which in turn reduces the chances that Iran will be isolated in the Middle East.[10]

Although there are some gaps with regards to empirical evidence, past behaviour suggests that Hizballah would not conduct an operation as significant as the 12 July 2006 kidnappings without Tehran's approval. Further, the close ties between Hizballah and Iran's theocrats have probably emboldened the former. Even if Israel manages to destroy much of Hizballah's missiles and facilities, Iran will replenish its stocks. However, Hizballah is more than an instrument of Iranian foreign policy. Its leader, Hassan Nasrallah, enjoys far more prestige in the Arab world than any of Iran's current leaders. Further, the organization's increased strength in Lebanon since the Syrian withdrawal has boosted its confidence.[11]

Iran instead uses terrorism as a way to deter Washington. Terrorists give Tehran a way to strike at the United States in Europe, Asia, Latin America and elsewhere. Iran has cased US embassies around the world and has off-the-shelf options for striking US targets. Washington recognizes that if it pushes Iran's leaders, they can push back. As such, terrorism complicates US planning for stopping Iran's nuclear programme and other top priorities.[12]

Byman believes that support for terrorism offers Iran what it craves most today: options. He claims that Iran is at best a middleweight economic power, and its military is in a state of disrepair. Terrorism, however, offers Iran a role in the fight against Israel, a strong voice in Iraq's future, and a way to deter the United States. In the end, he feels that Iran may decide to push Hizballah away from the brink or to be a constructive player in Iraq. Nonetheless, Iran's ties to terrorist groups also give Tehran options to escalate such conflicts.[13] While the context in the Middle East in markedly different from what is witnessed in Kashmir, the strategic rationales used by both Tehran and Islamabad are remarkably similar in many ways, especially with regards to achieving deterrence against much stronger adversaries.

Developing organized crime–terrorist nexus in South Asia

Engagement in criminal activity by terrorist groups is not new and has been witnessed in a wide range of geographic locations as well as conflict theatres. While the relationship between arms and narcotics trafficking cannot be classified as symbiotic, conditions that promote one kind of trafficking often promote the other.[14] As many terrorist groups rely on the black market for arms, it should not surprise analysts that terrorist groups come to engage in narcotics trafficking and other smuggling-related activity regardless of their background, goals and ideology. While such activity tends to have its roots in fundraising purposes, it has the ability to steer a group in directions that its leadership had not initially intended. This can both be beneficial, as is the case with LeT as its ties with Indian organized crime enabled it to strike throughout India, or it can cause a massive breakdown in discipline thus rendering a group virtually unable to achieve its stated aims. While there are many examples, the most prominent is the Fuerzas Armadas

Revolucionarias de Colombia (FARC), a group which has Marxist-Leninist roots and initially aimed to overthrow the democratic, capitalist Colombian government. However, FARC now resembles a criminal syndicate more than any kind of revolutionary movement and lacks ideological coherence.

Sharp investigators previously noted marked similarities in the behavioural and operational methods of both terrorists and organized criminals. Yet they saw no reason to change their long-held view that different goals – personal profit for criminals and political upheaval for terrorists – would keep the two types distinct. Both law enforcement and intelligence continued, therefore, to rely on the established maxim of examining 'methods, not motives' in attempts to observe and identify the two criminal types.[15]

Recent research conducted by Shelley and others demonstrates that this is too narrow a view. They support the notion that terrorists and criminals often use the same methods, although most often for divergent motives (but not always). In some cases, the terrorists simply imitate the criminal behaviour they see around them, borrowing techniques such as credit card fraud and extortion in a phenomenon which they refer to as activity appropriation. In order to highlight the subsequent steps, they point to the situation in regions of the world where combinations of poor governance, ethnic separatism and/or a tradition of criminal activity that are most likely to support crime–terror interactions, such as failed states, war regions, penal institutions and some neighbourhoods of urban centres.[16]

Once terrorists and other criminals begin to work together, they have moved beyond activity appropriation to a different and closer form of interaction. As such, Shelley and others devised an evolutionary system showing five different stages in the terror–crime relationship. This linear scale is termed the terror–crime interaction spectrum.[17] Starting by borrowing each other's methods (activity appropriation), terror and crime groups naturally begin to buy and sell services and goods from each other instead. The researchers claim that it is clearly more efficient to outsource a service, such as passport forgery, to an established specialist than to try and master the necessary techniques on their own. These business relationships, which are termed nexus, tend to be focused on individual transactions and may not persist beyond the short term. The next stage of convergence is a natural progression from that point: the two groups begin working together more regularly and begin to share each other's goals as well as working methods. This stage is called a symbiotic relationship.[18] As will be demonstrated in this project, the current dynamic between LeT and D-Company can best be described as a symbiotic relationship although D-Company's goals and methods of operation have been impacted more than those of LeT. While D-Company's core business remains organized crime, it also diverts resources and personnel for terrorist activity and although members of LeT are believed to be involved in organized crime as well, it has not altered the strategic focus of LeT like terrorism has with regards to D-Company. Put simply, the influence that both groups have on each other has not been equitable as suggested in Shelley's definition of symbiotic relationship. As such, this research will introduce this new dynamic within Shelley's model.

Regions such as Chechnya and the tri-border area of Paraguay, Brazil and Argentina are so saturated with all kinds of organized crime as well as terrorist activity that it is often difficult, if not outright meaningless, to draw a distinction between groups. Many individuals belong to both terror and organized crime groups, and conduct a variety of tasks for both. In those circumstances, the process of convergence continues until the two groups become one, which is referred to as a hybrid group. Organized crime and terrorism are more or less equally important to the group, which also needs to commit fraud, extortion and other staple activities of organized crime in order to fund its terror operations. In a few cases, a hybrid group becomes fixated so keenly on one activity that it drops the other altogether. This process is called transformation.[19] Shelley and others emphasize that while convergence is a dynamic process, many terror–crime links do not ever progress to close cooperation, let alone merge. In fact, close proximity does not even guarantee that crime and terror groups will collaborate and the researchers claim that the true utility of the terror–crime interaction spectrum is to suggest the possibilities to investigators and analysts.[20]

Makarenko also provides a model and theoretical framework although her Crime–Terror Continuum, although it has some limitations when applied to the triangular relationship between Pakistan, LeT and D-Company and is also not as detailed as the model put forward by Shelley. For example, Makarenko's model notably lacks a symbiotic stage. However, Makarenko was the pioneer of this type of modelling and her influence is clear in the development of Shelley's more advanced model. She writes that since the end of the Cold War and the subsequent decline of state support for terrorist organizations, many terrorist groups have come to rely on organized crime in order to fund their activities. These types of activities increased throughout the 1990s with the end result being new working relationships which developed between terrorist groups motivated by ideology and organized criminal groups, who she believes are motivated primarily by profit.[21]

Makarenko begins discussing the various links by stating that the first level of relationship that exists between organized crime and terrorism is that basic alliance which can involve criminal groups forming alliances with terrorists or vice versa. The nature of these alliances often varies and can include one-off, short-term or long-term relationships. In addition, she believes that motivations for the alliance vary. For example, some relationships may be formed to gain access to specialized knowledge such as money laundering, counterfeiting or bomb-making. On the other hand, others form partnerships for operational support, such as access to smuggling routes. Many of these relationships share similarities to relationships formed in legitimate business environments. She points to the example of the Medellin cocaine cartel in Colombia soliciting the services of the paramilitary Ejército de Liberación Nacional (ELN) to plant car bombs in 1993 as the Medellin cartel did not possess the capabilities to conduct such activities themselves. Makarenko also states that Ibrahim is suspected of having links to the LTTE in Sri Lanka.[22] If the latter example is true, it could be argued that this demonstrates that Ibrahim indeed views weapons trafficking as one of his primary activities and has no issue with supplying weapons to conflict zones.

Makarenko notes that both criminal and terror groups capitalize on instability in that it allows criminal groups to engage in a wide range of activities without fears of reprisal and it also helps terror groups to diminish the legitimacy of a particular government, the very people whom they are often seeking to overthrow. She asserts that many organized criminal groups and militant organizations in the past have tried to avoid forging alliances if possible in order to develop their own individual in-house capabilities and maintain operational security. This represented an attempt to prevent future alliances from becoming jeopardized by differences over priorities and strategies, distrust, the danger of defections and the possibility that the alliance could create competitors. As a result, Makarenko believes that most organized crime and terror groups that were active in the post-Cold War period have the capacity to engage in both criminal and terrorist activities.[23]

Makarenko asserts that organized criminal groups have utilized terrorist methods throughout history but that terror groups engaging in organized criminal activity is a relatively new phenomenon that began to emerge as a matter of concern in the early 1990s. Further, she states that organized criminal groups have typically used terrorism not to alter the status quo, but to 'secure their operational environment'.[24] On the other hand, terror groups who engage in criminal activities view it as an illegitimate means to a legitimate end and hold their ideology in a much higher position. She is also of the opinion that many groups lost their initial focus, motivations and aims as they begun to incorporate economic factors into their agenda. As a result, Makarenko states that there are a growing number of groups in the twenty-first century that display characteristics of both organized crime and terrorism.[25]

Makarenko discusses the 'convergence thesis', which addresses the possibility that criminal and terrorist groups could possibly merge into a single entity that displays characteristics of both organizations but also has the potential to transform itself to any other type of entity situated on the opposite end of the spectrum from which it began. The convergence thesis includes two independent components. First, it incorporates organized criminal groups who change their motivational paradigm and begin to display political tendencies. Second, it involves terrorist groups who have eventually become equally interested in criminal profits but who utilize their public rhetoric as a 'façade for perpetuating criminal activities'.[26] Within the first group, there exist two subsets. One subset is the criminal group that uses terror tactics to gain influence above the disruption of the judicial processes or attempts to block anti-crime legislation. She states that these types of groups seek to maintain political control by means of direct involvement in the judicial process and state institutions. The second subset consists of criminal organizations that initially use terrorism to establish a monopoly over profitable economic sectors that are under the control of the state. The logic of these groups is that in a global society that is largely characterized by a free market economy, economic influence is a necessary prerequisite for political power.[27]

The second part of Makarenko's thesis touches upon terrorist groups that engage in criminal activity but use political rhetoric as a front to provide cover for their criminal activities. She states that, in recent times, there are an increasing amount of these groups developing and engaging in terrorist actions for two primary reasons: first, to ensure that the government and law enforcement bodies maintain their focus on political issues and problems instead of opening criminal investigations. Second, terrorist tactics can be used as a means to intimidate rival criminal groups and to assert themselves as the primary player. Further, by continuing to portray their political ideology as their sole motivator to the public, 'these groups will be able to use the previously-established terrorist support network'.[28]

Last, Makarenko discusses her 'black hole' thesis, which refers to situations in which weak or failed states facilitate the convergence of organized crime and terrorism and eventually create a safe haven for these hybrid groups. The black hole syndrome consists of two situations: the first is where a civil conflict switches its focus from political aims to criminal ones. The second situation is where a hybrid group is successful in taking over an entire nation, which Makarenko refers to as a 'black hole state'.[29] She notes that these two situations share a commonality in that they both demonstrate the dangers of convergence between organized crime and terror groups and the situation that it could create; the potential formation of conditions that could spark a civil conflict, or even a regional war, to secure economic and political power. She cites examples such as Afghanistan, Angola, Burma, North Korea, Sierra Leone and Tajikistan as past experiences and points to the Northwest Frontier Province (NWFP) in Pakistan, Indonesia and Thailand as places that could become black hole states in the future.[30]

Makarenko finishes her argument by offering words of caution for the future by stating that as many groups have come to realize that political and economic power enhance one another, an increasing number of groups will become hybrid by nature. It also appears that criminal and terrorist groups have begun to learn from the others' experiences and have adapted their operating structures accordingly. Further, she notes that ungoverned territory such as the NWFP, parts of Tajikistan and the tri-border region in South America continue to facilitate strengthened relations between organized crime and terrorism. Finally, she offers criticism by alleging that there has been an over-focus on political aims and motivations in regard to the formation of terrorism policy at the expense of issues relating to criminality and firmly claims that no matter which end of the spectrum a group finds itself, the one consistent factor amongst them is criminality.[31]

Stern, of Harvard, analyses the growing relationship between terrorist and organized criminal groups although she does not provide analytical frameworks like Shelley and Makarenko. Rather, she takes a more simplistic view and states that terrorist often hire criminals to conduct activities that Stern refers to as 'dirty work'.[32] She alleges that some terrorists even become involved in organized crime themselves and that criminals are often used to transport weapons and explosives or to carry out more extreme acts of violence that a militant group is either unwilling or unable to perform. Stern states that a prime example is the 1993 bombing of the Mumbai Stock Exchange as the attack was conducted by then Dubai-based D-Company that had travelled to Islamabad a month before the attacks and had received training on how to fire Kalashnikov assault rifles and throw hand grenades from Pakistani militants. Further, it was noted that none of the criminals' passports contained Pakistani stamps, thus suggesting government complicity.[33] Treverton takes it a step further by claiming that D-Company appears to have morphed from a traditional criminal syndicate motivated by money to a terrorist group motivated by a political agenda funded at least in part with the proceeds of crime.[34] However, both of these scholars have neglected the fact that organized crime remains the primary activity of D-Company and that its involvement in terrorism is almost a secondary consideration and largely the result of Ibrahim's residence in Pakistan and his desire to see his syndicate continue to be viewed as the defender of Indian Muslims, particularly in Mumbai.

Stern also believes that criminals often join terrorist organizations for the sake of violence itself or for financial reasons and they tend to be less committed to the ideology of the group. However, she states that when criminals enlist in private armies traditional political and moral restraints tend to erode. This is problematic as these restraints often serve as a check on the behaviour that results in mass-casualty, random attacks. Stern also believes that the involvement of criminals in a particular militant movement makes it more difficult for nations such as Pakistan to effectively contain the group as mercenaries are oftentimes harder to control than militants whose goals are at least somewhat parallel to the state.[35] However, while the goals of Pakistan-backed terrorist groups such as LeT have been parallel in the past, actions such as the November 2008 Mumbai attacks clearly demonstrate that this is no longer the case.

1 Analysis of current research

The Kashmir conflict has sparked much interest amongst academia and policy-makers alike as it is viewed as a major Asian flashpoint that could abruptly bring two regional rivals to the brink of large-scale conventional warfare or even a nuclear conflict. As this conflict is extremely complicated and multifaceted, there is a plethora of information available on the subject.

This section will focus on the literature regarding the history and overview of the conflict, the dynamics of the relationship between India, Pakistan and the People's Republic of China, Chinese arms sales to Pakistan and the triangular relationship between states, terrorist groups and organized criminal syndicates and how it manifests itself in India and Pakistan.

While researching these particular topics in international relations, it is often difficult to find truly balanced analysis. Because of this, it is necessary to survey material from a wide spectrum such as international and regional think tanks and policy institutes, academics, newspaper articles (although the newspaper must be carefully researched) and well-established journals.

Introduction and historical overview

History commonly states that the hostilities over Kashmir stem from the partition of British India in 1947 and that the main sticking point is that Pakistan feels that India acquired Kashmir through fraudulent means by influencing the then Hindu leader to choose to have Muslim-majority Kashmir become part of the Indian Union. Many voices in India and throughout the world counter this by stating that Pakistan had already begun to send militants and regular military units to Kashmir to pressure the ruler of the kingdom to side with Pakistan and that the ruler of Kashmir made the decision to join India either through his own free will or because of the need to be shielded from Pakistan. However others are careful not to view the conflict in solely political terms. For example, Badmus is of the opinion that the Kashmir conflict is not necessarily so much a political struggle, but an extension of much older Hindu–Muslim tensions in the region and that the conflict centres much more around religion despite being conducted under the guise of politics.[1]

Misra, of the Institute for Defense Studies and Analyses (IDSA), a prominent New Delhi-based defence think tank, takes the path of most historians and claims that Pakistan still views Kashmir as unfinished business stemming from the 1947 partition while India views the issue as over and the problems in Kashmir as being an internal matter. As such, he states that India has attempted to address the problems in IHK through a constitutional framework and has focused on government at the local level all while stressing economic development, law and order, and instilling democratic principles. India has also officially granted limited autonomy to IHK and the province is supposed to have the ability to draft its own legislation on various subjects. Meanwhile, Pakistan supports terrorist activities within Jammu and Kashmir and ex-President Musharraf has even been accused of using Pakistan's tribesman from the Northwest Frontier Provinces (NWFP) and Afghanistan, namely Pashtuns, with the help of Osama bin Laden to suppress a Shia rebellion against their Sunni-dominated government in Gilgit in PHK.[2] This particular claim has also been supported by Palit, of IDSA, who claims that prior to 9/11, Pakistan commonly used Afghanistan-based Al-Qaeda terrorists to fight in Kashmir.[3] Misra also alleges that Musharraf used terrorist groups to kill or displace Kashmiris and brought in other non-Kashmiri groups to replace them and that these types of actions have brought normal life in IHK to a standstill. Warikoo, who is also a researcher at IDSA, supports these claims by stating that Pakistan has engaged in religious and ethnic cleansing in the Kashmir Valley.[4] Misra cleverly sums up the difference in approaches by stating that India views the conflict as the 'problem in Kashmir' while Pakistan views the situation as the 'problem of Kashmir'.[5] Although the voices of these IDSA researchers are not without merit, it must be noted that IDSA is funded by the Indian government, is located near an army base, and consists only of Indian researchers, many of whom served in the armed forces. As such, their research cannot necessarily be classified as objective.

Misra also addresses another sore spot in Indo-Pakistani relations: the implementation of previous UN resolutions. He writes that Pakistan consistently calls for the implementation of the UN resolutions that state that the status of Kashmir should be determined by the Kashmiri people (although in late 2006 Musharraf hinted that Pakistan may drop this stance). However, he is sceptical about Pakistan's sincerity towards the self-determination of the Kashmiri people and believes that Islamabad actually feels that Kashmir should be part of Pakistan because it has a Muslim majority and should not be part of a Hindu-majority state. He also feels there is a sense of irony in Pakistan's citation of previous UN resolutions due to the fact that Pakistan still has not complied with many of the UN demands (which are part of the Kashmir resolutions) that state that Pakistan must remove all of their regular and irregular forces from the area. Misra also claims that Pakistan illegally ceded part of occupied PHK to China in 1963. Further complicating the matter is the fact that India feels that the Kashmir resolutions are outdated and can no longer be placed into a modern context. Lastly, Misra finishes his argument with a rather negative prognosis for the future by stating that neither Pakistan nor India is likely to make significant concessions on Kashmir, seemingly suggesting that a stalemate will remain for the near term but a major military conflict is a very real possibility.[6]

Jamwal, yet another scholar from IDSA, also takes a more conventional view of history by stating the Pakistan's *raison d'être* was based upon a two-nation theory that stated that Hindus and Muslims cannot live together in one nation. He states that this basic belief amongst many Muslims in British India led to the 1947 partition and the creation of the Pakistani state. Jamwal goes on to assert that Pakistan believes that because India is a secular state, Muslims are not safe and that many apprehended Pakistan-backed terrorists claim their motivation was to kill as many Hindus and security force personnel as possible, despite Indian Muslims suffering the most casualties.[7] Though Jamwal's views are not without merit, it should be noted that many Indians view Kashmir as central to the concept of the Indian nation state as they feel that if Hindu-majority India can successfully govern Muslim-majority Kashmir, then it proves India's democratic credentials while simultaneously undermining Pakistan's reason for existence. Though nationalism runs high in this dispute, religion also plays a major role.

Jamwal believes that post-1989, Pakistan gained confidence after its successful Afghan jihad and, thus emboldened, decided to begin a low-intensity conflict in Kashmir.[8] However others, such as Samii, disagree with Jamwal regarding the roots of the 1989 spark of terrorist activities and believes that the separatist struggle emerged in Kashmir as the result of 'decades of heavy-handed and corrupt rule by New Delhi and state politicians'.[9] Samii appears to feel that terrorist activities in IHK were more of a backlash against authoritative Indian rule rather than state-sponsored terrorism designed to further Pakistani state interests. Also, Bhatt claims that the ISI capitalized on the frustration of Kashmiri youths towards New Delhi by organizing, training and funding them to become Islamic terrorists.[10] Another theory has been put forward by Malik claiming that the Chinese provision of a nuclear and missile shield to Pakistan during the late 1980s and early 1990s led to the emboldenment of Pakistan and encouraged them to engage in a proxy war in IHK without the fear of a major Indian military response.[11] As this project will demonstrate, the actual answer is a combination of the first two mentioned explanations although this is not to say that the Chinese provisions were irrelevant.

Jamwal continues on to say that Pakistan's ISI funds roughly 75 per cent of militant activities in IHK and has established training camps in PHK and indoctrinates fighters to kill Indian *kafirs*, or non-believers. Jamwal also writes that many terrorists in IHK, both foreign and Pakistani, have criminal backgrounds and are promised that their charges will be dropped once they return from fighting Indian security forces. He claims that they also often receive payment or a monetary reward is given to their families in the event that they do not return.[12] Marwah (IDSA) is in agreement with Jamwal, alleging that many militant groups are not driven by ideology, but rather by greed. Marwah also states that the ISI provides legal protection within Pakistan to drug cartels that raise funds for militant groups not only in IHK, but in northeast India as well. He continues on to say that Pakistan cannot accept the fact that not only is India a democratic, plural and multi-religious society, India also has more Muslim citizens than Pakistan does. Therefore, the main goal of Pakistan's foreign and domestic policy is the destruction of the Indian Union.[13] In these statements, the overt bias of these IDSA researchers becomes evident. For example, it would be impossible for Jamwal to legitimately determine what percentage of militant activities are sponsored by ISI and that insurgent groups in IHK are mostly mercenaries driven by monetary benefit. In regards to Marwah, he appears to have overstated the functionality and pluralism of the Indian system and views the differences between India and Pakistan in black and white terms. Although the democratic project in India has been more successful than in Pakistan, Indian politics are notoriously corrupt, the caste system is still present in everyday society, and religious tensions that culminate into riots are not uncommon.

Kartha (IDSA) focuses much of her research on Pakistan-backed militants operating in India. She states that terrorism in India has three main objectives: acquiring territory, over-expending the resources of the Indian armed forces and to generally destabilize India. Simply put, attempting to accomplish conventional objectives that are attained in an unconventional manner through the use of irregular guerrilla tactics.[14] Ganguly, a well-known South Asia scholar, seems to be in agreement by stating that Pakistani strategy is a 'war of a thousand cuts' against India.[15] Others, such as Racine, believe that Pakistan's strategy of 'bleeding India' is no longer valid as most of the Pakistani military leadership are careful not to openly contradict Washington's agenda and are keen to avoid being labelled a rogue state or to be 'demonized' by Washington.[16]

Warikoo provides an in-depth analysis of the recent history and current status of Pakistan-sponsored terrorism in IHK. He starts by stating that many extremist groups initially came at the call of Pakistan to wage jihad in Afghanistan in addition to Kashmir but have now adopted their own agendas independent of Islamabad and have begun to destroy Pakistan from the inside and exacerbate already-tense sectarian divisions in the process. He also claims that militants in IHK consist of Islamic extremists, terrorists and foreign mercenaries, all of which have been trained in Pakistan since 1989. Many of these fighters subscribe to radical Islamist ideology and view India's multi-ethnic secular democracy as un-Islamic. Warikoo blames political parties such as Jamaat-e-Islami for laying the groundwork for overt Pakistani involvement in Kashmir by funding extremist institutions, madrassas, mosques and circulating radical literature throughout Pakistan.[17]

Warikoo also believes that the ISI has used Afghan rebel leaders such as Gulbadin Hikmatyar and his Hizb-e-Islami group to foment unrest in Kashmir, thus providing Islamabad with deniability. Lastly, Warikoo points to two major events that greatly influenced the Kashmir conflict and further connected the issue with Islam. One event was the 1979 Islamic Revolution in Iran while the other was the Soviet invasion of Afghanistan that same year. He believes that the Iranian revolution inspired many Asian Muslims and the Soviet invasion reminded these populations that threats still existed to Muslim societies.[18] Although Warikoo, like Kartha, provides a solid overview, there is still no significant mention of other key developments such as the sharp increase of arms to the region by both the Soviets and the United States (funnelled to the Afghan militias through the ISI) nor the devastation of Afghanistan following the Soviet withdrawal that gave further rise to extremist groups such as the Taliban. Although the Iranian revolution and Soviet invasion provided the ideological support, these events provided the necessary materiel.

Despite the fact that the vast majority of scholars and analysts feel that the activities undertaken by Pakistan-supported terrorists falls under the realm of terrorism, there are a small minority that seem to challenge that notion. Mazari, of the Institute for Strategic Studies (ISS), an Islamabad-based policy and defence think tank with close links to the security establishment, claims that Kashmir is an 'indigenous Kashmiri struggle against Indian occupation'.[19] Mazari also states that although terrorism is going to be the next major unconventional challenge to the international system, many individuals who were formerly referred to as terrorists are today viewed as freedom fighters and national heroes.[20] Though it is unclear whether or not Mazari is specifically referring to terrorist activities in Kashmir and it is important that the quote is not taken out of context, it possibly provides interesting insight into the thinking of some Pakistani strategists. Is it possible that some of Pakistan's senior leadership believe that history will forgive them if they are successful in capturing Kashmir? Although it would be a difficult task to answer this question, it is nonetheless well worth asking.

Samii also focuses on Pakistani strategy and its use of terrorist groups in IHK as well as other areas. He writes that Pakistani strategists believe that by keeping the terrorists strong, Indian military and civilian thinkers will come to realize that they cannot impose a military solution. He continues on to say that Pakistan's support for terrorists is part of an asymmetric strategy to balance against India's clear conventional superiority in both numbers and equipment. He finishes by stating that even if Pakistan wanted to dismantle the entire terrorist structure, they would unlikely be able to accomplish it because Samii, like many other researchers, believes that many of Pakistan's extremist groups now have funding from international sources, such as Islamist organizations, and independent commercial and fundraising ventures. Another reason given for Pakistan's inability to reign in their militant groups is the fact that Musharraf was in an embattled state and was under attack from political parties on all sides of the spectrum in Pakistan. Because of this, he was unlikely to have wielded the power that is necessary to take meaningful action against terror groups.[21]

Sino-Pak ties in relation to India

There exists a fair amount of literature regarding the strategy of China towards India, some of which discusses arms sales to Pakistan as central to Chinese strategy. Many Indians feel that Chinese involvement in Pakistan's military and economic programmes combined with Beijing's efforts to develop warm ties with Bangladesh and Burma, are part of a strategic plan to encircle and contain India.[22] In addition to loans and assistance with infrastructure projects, a main staple of China's relations with both Burma and Bangladesh has been the provision of weapons.

Gill notes that Chinese naval modernization is viewed by some as a threat to India's primacy in the Indian Ocean, but stops short of stating whether or not the Chinese Navy (PLAN) plans to use the Gwadar port in Balochistan.[23] Tellis furthers this argument by stating that Indian leaders cited challenges posed by China as one the main justifications for India's 1998 nuclear tests. He also states that Sino-Pakistani relations go back to the 1962 Sino-Indian border war, which led China and Pakistan to increase ties based on mutual interests, centred primarily on containing what they viewed as Indian dominance in South Asia. Tellis also notes that China was sharply critical of India's actions in the Pakistani civil war in 1971 but China did not intervene militarily despite requests by Islamabad. Because of this, he feels that this demonstrated that China would provide Pakistan with moral and diplomatic support and even provide Pakistan with arms but it would not provide Pakistan with security guarantees. Tellis also points to other trouble spots in Sino-Indian relations in India's maintenance of diplomatic relations with Taiwan, India's providing asylum to thousands of Tibetan refugees and the Dalai Lama, and the fact that China has also targeted India with its superior nuclear arsenal.[24]

Subrahmanyam takes these points a step further and sums up China's relations with Pakistan by stating that 'for China, Pakistan is its Israel'.[25] Subrahmanyam seems to suggest that China views Pakistan as almost a subservient strategic hammer in South Asia that can be strengthened and utilized in the event that China feels that India is becoming too powerful. He also believes that China can provide as many or as few arms as it feels is necessary to maintain a strategic balance in the region and can discourage or encourage Pakistan to take aggressive action against India as it deems fit. However, Subrahmanyam has grossly overestimated China's ability to influence Pakistan's behaviour. For example, events in Pakistan's tribal areas and Islamabad's support for terrorists in Afghanistan and India have serious implications for China's Xinjiang province and, like NATO, China would likely prefer to see Pakistan shift its military focus from the border with

India to its unstable western regions. However, Pakistan still refuses to shift its strategic paradigm. Second, in recent years the United States has showered Pakistan with billions of dollars and a wide range of military equipment while also playing the key role in rescuing Pakistan from devastating loan defaults yet Washington's leverage with Pakistan still remains somewhat limited and has not persuaded Pakistan to cease its support for irregulars in Afghanistan. These events demonstrate that even if it behaves irrationally and in a self-destructive manner, Pakistan closely defends its sovereignty, is sensitive to public perceptions depicting it a junior partner or mercenary, and is highly unlikely to become subservient to China.

Pillsbury discusses Chinese views regarding the threat from India. He states that many Chinese strategic analysts have accused India of embarking on a major military expansion in order to become a dominant military power and to unilaterally control South Asia and the Indian Ocean. Pillsbury also writes that many in China are concerned that India could join the United States in assisting Tibetan independence. Further, he asserts that the late Chinese Premier, Zhou Enlai, discussed India's 'blood relationship (interbreeding)' with the British and stated that the Indian middle classes continued on the imperial British concept that India is the dominant power and centre of Asia.[26]

Pillsbury believes that few Chinese thinkers welcome the idea of India or Japan as a major strategic partner in Asia, that there is concern within China that the Bharatiya Janata Party (BJP) will take control of India and introduce hard-line 'Hindu chauvinistic policies', and that Beijing is worried that India and Japan could develop sufficient economic and military strength, play the China threat card, and forge an alliance with the United States, thus forming an anti-China bloc in Asia.[27] Lastly, Wenmu, a well-known and influential Chinese analyst, believes that India has the intention to remove Tibet from China in order to create a buffer zone between China and India and that this would enable India to engage in bolder activities in South Asia and in the Indian Ocean without fear of a Chinese military response.[28]

Mannan seems to continue on to the points made by Pillsbury and others by stating that China seeks to see a South Asian region that is free from external hegemonic power, namely the United States, that opposes China's rise to world power status and that China would undertake efforts to forge strategic alliances in Asia to encircle and contain India.[29] This comment made by Mannan is interesting as US–Indian ties are steadily improving and expanding in many areas, namely defence and civilian nuclear cooperation after the signing of the Indo-US Civil Nuclear Cooperation Agreement. Mannan continues on to say that China forges relations with nations such as Pakistan and Bangladesh because Pakistan's interests coincide with China's by seeking a regional order with multiple actors and reflecting China's importance.[30] Also noteworthy is the fact that China needs Pakistan's assistance in combating Uyghur separatist groups in Xinjiang, some of which have bases in Pakistan.

Budania (IDSA) believes that not only is China attempting to use Pakistan as a counterweight to India in South Asia, but that China also aims to tip the nuclear balance in favour of Pakistan but still notes that China's Kashmir policy is now 'careful neutralism' and stresses a resolution through bilateral negotiations.[31] Although China seems to have declared a neutral stance on Kashmir, it still continues to supply arms to Pakistan, a well-known state sponsor of terrorism in IHK, Afghanistan and within India. Is this an example of intentional strategic ambiguity or a demonstration of a lack of a comprehensive, developed policy? Had Budania commented on these types of questions, his research would have likely been much more insightful.

Racine believes that China's policy regarding India will likely be significantly influenced by the PLA.[32] If true, this is highly problematic as there are several security issues between China and India such as at least 90,000 square kilometres of disputed territories, Tibet and India's accommodation of the Dalai Lama, and India's ties with Taiwan. It is very probable that the PLA views arms sales to Pakistan (that likely end up in regional conflict zones where Pakistan has a state interest) as not only providing a valuable source of funding for their modernization efforts, but that it is also a relatively inexpensive way to keep the military might of India checked by keeping them occupied in IHK and in northeast India. It is also probable that the PLA lobby could greatly inhibit future efforts by the Communist Party to exert greater control over Chinese defence companies.

Chinese arms transfers with special reference to Pakistan

Chinese arms transfers to Pakistan are viewed by Beijing as a low-cost investment as the sales increase Pakistan's defence capabilities but do not require any public commitment to transfer technology to Islamabad or to make defence agreements.[33] However, analysts have not addressed where Chinese weapons go after their transfer. Pakistan's defence capabilities would be directed at India, as Pakistan lags far behind India in terms of military strength and one of Pakistan's only means of hitting India is through state-sponsored militancy in IHK. Nonetheless, Tellis continues claims that China's assistance to Pakistan yields three key results: it ensures that New Delhi stays focused on Islamabad; it limits India's freedom of action in South Asia; and it helps to prevent India from becoming a major competitor to China in Asia. Pakistan has also been granted access to the best conventional Chinese arms and technologies available. Although Chinese arms and technologies lag behind many Western weapons, Chinese arms are easily available, relatively inexpensive and easier to maintain. Therefore these weapons have been used to 'beef up the "low" end of the "high-low" mix of capabilities' the Pakistani military possesses in regards to India.[34]

Tellis believes that the Chinese military-industrial complex is very likely to become Pakistan's primary partner in future product improvements, joint production ventures and exports of low-end conventional weapons.[35] If true, the development of this type of relationship between Islamabad and Beijing would likely guarantee a steady flow of hard-to-trace small arms to Pakistan in order to continue to strengthen the lower end of Pakistan's defence capabilities in order to keep pace (or at least attempt to) with India.

Researchers at the Center for Nonproliferation Studies provide a possible reason for the high number and seemingly indiscriminate arms sales by Chinese companies. They state that as China began its capitalist reforms in the early 1980s, there was intense pressure on Chinese defence industries to become involved in the potentially lucrative international arms market. They also state that Pakistan became one of China's most valued customers.[36] Although this push to export began in the 1980s, it likely has continued on to the present day. Although a great many variables have changed since this time period, three key facts remain: there are still a range of conflicts across the region whose actors need weapons ranging from small arms to conventional weapons, arms sales is still a very lucrative, low-cost business, and China still needs large sums of hard currency and resources to fund its many modernization programmes.

Spector, Yuan and Saunders, all from the Center for Nonproliferation Studies, further the point made by their fellow researchers by stating that Chinese economic reforms in 1979 not only loosened export controls, but also reduced government support for the Chinese defence-industrial complex. The consequence of these occurrences was a spike in Chinese proliferation activity as Chinese defence companies capitalized on new opportunities to engage foreign markets, including exporting ballistic missiles, nuclear technology and precursor chemicals and equipment that can be used to make chemical weapons. Further, Spector and his associates believe that the Chinese government approved of many of these deals as they were viewed as a way of funding China's defence modernization programme and they feel that it is also very likely that some Chinese politicians personally profited as well. Spector and others point to another problem regarding Chinese arms sales in government corruption.[37] Many scholars choose to focus on the lack of Chinese institutional and legislative capability to deal with weapons trafficking, often while neglecting the fact that even with these controls in place, corruption amongst low-to-mid level Communist Party officials still serves as a major impediment to controlling clandestine arms sales.

Spector and others also believe that China's domestic export control system is underdeveloped and that Beijing does not have the ability to adequately monitor, much less control, Chinese arms companies that are engaging in proliferation. Over the past decades, they believe Chinese arms exports have skyrocketed and are no longer under the control of the Communist Party. Further, they state that Chinese companies are driven by market opportunities rather than government plans or other political factors and although export regulations were established in 2002, the Chinese system still suffers from a lack of resources and training, inadequate and unclear interagency coordination procedures, and a conflict over the relative priority of non-proliferation versus commercial interests. Further, Spector and others state that factors such as WTO membership, the decentralization and diversification of export-focused companies, the trade in dual-use technology and increasing globalization have also contributed to further increased arms sales by Chinese defence companies.[38]

Lastly, Chalk (RAND) discusses Pakistan's long history of diverting weapons routes to unintended sources in addition to Chinese small arms sales to Islamabad. He claims that during the Soviet invasion of Afghanistan, tens of thousands of tons of weaponry and ammunition flowed into Pakistan, with Washington dedicating US$6–8 billion to supplying the ISI with arms meant for the Afghan militias fighting the USSR. However, Chalk alleges that many of these weapons never made it to the frontline and that some estimates claim that up to 70 per cent of the weapons sent to Pakistan never reached their intended destination. He continues on to say that China currently has at least 15 factories that produce small arms and that these companies have been encouraged to make illicit transfers to account for capital losses resulting from a significant decline in the legal demand for small arms. He notes that official corruption, an absence of strong controls over surplus weapons stocks, and 'massive social dislocation and disparities in wealth caused by runaway economic growth' have also greatly contributed to Chinese small arms trafficking.[39]

Links between terrorism and organized crime in Iraq: lessons for South Asia?

Organized crime, by and large, has been a neglected dimension of the conflict in Iraq. Yet, its importance is difficult to overestimate as both criminal enterprises and activities had a debilitating impact and made the attainment of US objectives much more difficult. Organized crime inhibited reconstruction and development and became a major obstacle to state-building as the insurgency was strengthened and sustained by criminal activities. Further, sectarian conflict was funded by criminal activities and motivated by the desire to control criminal markets and the more traditional criminal enterprises created pervasive insecurity through kidnapping and extortion. Organized crime also acted as an economic and political spoiler in an oil industry expected to be the key driver for growth and reconstruction in post-Ba'athist Iraq.[40]

The rise of organized crime after the US invasion came in two distinct waves: the first wave followed the collapse of the state and was accompanied by the breakdown of social control mechanisms and the development of anomie while the second wave was driven by anarchy, insecurity, political ambition and the imperatives of resource generation for militias, insurgents and other groups.[41]

Williams believes that members of criminal organizations tend to be interested first and foremost in profit, but this is not always an exclusive focus.

Indeed, it is possible to identify a range of criminals that includes those whose only concern is profit as well as those who are interested in both personal profit and obtaining money for political causes. As a result, clear distinctions between criminals on the one side, and terrorists, insurgents and militia members, on the other, are not always compelling.[42] There are several reasons for the blurriness. First, individuals often have roles which are multiple, overlapping and compatible rather than those that are single, distinct and mutually exclusive. Further the greater the proceeds that can be obtained through criminal activities, the less the tensions between personal enrichment and the cause and it becomes easier for multiple roles to coexist. Second, distinctions between political and criminal organizations are sometimes fuzzy because even though motivations may be different, their actions are similar. Third, criminals are highly opportunistic and if there are clear advantages (and limited risks) to working in one way or another with politically motivated individuals and groups, then cooperation will occur (sometimes in ways which make it difficult to disentangle motivations). Fourth, both individual and group roles can change over time. Sometimes, basically mercenary criminals become politicized, so that activities initially designed for personal profit become enmeshed in larger political purposes.[43] Sometimes, the movement is in the other direction, with ideological causes and political agenda becoming less important than profit.

It seems that at least four major kinds of criminal organizations operate in Iraq: traditional criminal enterprises, tribal-based criminal organizations, foreign jihadi groups and militias which include splinter or rogue factions. The foreign jihadi groups and some of the Sunni tribes were also the main participants in the insurgency, and many commentaries refer simply to insurgent funding.[44] There are two reasons why Williams distinguishes between different groups within the insurgency rather than treating it as monolithic. First, the insurgency has changed over time. Initially, it was composed of former regime elements and Ba'athists and it soon extended to include other members of Sunni tribes whose objective was primarily to eject foreign occupiers. As former regime elements became more concerned with the resettling of their families and maintaining them in a manner which they had been accustomed to during the Hussein years, the tribes along with the foreign jihadis increasingly drove the insurgency. Consequently, the revenue streams also changed. Not surprisingly, these streams vary over time according to circumstance and opportunity and they are both dynamic and adaptable, making them difficult both to dissect and to block.[45] One official noted:

> The financing challenge related to Iraq terrorism and insurgency is a complex, formal, and informal multidimensional phenomenon involving external money flows and internal revenue generation and distribution networks. These numerous revenue generation and distribution structures are mostly decentralized, with different funding sources and streams overlapping and mutually reinforcing each other. Some

> networks that finance terrorists and insurgents are self-regenerating, especially networks and revenues sources that are internal to Iraq. Finally, terrorists and insurgents are adaptive. In the past, as we've affected one stream of financing, we've observed terrorists and insurgents transition to other areas in response.[46]

Al-Qaeda in Iraq (AQI) members have been heavily engaged in criminal activities as a source of funding. AQI has also been heavily dependent on human smuggling organizations and their brokers to bring new members into Iraq. Yet, Williams notes that the process has not been entirely smooth. It appears that while some of the necessary networks are supportive of, if not affiliated with, the insurgency in Iraq, others are simply criminal businessmen who are not scrupulous about whom they smuggle, only about whether it is profitable. Since many such coordinators, smugglers and other middlemen are criminals concerned more about cash than cause, AQI has not been entirely comfortable with them. Although AQI has been concerned that its fees to these smuggling networks are excessive, it has continued to pay them because the flow of fighters depends on the smugglers' cooperation.[47]

Though the relationship with the Syrian smuggling network has been characterized by a lack of trust, it has been much smoother than the relationship between AQI and the Sunni tribes. The dramatic change in the relationship between tribal organized crime and AQI has been well-documented by Austin Long.[48] In his view, AQI's attempt to obtain control of revenue sources, such as banditry and smuggling, that had long been the province of the tribes, was the key factor in creating dissension. He notes that the tribes actually began to fight with AQI in early 2005 before most of AQI's violence towards civilians and tribesmen in Anbar occurred. The primary motive was not moral but rather self-interest. Long claims that the first tribe to break with AQI was the Albu Mahal tribe around the city of Qaim which resented AQI's challenge to its lucrative smuggling operations. Supported by members of the Albu Nimr tribe, the Albu Mahal formed the Hamza Battalion and sought help from the US Marines. For a variety of reasons, US assistance was not timely or decisive enough to make a difference. However, while AQI seemed to have emerged victorious, there was a US offensive against AQI in and around Qaim coordinated with the Albu Mahal in November 2005. Cooperation continued to improve following this operation and Marines and Iraqi army personnel stayed behind to support the Albu Mahal in providing security.[49]

As briefly mentioned earlier, AQI capitalizes on the extensive tribal smuggling networks across the Syrian/Iraqi border, much of which has traditionally received explicit or tacit support from Syrian and Iraqi officials. The smuggling takes a number of forms, each of which requires a unique set of expertise. Livestock smuggling is the most prevalent and usually occurs on unmarked trails away from established border crossings.[50] Cigarettes and other bulk items are often moved in trucks through border crossings, something which requires bribing border guards. High-value items such as electronics require larger bribes and better intelligence about border officials while human smuggling often takes place on the same trails as livestock smuggling. There is ample evidence that AQI uses criminal smugglers, who they do not fully trust, to cross the border. AQI's effort to monopolize smuggling networks, which impeded Sunni tribal leaders from much of their traditional livelihood, was an important element convincing Iraqi tribes to cooperate with US forces.[51]

AQI's permanent Border Sector personnel are vulnerable to coercion as family men with property dominate the Border Sector's permanent establishment. Many are purely motivated by financial gain rather than ideology. Bergen and others believe that to the extent that they can be identified, such individuals are highly vulnerable to pressure and may be susceptible to being turned and used as agents. They also notes that AQI's reliance on criminal and smuggling networks exposes the group to the greed and the uncertain commitment of mercenaries. Governments may be able to use financial incentives and creative security guarantees to gain cooperation from these criminal networks.[52] Offering a large bounty for foreign fighters may be more attractive than the payments Syrian coordinators/smugglers can expect to receive from AQI, or the cash they can take from the fighters travelling to Iraq. It is likely that individuals who provide logistical support are less committed to the cause than the group's permanent staff in Iraq or traveling jihadis. This difference in commitment can be exploited. One way to do so is to encourage Syrian authorities to offer amnesty or reduced punishment for known Syrian coordinators in exchange for cooperation.[53]

While this analysis of the links between state actors, insurgents/terrorists and organized criminal syndicates in Iraq provides some very useful insight regarding this particular insurgency, its dynamics, key enablers and drivers, and points of vulnerability are quite different from what is witnessed with regards to the triangular relationship between Pakistan, LeT and D-Company. First, unlike what is witnessed in Iraq, members of LeT and D-Company are almost all Pakistani and Indian and, while both groups have been influenced by Al-Qaeda (a foreign force), neither is likely to come under Al-Qaeda's umbrella and, as will be demonstrated in this project, LeT will not sacrifice its independence like other terrorist groups have in Pakistan and the Middle East. Second, while LeT relies on criminals within D-Company for logistical (and occasional operational) support for terrorist activities in IHK and throughout India, this partnership does not suffer from the same vulnerabilities as its counterparts in Iraq as there is considerable ideological overlap between LeT, D-Company and the Pakistani state despite differences in core business practices. Third, as D-Company is the undisputed kingpin of organized criminal activity in India, Pakistan and the rest of South Asia, LeT likely does not have to worry about clashes with smaller, less powerful syndicates that could potentially jeopardize its interests and/or abilities to carry out uninterrupted operations within India. In addition, unlike Al-Qaeda, whose presence in Iraq was resented by many, LeT and D-Company enjoy a positive image amongst many everyday Pakistanis due to their carefully crafted images depicting them as being on the frontline against a hostile Hindu India in Kashmir. This is especially true regarding LeT and played a critical role in enabling the group to operate in the open while receiving state patronage for decades.

2 Misgovernance and proxy warfare in Kashmir

Laying the groundwork for the crime–terror nexus

Introduction

Kashmir has served as the key source of tension between Islamabad and New Delhi since British India's 1947 partition. Both nations have fought several wars over the former kingdom and the region still serves as South Asia's most volatile flashpoint. The conflict has inflicted tremendous social, political and economic damage on all three parties (the Indians, Pakistanis and Kashmiris) and no solution is in sight. As such, Kashmir remains perennially unstable despite the presence of nearly 700,000 Indian troops. Human rights abuses such as rape, extrajudicial killings and forced disappearances by Indian troops are not uncommon while attacks staged by Islamabad-backed terrorist groups rarely miss civilians and often target them directly. The end result has been an alienated local population and small-scale power vacuums due to ungoverned space that greatly facilitated the development of the trilateral relationship between organized criminal syndicates such as D-Company and Pakistan-backed LeT.

The Kashmir conflict developed out of competing ideologies and approaches to nation-building with New Delhi maintaining its claim on Kashmir to demonstrate its secular credentials while Islamabad feels that, as a Muslim-majority state, the territory is a natural part of Pakistan, the supposed homeland for South Asian Muslims.[1] However, some feel that despite the fact that Pakistani leaders often cite Kashmir as the primary issue between India and Pakistan, Pakistan's policy is actually driven by a deeper fear of India and by Pakistan's national identity. Former Boston University professor and Pakistan's current ambassador to the United States, Hussain Haqqani, elaborates:

> The growth of Islamic militancy and the pre-eminence of the military in Pakistani society and the rise of Hindutva in India have rendered the conflict more intractable. In short, Pakistani nationhood has become predicated on balancing the perceived Indian (or Hindu) domination of South Asia, and Kashmir has become a symptom rather than the fundamental cause of Pakistan's troubled relationship with India.[2]

The International Crisis Group seems to forward this view by claiming that when relations between Islamabad and New Delhi improve, the conflict is placed on the backburner. However, some Pakistani governments have utilized the Kashmir conflict to reinforce Pakistani nationalism, encourage pan-Islamism, raise domestic support or ensure regime survival.[3] The think tank also believes that the potential for another crisis in Kashmir remains high as mutual distrust and hostility continue to exist and both nations remain rigid on their positions and are averse to flexibility.[4] Misra cleverly highlights the disconnect between the two by stating that, for Pakistan, the dispute is the 'problem of Kashmir' and is part of an 'unfinished agenda' of Partition. On the other hand, India views the situation as the 'problem in Kashmir', thus suggesting that the accession of Indian-Held Kashmir (IHK) to India is final and that the main issue is now combating cross-border terrorism and addressing development issues and the grievances of the people within a constitutional framework.[5]

The dispute subsided temporarily following Islamabad's defeat during the 1971 Indo-Pakistan war and the subsequent development of Indian conventional superiority. Between 1971 and 1989, Pakistani leaders only made verbal references to the disputed territory. As such, many in New Delhi erroneously believed that the issue was quashed. However, these assumptions proved false in 1989 when a predominantly indigenous insurgency exploded in the Kashmir Valley. This development was largely attributed to the growing political awareness of Kashmiris, improved educational opportunities and access to mass media, thus producing a generation of young Kashmiris who refused to accept the Indian shadow over most of the elections in the state. The National Conference, the then dominant political party in IHK, frequently intimidated political opponents, stuffed ballot boxes and coerced voters – often with approval from New Delhi. Pakistan seized upon this opportunity to undercut the Indian government and to avenge their loss in 1971 and began training terrorists and providing them with supplies and refuge.[6] Further assisting this effort was the fact that by 1989, the authority of the Indian state had virtually collapsed in Kashmir while at the same time Pakistan received a nuclear and missile shield from China, which emboldened Pakistan and encouraged them to engage in a proxy war in Kashmir without the fear of a major Indian military response.[7]

Ganguly reckons that Islamabad's involvement in Kashmir transformed the conflict as it began to attract fighters that were driven by more extremist ideology and greed rather than the desire to safeguard the self-determination of Kashmiri Muslims. He writes:

> During the 1990s, the insurgency in Kashmir became a well-organized, ideologically charged extortion racket and, in the process, lost support of much of the local populace. The insurgents lost popular support because of their willingness to harass, and sometimes even terrorize, the Kashmiris regardless of their religious affiliation.[8]

India was able to utilize this alienation of the local populace to turn the tide against the terrorists by adopting sound counter-insurgency tactics and by holding free and fair elections in 1996 and 2002.[9] However, although there is currently a ceasefire along the Line of Control (LOC), the region continues to be plagued by instability and low-intensity violence characterized by occasional flare-ups. An average of three people die per day in the state, largely as the result of small arms fire, and Kashmiris remain split between pro-India, pro-Pakistan and pro-independence groups.

Raju illustrates the complexities of the conflict in Kashmir:

> The voices are many and varied. One section believes in acceding Kashmir to Pakistan, another group articulates the idea of remaining independent both from India and Pakistan, while some other section desires to be part of India. In this pluralistic game, guns are superseding politics.[10]

Between 1990 and 2006, there have been over 64,200 violent attacks by terrorists against civilians and around 29,600 against Indian security forces. In addition, almost 16,000 civilians have been killed and over 20,000 injured while India's security forces claim to have suffered 4,850 casualties and more than 11,650 wounded.[11] However, despite the gradually decaying socio-political environment and unacceptably high level of violence, some in India still do not feel that a troop withdrawal or redeployment is the appropriate solution. They believe that if India were to pull back its troops from Kashmir, the over 2,000 estimated militants in IHK and the hundreds more ready for infiltration across the LOC would slip into urban centres and could only be evicted by messy urban warfare that would produce heavy civilian casualties.[12] Also, Lieutenant General A.M. Vohra, the former Vice Chief of the Indian Army, has termed ex-President Musharraf's offer of joint Indo-Pak management of Kashmir 'unimaginable'.[13]

Major motivations for India's insistence upon holding onto Kashmir are related to both economic and stability issues whereas Pakistan's are mostly ideological though some strategic issues, such as water security, also factor in. Governing a Muslim-majority state puts forth an image of secularism and thus deflects Western criticism away from India's rising Hindu nationalism. This image facilitates trade and investment and presents India as a modern, stable nation with a friendly business climate. In addition, India is home to 150 million Muslims that are dispersed unevenly throughout Indian territory and, as such, the potential for sectarian violence is always present. If India were to relent on Kashmir, other separatist movements could emerge from other minority groups such as the Sikhs, Tamils or a myriad of groups in the northeast. Also, any concession on Kashmir could likely bring about anti-Muslim violence by right-wing Hindu groups and even some elements within the Indian security apparatus.[14] Conversely, Pakistan seems equally determined to retain their claim on Kashmir as Pakistan was carved out of

British India in order to serve as a homeland for South Asia's Muslims. If a Muslim-majority Kashmir can continue to exist on Pakistan's borders, it implies that Muslims can also find a home in India, thus undermining Pakistan's fundamental reason for existence.[15]

Indian misrule

Indian-American scholar Ganguly argues that the insurgency that began in Kashmir was due to a lack of appropriate channels to air grievances and address concerns, a clear example of Indian misgovernance. Also, as Kashmiris became more educated, they became more keenly aware of their situation, especially vis-à-vis the rest of India. Ganguly writes:

> The insurgency is fraught with considerable theoretical and policy significance. At a theoretical level it demonstrates the dangers that states face when political mobilization occurs against a backdrop of institutional decay. The failure of governments to accommodate rising political demands within an institutional context can culminate in political violence.[16]

It is interesting to note that in 1965 Ayub Khan, Pakistan's first military dictator, launched Operation Gibraltar with the intent to spark an insurgency in Kashmir by taking advantage of the less-than-ideal conditions of the state. The state had experienced rioting and anti-Indian sentiment was undoubtedly present. However, despite the well-organized effort, no insurgency took place. It is also noteworthy that Hindus and Muslims had lived side by side in Kashmir for hundreds of years and had experienced three wars between India and Pakistan (1947–8, 1965 and 1971) without significant inter-religious violence. In regards to Operation Gibraltar, Ganguly wonders if the Kashmiris were indeed a 'captive' ethno-national group as many Pakistani decision-makers believed, then why did the Kashmiris not revolt against New Delhi when presented with such an opportunity?[17] A new and untested prime minister was in office, southern India had experienced riots over the declaration of Hindi as the national language, and the Indian Army had just been recently humiliated by China. On top of this, arms and other forms of assistance were available from the thousands of Pakistani troops who had infiltrated into the state.[18]

A lack of political sophistication, literacy, education and exposure to mass media all explain the missing motivation to engage in armed rebellion despite the fact that abuses of the democratic system, such as vote rigging, were occurring much as they were in the late 1980s. Although the political mobilization of the Kashmiris began later than in the rest of India, its institutional decay began much earlier in the 1950s. As Kashmiri political awareness dramatically increased after the 1970s, these 'two trends intersected as a new generation of Kashmiris emerged on the political scene'.[19] Further, as the authority of New Delhi over Kashmir began to erode, the Hindu community began to fear attacks from Muslim insurgents while many Muslim civilians that were not involved in the insurgency started to fear retaliation attacks from displaced Hindus.[20] This mutual suspicion and fear of the intentions of the other can cause members of a particular group to act irrationally, thus potentially tipping off a dangerous reciprocating cycle of violence that further polarizes communities and adds to destabilization. As has been demonstrated by Ganguly, this ethnic–religious divide is a recent development in Kashmir and is partially attributable to Indian misrule.

Some believe that the Kashmiris still lack viable representation: 'Politics in the Kashmir Valley and other Muslim-majority areas of IJK (IHK) are marked by gamesmanship, fleeting alliances of convenience, and personality politics. Means for aggregating collective Kashmiri political interests have been elusive'.[21] This lack of a viable alternative to Islamabad or New Delhi only adds to feelings of hopelessness and an absence of the right to self-determination. Faced with poverty and the prospect of their home serving as a battleground for India and Pakistan's competing ideologies and interests indefinitely, many young Kashmiris may be the only ones who not have much vested interest in the fate of Kashmir. This will undoubtedly cause some to conclude that the current mainstream political and economic arrangements are dysfunctional and beyond repair and they will seek to move in a new direction, which is likely to be independence. As such, groups that at least claim to share this view and are perceived to have the motivation and means to achieve their objectives are set to benefit. In this case, these groups are outfits like LeT as well as D-Company. Further, these groups can serve as a source of employment and income generation as their logistical networks require continuous maintenance and diversification.

This fragmentation is at least partially due to interference by New Delhi and Islamabad as both have jostled for influence in IHK. The rigged elections in 1987 discouraged many Kashmiris from participation in democratic politics and the brutal crackdown executed by the New Delhi-backed Governor of IHK during the initial stages of the insurgency furthered that alienation. Although India often points the finger at Pakistan regarding the human rights abuses of dissenters in the state, India's use of arbitrary arrests, extrajudicial and custodial killings, torture and the use of violent irregular outfits are well documented.[22] Also, the rigged 1987 elections radicalized Kashmiri youth and sparked cross-border exfiltration into Pakistan-Held Kashmir and eventually the largely indigenous Hizbul Mujahedeen and other Kashmiri groups came back across the LOC along with foreign fighters to wage an insurgency in the state. These occurrences laid the groundwork that would later be seized upon by other jihadi groups following the termination of the proxy war against the Soviet Union in Afghanistan as well as D-Company and their state backers in Pakistan thus facilitating this trilateral nexus.[23]

Many Kashmiris, especially those in the Valley, still choose not to take part in elections due to perceptions of bad governance and suspicion of vote rigging. According to a study conducted by the Institute of Peace and Conflict Studies in August 2002, 81 per cent of the Kashmir Valley felt that the 2002 state elections were going to be rigged.[24] However, in late 2008 IHK witnessed relatively clean elections which saw the election of Omar Abdullah of the pro-India National Conference Party. Turnout in most Muslim-majority constituencies was over 50 per cent, slightly higher than in 2002.[25] Nonetheless, Srinagar saw a turnout of around the same rate at the 2002 elections: 10 per cent.[26] This clear lack of trust in the Indian democratic system within critical segments of the Kashmiri population is a major challenge for New Delhi's counter-insurgency strategy in the state. Unless New Delhi can make headway with the Muslim population in IHK and convince them that they have a viable partner in New Delhi, instability will remain and disaffected Kashmiris, namely youths, will continue to join militant groups or criminal syndicates and a section of the local population (and critically, the middle classes) will at least remain apathetic to these activities. Further, while India's policy and approach towards IHK may remain static, LeT, D-Company and their supporters in the Pakistani security apparatus certainly are not. Recognizing that fighting in Kashmir is an indispensable component of its image, LeT is continuing to expand its operations in the disputed territory and throughout India using D-Company infrastructure in India and, at a minimum, Pakistan's tolerance of LeT's activities inside the country. As will be shown, this three-way dynamic is very fluid and power is shifting in the direction of LeT and away from Islamabad, LeT's former patron, and is taking D-Company along with it as almost a type of junior partner when it comes to terrorist activity while not raising any issues over Ibrahim's primary concentration on organized criminal activity. While elements of Shelley's symbiotic relationship are certainly present, this is a new dynamic that has not been analysed before.

Political engagement between Islamabad and New Delhi has been half hearted at best and hampered by impatience on behalf of New Delhi accompanied by demands for immediate, but impossible, results from separatist leaders. The reason for this haste is that many Indian strategists view Kashmiris as agents of a larger proxy war between India and Pakistan. This approach completely ignores IHK's unique status within the Indian Union and also violates the state's terms of accession. As a result, the issue of the restoration of IHK's special status is possibly intentionally confused with the debate over the legitimacy of India and Pakistan's respective claims over the whole of Kashmir.[27] Also, any concession to the requests of the local populace is considered by New Delhi as a concession to Pakistan.[28] The notion of being used as a pawn in a larger strategic chess match can not only lead to frustration and humiliation, but can also greatly weaken, if not detach entirely, psychological connections to the state. If this crucial connection is somehow severed, this factor combined with a lack of legitimate upward mobility and a sense of hopelessness regarding the future will undoubtedly result in at least a segment of the population serving as a ready pool of recruits for acts of terrorism as well as criminal activity.

There is also concern that some governments in New Delhi will not honour the promises made by previous administrations. For example, in 1999 and 2000, the state government submitted proposals to the National Democratic Alliance in New Delhi for ways to restore IHK's autonomy within the Indian Union. These proposals were rejected on the grounds that they were not bound by the promises of previous governments to re-establish the autonomy of Jammu and Kashmir. If negotiations for autonomy do take place, can any current Indian government provide credible assurances that a future regime will not backtrack and renege on previous agreements?[29] In addition, National Conference President, Omar Abdullah, has even claimed that New Delhi actively seeks instability in Kashmir and has backed unstable regimes in order to justify its continued presence in the state.[30] However, by refusing to allow legitimate opposition parties, the National Conference played a role in stoking instability themselves.[31]

Since 1990, Jammu and Kashmir has witnessed wide-scale human rights abuses by the Indian security forces, which include the Army, the Central Reserve Police Force and the paramilitary Border Security Force. Torture is frequently used during combing operations[32] and also occurs frequently in Army camps, interrogation centres, police stations, as well as prisons. Further, indiscriminate beatings and rape are routine and rape has been systematically employed in order to humiliate and intimidate the local population into submission.[33] Also, there are widespread accusations regarding the existence of up to 1,000 mass graves, something that is particularly appalling to Muslims.[34] Abuses by Indian security forces, although they are aimed at subduing the local civilian populace and forcing them to accept Indian rule, actually run counter to these aims and assist the recruitment efforts by Pakistan-backed militant groups. Much as Pakistan was able to capitalize on the frustration of Kashmiris regarding their exclusion from the democratic process, victims of violent abuses often provide motivated, revenge-hungry insurgents. Even if Pakistan does cease its involvement in IHK, if criminal acts by Indian security forces such as rape and torture continue unabated, an indigenous insurgency and general resistance to Indian rule will remain. This will result in continued instability and a favourable working environment for organized crime as well as terrorist groups that engage in illicit activities in order to finance their operations.

Fake encounters[35] by Indian security forces continue to plague the state, thus harming counter-insurgency efforts. In addition, official enquiry into custodial killings is hampered by a number of factors. First, the Armed Forces Special Powers Act makes it compulsory to gain permission from the central government before beginning proceedings against any Army personnel involved in human rights abuses but permission is rarely granted. Also, the Special Operations Group (SOG), despite the fact that it has officially been disbanded, continues to exist and it is unclear as to whom they are accountable. The SOG's organizational structure and operating methods are not transparent and there is concern that it can continue to function even if the special powers of the armed forces are suspended. Further, sections of the police have become involved in fake encounters with the most likely motivation being to obtain awards.[36] A security force that can operate with impunity combined with a profit/benefit driven police force could cause many Kashmiris to turn to terrorist groups not because of shared ideology, but due to necessity. It can also lead many Kashmiris to conclude that the Indian security apparatus in the state is corrupt and/or ineffective and prompt them to take the law into their own hands. This will inevitably lead to inner-communal rivalries and increased violence; something that is highly ironic given the initial intent. Human rights abuses such as fake encounters greatly erode the credibility of New Delhi as well as the Indian security forces, thus leaving a space to be filled by terrorist groups, criminal gangs and other non-state actors, some of which are backed by Pakistan. As this situation continues, the roots of this dynamic continue to grow deeper and become more ingrained in the basic fabric of society. However, unlike in the past, Islamabad now often finds itself on the outside looking in when it comes to LeT's decision-making and its coordination with D-Company thus removing a critical inhibitor on extreme acts of violence, such as the November 2008 Mumbai attacks, and a degree of predictability and control regarding terrorist activities in IHK.

Happenings outside of Kashmir also impede New Delhi's counter-insurgency efforts. For example, LeT sought to capitalize on events such as the demolition of the Babri Masjid in Ayodhya in 1992 and the anti-Muslim riots in Gujarat in 2002 to rally Indian Muslims towards a pan-Islamic cause.[37] In both of these incidents, the central and state governments were accused of apathy in taking adequate steps to protect Muslims. In the case of Gujarat, there were even signs of active government complicity with the Hindu mobs. Although these events occurred outside of Kashmir, they nonetheless dealt blows to India's claims of secularism and equal protection under the law.

Surprisingly, within IHK there exist isolated areas that remain out of New Delhi's reach, something which is quite paradoxical considering the heavy presence of Indian troops. However, as opposed to making efforts to extend the writ of the Indian state to these areas through the construction of roads and other infrastructure projects, New Delhi raised Village Defense Committees (VDCs) and has provided them with arms. This is problematic for a wide range of reasons. For one, involving civilians expands the scope of the conflict and also makes them targets for terrorist attacks. Second, arming and training the local population militarizes society through increasing the flow of arms from both legal and illegal channels. Lastly, by asking citizens to defend themselves, the state is admitting its inability to protect its own citizens.[38]

Another problem scenario for the Kashmir impasse is the potential rise of the Bharatiya Janata Party (BJP) into power by gaining either a majority in parliament, successfully placing its candidates into top leadership positions, or both. Despite having engaged in a comprehensive dialogue with Pakistan during its previous stint in power, the BJP has traditionally favoured a military solution over a political resolution to the Kashmir conflict and has been unwilling to compromise.[39] If the BJP is to gain influence or even top leadership positions in future elections, it could very well set back years of painstaking diplomacy between India and Pakistan to provide at least a degree of stability in Kashmir while also accelerating the trend of LeT expanding its activities throughout India by using D-Company infrastructure without bothering to consult Islamabad, as was the case in the past. There are elements within the BJP that are virulently anti-Pakistan and many argue that they advocate Hindu-favoured policies and do not view Muslims as legitimate citizens of India. If the BJP does indeed take control of parliament and the armed forces, they will likely implement more aggressive policies in Kashmir that focus more on physically eliminating terrorists and enhancing security across the LOC rather than addressing the political, economic and social grievances that are critical components of any counter-insurgency strategy and have served as critical enablers for LeT, D-Company and their Pakistani state patrons in the past. Unfortunately, based on previous behaviour, it appears that the BJP views the Kashmir issue through a more narrow, nationalistic lens and does not possess the comprehensive vision necessary to achieve sustainable progress towards the resolution of this issue. If the BJP comes into power again without an evolution in its thinking towards the Kashmir dispute, it could prompt LeT to further expand its campaign throughout the whole of India and the few rational voices in Pakistan who warn of the dangers associated with LeT and D-Company would be silenced by the groundswell of jingoism and anti-India sentiment.

If the BJP's past actions can be used as a precedent, their policies will likely lead to further destabilization of the disputed territory and will actually in many ways assist D-Company and LeT. Poorly trained and undisciplined Indian troops and paramilitaries with a more aggressive mandate will inevitably result in increased abductions, rapes, torture and civilian casualties as Indian forces comb civilian populations while searching for terrorists. These actions will also seemingly validate Pakistan's claim that the Indian Army is a Hindu-dominated occupying force that is not as interested in the well-being of Muslims as they are in securing the strategic interests of New Delhi. They may also infringe upon the already-fragile democratic process in IHK. As a result, LeT and, to a lesser extent, D-Company could be viewed as a lesser of two evils within critical segments of the Kashmiri population, namely in Srinagar, and this would prove disastrous for India's counter-insurgency efforts.

Despite the generally negative prognosis, there is one potentially positive development within India that could at least cool the flames in Kashmir. After conducting hundreds of field interviews with individuals across various occupations in the Indian cities of New Delhi, Kolkata, Mumbai and Hyderabad, Raju concluded that although many first and second generation Indians place a strong emphasis of regaining the whole of Kashmir, the younger generation prefers to see the issue resolved peacefully and feel that Kashmir-associated military spending would be better spent on economic development. He also feels that the third generation is less emotional about the issue and do not feel the same animosity towards Pakistan.[40] This new, younger generation of leaders could very well produce more rational policies that are driven by pragmatism rather than nationalist/religious fervour. Nonetheless, during the 15 to 20 years that will elapse while this third generation develops as leaders, there is plenty of time for continued mismanagement and proxy warfare that results in further destabilization and a more ingrained culture of violence and terrorism, organized crime and a general sense of hopelessness regarding the future. The current leadership on both sides of the border must be careful not to damage Kashmir beyond repair. However, as long as the policies of New Delhi and Islamabad remain hostage to domestic pressure and greater strategic objectives at the expense of Kashmiris, the continuation of a distressed state is a very real possibility.

Pakistan's proxy warfare

In addition to importing foreign fighters into Kashmir, Pakistan also introduced fundamentalist imams into many mosques for *tabligh* (religious indoctrination) and thus displaced many local Kashmiri imams who largely advocated an indigenous culture and tolerant view of Islam. Eventually, a wider network of mosques fell under extremist influence and began to galvanize Kashmiri Muslims for jihad against Indian rule. After having largely cleared Kashmir Valley of Hindus, gained control of the local media and damaged many administrative and political structures, terrorists began to exert their influence over the local Muslim population. Warikoo claims that thousands of young Kashmiri Muslims were forced across the LOC to undergo training in camps in PHK, Pakistan and Afghanistan, with select groups being taken to advanced training camps on the Pak-Afghan border. He claims that thousands of Kashmiri youth that resisted were tortured or even killed while a series of assassinations and bomb attacks on moderate Kashmiri leaders claimed the lives of many more. These attacks sought to destroy the established political structures and to thwart the process of the restoration of democracy. They have even attempted to banish 'un-Islamic' practices such as visiting ancient holy shrines of *sufis* and *rishis*, traditions that have long been part of the Kashmiri form of Islam.[41] However, in Warikoo's analysis, he seems to assume that there was indeed an established, functional political structure as well as a general effort to revitalize democracy in the state. As has previously been seen, this was not the case.

The possibility of the establishment of an Islamic caliphate that spanned from Kashmir to Pakistan through Afghanistan and Central Asia was actively being discussed by terrorist groups in Kashmir at the time of the Soviet withdrawal and the emergence of the Muslim-majority Central Asian Republics from the ruins of the USSR. This idea of pan-Islamism is what strengthened the bond between Islamic terrorists in Kashmir and the Afghan militias.[42] During this same period, the relationship between the extremist mullahs and the Pakistani Army was beginning to become solidified under the Islamic hard-line military dictator, General Zia ul-Haq.[43] However, at this point in time none of Pakistan's irregulars had a local partner like D-Company or access to a logistical network that spanned throughout India. It is largely through the introduction of D-Company into the equation that inadvertently prompted the decline in Islamabad's influence over their proxies such as LeT.

IHK is most likely to remain a stalemate for the foreseeable future. Reinforcing this stalemate is the fact that a standstill is actually more attractive to some of the involved parties than bringing about a solution. For example, the Kashmir dispute has allowed the Pakistani military to tie down Indian forces in order to offset India's conventional superiority and to equalize the military balance. Stephen Cohen has said that 'Pakistan is willing to fight India to the last Kashmiri'.[44] Pakistan's willingness to sacrifice the security of a population that they claim to defend in order to further Islamabad's foreign policy objectives vis-à-vis India will only lead to the further destruction of the former kingdom. As Pakistan refuses to halt its use of proxy terrorists and as religious zealots in the Pakistani political and military establishment advocate continued low-level hostilities, a steady process of destabilization will continue. With no end in sight and no reliable peace partner in the region, Kashmir will remain fertile ground for not only terrorism, but also for weapons trafficking and organized crime. Similar developments have been seen in places such as Russia's breakaway provinces of Ingushetia, Chechnya and Dagestan. Although these conflicts claim to have their roots in the fight for Muslim self-determination, the continued fighting with neither side able to claim a victory has allowed organized crime, narcotics and weapons trafficking, and targeted killings to flourish. These developments are associated with the subsequent political and security fallout that tends to follow indecisive bloodletting. Low-intensity conflicts (LICs) such as those in southern Russia and Kashmir devastate civilian infrastructure, including their often-fragile economies, but do not bring about positive outcomes or better prospects for the future.

Ironically, Islamabad's attempts to 'free' the Kashmiris have done more to ensure their continued marginalization and second-class bystander status rather than increase their chances of having a say in their own affairs. Further, as Pakistan's non-state instruments in IHK continue to evolve, develop their own agendas and become more openly hostile to any hint of secularism in Pakistan, it would be advisable for Islamabad to cut its losses and make sincere efforts to stem the flow of materiel, funding and training to LeT and cease its tolerance of D-Company in the country; even if it involves tackling high-ranking ISI officials and their allies in other government bodies and parliament. This task may be a mountain in itself and will likely bring about additional instability (at least initially) but the benefits greatly outweigh the costs as the threats that the Kashmir-centred jihadi groups pose to the state of Pakistan itself have only just begun to materialize. The existence of groups such as LeT are now a reality, especially since they have expanded their spheres of influence and have developed partnerships with criminal syndicates. However, if Pakistan slows or ceases its supplementation of resources to these groups, Islamabad would be able to buy itself enough time to develop an effective counter-terrorism strategy that will prevent its former proxies from devouring Pakistan itself. The warning signs, such as the presence of JeM militants holed up inside the vigilante Lal Masjid in the centre of Islamabad and several assassination attempts on senior Pakistani leaders, are already present. Further, LeT's involvement in the November 2008 attacks in Mumbai could have triggered a major conventional conflict with India. Pakistan must attempt to at least minimize domestic support for these militant groups, even if it is in its own self-interest rather than a more ambivalent desire to ease tensions with India over Kashmir. Pakistan is still paying the price for its use of militants, both foreign and domestic, against the Soviet Union in Afghanistan. To repeat such a mistake is inexcusable and should invoke the sympathies of none.

The insurgency in IHK has also allowed the Pakistani Army to temporarily disengage from the Kashmir front and to focus their firepower on the insurgency in Balochistan and the Pakistani Taliban movement in FATA.[45] As neither of these internal security issues shows any signs of evaporating in the near future, Pakistan will continue to rely on terrorists who attack civilians along with the Indian security forces. Islamabad has also come to rely on Dawood Ibrahim and his Mumbai and Karachi-based D-Company to provide funding and logistical support to groups such as LeT. The use of non-state actors, who are not bound by the same constraints and deterrents as nation states, is a highly dangerous tactic that will result in indiscriminate acts of violence against civilian populations and soft targets, rights abuses and the development of alternative agendas. Also troublesome for Pakistan as well as the region, are the ethnic and linguistic commonalities between militants operating in Kashmir and in FATA. In the event of a consolidation, Pakistan would be faced with its greatest internal security challenge since independence as Islamabad would have to fight Islamist extremism not only in the NWFP, FATA and the Punjab, but also in Sindh, an area prone to sectarian, communal and other forms of political violence that is home to Karachi, Pakistan's most vital port (although the Chinese-built Gwadar port will compete in the future) and economic hub. If these events were to occur, they would be an assault on the primary pillars of the Pakistani state.

ISI has several objectives in its backing for terrorists in IHK. For one, ISI is attempting to gain more exposure for the Kashmir issue on the international scene. In addition, it appears that ISI feels that with enough backing, the terrorist groups can actually wrestle Kashmir away from Indian control. Further, transporting and arming militants, many of whom are veterans from other conflict theatres, keeps them occupied and thus prevents them from posing an internal law and order problem for Pakistan.[46] This last point is critical in that Pakistan cannot allow a situation such as the predicament in FATA and Balochistan to occur in the Punjab, Pakistan's political powerhouse and home to Pakistan's most wealthy and influential ethnic group. Although areas such as FATA and Balochistan have historically been lawless and not under effective control, the blowback that followed the Soviet withdrawal greatly exacerbated the situation. After these former 'freedom fighters' ceased to serve a purpose, they became highly trained, well-armed undesirables almost overnight. Today, kidnappings and attacks on military and police checkpoints are common occurrences in western Pakistan as the Pakistani Army still struggles to establish the writ of Islamabad over an assorted band of Pashtuns, Balochis, Uzbeks, Chechens, Arabs and various other ethnic groups who are in possession of considerable firepower. If an Afghan-type blowback were to occur in the Punjab, it could bring the Pakistani state to the brink. As such, ISI and the Pakistani political and military establishment have a crucial strategic interest in ensuring that these transnational terrorists remain focused on the Indian Union and not looking back towards the Punjab or the rest of Pakistan. Pakistan's utilization of former Afghan militiamen to wage irregular warfare in IHK is yet another example of Kashmiris being treated as agents in a larger conflict. These actions also suggest that Pakistan is willing to use Kashmir as a dumping ground. These occurrences only fuel feelings of alienation and neglect and they also help to create a permanent state of instability in Kashmir as Pakistan will continually make efforts to make sure that these fighters remain in IHK and throughout India even if the fighters themselves are becoming less and less accountable to Islamabad.

Military and civilian leaders in Pakistan often hold opposing views regarding Islamabad's approach to Kashmir but the military tends to prevail. The Pakistani military has a vested interest in seeing the Kashmir conflict continue as it justifies its absorption of nearly 25 per cent of the national budget and its control over foreign policy.[47] Some even go so far as to say that 'Pakistan's Kashmir policy has been scripted and sustained by the Pakistani Army since 1947'.[48] Ever since independence, the Pakistani military establishment has played a dominant role in politics and has overthrown several democratically elected civilian leaders, such as Nawaz Sharif in 1999 by General Musharraf. In order to maintain this privileged position within Pakistani society, an external threat must exist that will turn attention away from domestic shortcomings and prevent dissent. Although there have been a range of declared threats ranging from the Soviet Union, Pashtun nationalists in Afghanistan, to the possibility of a large-scale American invasion of FATA, India has consistently been Islamabad's most dangerous perceived adversary. As the possibility of all-out conventional or even nuclear war is not particularly eminent at present despite several unfortunate regional developments, the Pakistani Army must hold on to Kashmir or risk losing its near monopoly on power and coming under civilian control like most armies in democratic nations. Because of this, the Army prefers to see IHK remain an LIC and is willing to use irregulars and even criminal syndicates to do so. However, Islamabad has made the mistake of viewing actors such as D-Company and LeT as static organizations that do not think or act independently. The Pakistani Army may have planted the seed, but D-Company and LeT have spread their roots everywhere. As this process continues, these vested interests in Kashmir will only become more deeply ingrained.

Haqqani believes that Pakistan's approach towards Kashmir has been incoherent, plagued by short-term thinking, and has always lacked a comprehensive strategy. The Pakistani Army is not accountable to the political establishment and to this day there is a debate as to whether Sharif and his civilian advisors were aware of General Musharraf's intention to invade Kargil.[49] As the Pakistani Army still seems to only answer to itself, it can act independently of the political process. This is highly problematic in that if India does not feel that it has a trustworthy partner on the other side of the border, it will not make concessions nor will it take anything more than token steps to find a sustainable political solution to the Kashmir conflict. Also, the Pakistani Army lacks the comprehensive vision necessary to bring about positive changes in the lives of Kashmiris, as has been demonstrated by its long and well-documented history of economic mismanagement, skewed priorities and misallocation of scarce resources within Pakistan.

Pakistan's crackdown on terrorism and Islamic extremism has been selective, only focusing on a few Al-Qaeda leaders wanted by the United States or sectarian groups, such as Lashkar-e-Jhangvi, that have targeted Pakistani leaders.[50] Nonetheless, despite these concerns, some believe that Pakistan may still use Kashmiri terrorists to occupy rear positions in the event of a larger conventional conflict with India.[51] If true, Pakistan seems to view irregulars in IHK as a sort of insurance policy against India in the event that peace negotiations fail or if the military balance tips too far in India's favour. As long as Pakistan feels the acute vulnerability of a much larger neighbour with conventional military superiority, Islamabad will try to ensure that there remains at least a minimal presence of terrorists in IHK, much to the detriment of stability while also, ironically, lessening Islamabad's influence over them.

Pakistan's support for terrorists has disrupted Kashmiri political organization as terrorists have often prevented political groups in IHK from reaching peace with New Delhi independently. The Pakistani military and ISI have intimidated and assassinated pro-India political figures with the most recent being the 2002 killing of moderate All-Parties Hurriyat Conference (APHC) leader Abdul Ghani Lone.[52] Further, terrorists have been involved in the killing of pollsters, namely in 1996.[53] Also, in 2005 several winning candidates in municipal elections resigned their positions before taking office and publicly apologized for taking part in the elections as a result of terrorists' threats. Pakistan's proxy fighters have also favoured IHK's accession to Pakistan and often target Kashmiris who advocate independence.[54]

Given Pakistan's political and social instability combined with stagnant economic growth, a mergence of Kashmir and Pakistan would only bring about further unrest as many terrorist groups would return as self-perceived victors and demand a say in the governance of Kashmir or even Pakistan itself. In addition, given Pakistan's track record of dealing with minority groups and its consistent failure to extend Islamabad's writ over its current territory, Kashmiris in IHK, although the situation under New Delhi's rule is not desirable, would be much worse off as part of Pakistan. As such, the intentions of Islamabad-backed groups do not appeal to Kashmiris as the majority prefers independence.

In the mid-1990s, the Jammu and Kashmir Liberation Front, the former heavyweight amongst Kashmir-based separatist groups, fractionalized as PHK-based leader Amanullah Khan fell out with IHK-based Yasin Malik over his decision to renounce violence and during the 2002 state elections many politicians in Muslim-majority areas of Jammu colluded with terrorists to assure electoral victories.[55] The trampling of the democratic process and the criminalization of politics are the first steps of a slippery slope that leads to civil unrest and perpetual instability. The 'means to an end' approach adopted by Pakistan-leaning politicians is extremely dangerous as it erodes the rule of law; the building block of any stable, prosperous society. If some segments of society are permitted to act with impunity due to certain political affiliations, it will breed resentment and eventual hatred and with no prospects for independence in sight and a questionable arrangement with India and Pakistan, there will not be many deterrents to violence, crime and other forms of subversive behaviour. However, none of this will benefit Pakistan and can actually cause its influence to wane even further if LeT is able to diversify its presence within India.

Some of the Pakistan-sponsored terrorist groups subscribe to the same radical ideology as Al-Qaeda and the Taliban.[56] Also, many apprehended militants have stated that they became terrorists in order to kill as many Hindus as possible.[57] This strict form of Wahhabi Islam is incompatible with the less austere and more tolerant version practised by many Kashmiris. Treated poorly by a Hindu-majority India and ostracized indirectly by Islamabad for following the 'wrong kind of Islam', many Kashmiris do not respect the writ of either party, thus paving the way for a future of internecine fighting as well as flare-ups between Kashmiris, Islamic extremists and the Indian security forces. It has even been alleged that prior to 9/11, Pakistan utilized Osama bin Laden's camps to train fighters for Kashmir.[58] It has also surfaced that some Kashmiri Indians have been trained to carry out suicide bomb attacks.[59] Further, Kashmiri and foreign militants are paid for various activities such as establishing bases, marrying local women, levelling false accusations against security forces, etc.[60] This profit-driven system combined with a similar system employed by the Indian security forces can result in deeply invested economic interests on both sides and a general reluctance by either to see the conflict come to an end. This 'kill-to-earn' system is largely blamed for fake encounters by Indian security forces and as a majority of both terrorists and Indian soldiers come from low socio-economic backgrounds, Kashmir could serve as an enticing opportunity to some.

Although Pakistan finances many terrorist activities in IHK, the groups themselves also generate revenue through criminal activities such as extortion of timber contractors and shopkeepers as well as narcotics trafficking.[61] With narcotics trafficking come a variety of social ills such as organized crime, corruption and addiction. In regards to the latter, as opium poppy grows naturally in Kashmir and as heroin abuse plagues its near-neighbours in Pakistan and Afghanistan, the Kashmiri populace is vulnerable. Heroin abuse would complicate an already precarious situation and could make the task of economic development and state-building even more challenging. Islamabad's approval of the use of drug money to finance its proxy war in IHK is not only unethical, it is counterintuitive. It also will result in 'business networks' being established in the region by opportunistic traffickers of Afghan, Pakistani, Central Asian or even Indian background. Once established, these traffickers will be difficult, if not impossible, to permanently uproot. Warning signs are already present with the arrest of Indians, Pakistanis and Afghans in South Korea that were manufacturing and smuggling acetic anhydride into Afghanistan, a precursor chemical that is needed to refine morphine into heroin.[62]

Some Indian analysts claim that ISI provides legal protection to Pakistan-based drug cartels that raise funds for militant groups in IHK.[63] While this is debatable and difficult to prove beyond a reasonable doubt, the flow of drug money into Kashmir has very dangerous potential because it greatly facilitates corruption and other forms of criminality. First, as Pakistan already finds itself in the international spotlight as a result of its role in the fight against Islamic terrorism and has been accused of state involvement in trafficking in the past, the smuggling of drug proceeds into Kashmir has to be highly sophisticated and undoubtedly moves through the underground hawala system. Also, if true, the longer Islamabad uses the services of drug cartels to fund its terrorist groups, the deeper the vested interests become and the more independent groups such as LeT become due to a diversified financial pipeline. Cartels in South Asia do not remain confined to one geographic area and many forge partnerships with other syndicates and/or terrorist groups to improve upon their operational capacities and to gain access to specialized knowledge. Any cartel in South Asia primarily smuggles opium poppy and as over 90 per cent of the world's supply comes from the Afghan Taliban strongholds in southern Afghanistan, it is hard to argue that some of Pakistan's protected cartels do not have ties with the Afghan Taliban. As such, by supporting drug cartels in this volatile region, Islamabad runs the risk of further shortening the gap between the conflict in Afghanistan and Kashmir, thus adding a wide variety of variables to a complex equation. Given Afghan warlord Gulbuddin Hekmatyar's past involvement in Kashmir, a return of his pro-Pakistan Hizb-i-Islami militia or other Afghanistan-based groups cannot be ruled out.

Lastly, many foreign militants that are imported into Kashmir have criminal backgrounds and are given a promise of their charges being dropped if they agree to fight against Indian security forces.[64] The use of criminals in Kashmir is dangerous in that criminals have less of an issue with carrying out extreme acts of violence against the civilian populace and engaging in 'extracurricular' activities such as extortion, smuggling and arms and narcotics trafficking. Although terrorists do indeed take part in these activities as well, they still do depend on a local support base and must be careful not to push too far or risk compromising their greater mission of removing Kashmir from the Indian Union. However, criminals, as they are motivated primarily by self-interest, are not subject to the same deterrents. The use of both militants and criminals likely confuses the common Kashmiri as it would be highly difficult to distinguish between the two, resulting in further confusion and a sense of powerlessness.

Conclusion

Through infringements upon the democratic process, poor governance, human rights abuses and proxy warfare characterized by a lack of strategic vision and short-term thinking, India and Pakistan have played a crucial role in the destabilization of IHK and the demoralization of its civilian populace. This dilemma is compounded by a lack of indigenous leadership and the established presence of terrorist groups such as LeT and transnational criminal syndicates like D-Company, both of which enjoy backing from Pakistan. As long as Islamabad and New Delhi each view this former kingdom as a vehicle to forward their interests against the other, this pattern is unlikely to change.

Levels of terrorism may decline in the state in the near term, but unless there is a fundamental shift in the approaches of both India and Pakistan towards the issue, any improvement in the security situation will only be temporary. Abductions, rapes and killings by Indian security forces and political meddling by New Delhi only serve to alienate the local population and create a pool of recruits for terrorist groups and criminal syndicates. Likewise, importing foreign terrorists that subscribe to radical Wahhabi ideology along with self-interested criminals sends the signal to Kashmiris that they do not have a genuine ally in Pakistan either. The end result is a vast area plagued by instability, pockets of ungoverned space that can be readily utilized by subversive elements, a lack of economic development, institutions and infrastructure, and a gradual evaporation of the writ of any sovereign government and the rule of law. India cannot station such a large force in IHK indefinitely and Pakistan's use of irregulars is already starting to backfire and threaten the state itself while greatly lessening Pakistan's influence over its former proxies thus altering the trilateral relationship substantially.

Many pleas have been made by scholars, politicians, activists and others to Pakistan and India to scale back their presence in IHK and to make meaningful moves towards a peaceful settlement. When making these demands, values such as freedom, justice and self-determination are often cited. Although these aspirations are indeed admirable, they alone usually are not enough to push states that are involved in a bitter conflict that is intertwined with history, religion, culture and nationalist ideology to alter their behaviour.

India and Pakistan should make meaningful progress on Kashmir because they have to. Pakistan will not be able to weather another massive influx of militants and the Rs.40 million that India spends every day on maintaining its troop presence in the state would be much better spent on economic and social development. Further, India's patience with the actions of Pakistan-backed militant groups in IHK and throughout India is nearing its end. As Pakistan's proxies become more transnational in character, they are beginning to exhibit more independence in their decision-making and the power dynamic is shifting dramatically. Another highly visible or symbolic attack on the Indian state by a terrorist group, even if it was not ordered by Islamabad itself, has the potential to trigger a large-scale conflict that would negate many gains made by both states in the contemporary period and will make the goals of regional integration and the development of SAARC as a powerful regional security and trade bloc even more distant and seemingly unattainable. Despite the fact that many frown upon the citation of self-interest as a primary reason for moving towards peace, it is the single greatest motivator in international relations.

This chapter has aimed to provide a comprehensive analysis of the actions and policies of the military and political establishment in both India and Pakistan as well as non-state actors in order to demonstrate how the groundwork was created for the establishment of the crime–terror nexus with Pakistani support in IHK. It has also demonstrated how what was an initially nationalist rebellion was gradually transformed into a violent Islamist insurgency and how Islamabad, with its aims to escalate the conflict to a certain level, actually inadvertently decreased its own relevance when it comes to LeT strategic decision-making and its activities not only in IHK, but throughout India. Now that we understand the context, the next chapter will get more into the 'nuts and bolts' of the arms trafficking network in IHK that is likely controlled by D-Company to ensure a continuous flow of small arms and light weapons to LeT. This will shed additional light on the nature of the symbiotic relationship between LeT and D-Company while clearly highlighting the fact that D-Company is still primarily driven by the profit motive, thus adding a new dynamic to Shelley's model.

3 The crime–terror nexus and Chinese arms in Indian-Held Kashmir[1]

Overview and history of organized crime in India

India has a long history of organized crime, contrary to the popular belief that it is a fairly recent, post-independence phenomenon. For example, throughout Indian history *Zamindars* kept private armies called *Lathaits* and *Paiks* that assisted in rent collection and forceful land acquisitions.[2] Interestingly, illegal land grabs, construction and evictions still constitute a major criminal racket in India today, especially in Mumbai. Modern-day organized crime in Mumbai has its roots in opium smuggling into China in the pre-colonial period (1790–1830) and two of the major ports involved were Mumbai and Karachi with Mumbai eventually assuming the role of primary hub of opium smuggling into China. Most firms involved in trafficking activities were indigenous and operated independently of the British though some dispute this claim.[3]

Prior to the 1980s, India's economy was highly regulated with restrictive national tariff and foreign exchange policies, thus providing extensive smuggling opportunities for organized criminal syndicates. However, after trade liberalization many former black market items were no longer profitable. Nonetheless, routes had been established and Indian organized crime groups adjusted to meet other market demands.[4] Today, organized crime groups in India engage in arms and narcotics trafficking, extortion, contract killings, protection money, numerous activities related to illegal real estate transactions, film financing, and have also now begun to become involved in sectarian and terrorist activity. Although syndicates operate all over India, the financial capital of Mumbai is home to the most powerful. Syndicates such as D-Company have extended their sphere of influence into a wide range of endeavours and are accused of fostering corrupt relationships with politicians, high-ranking government and police officials, as well as Mumbai's business leaders while also working with Pakistan-based LeT to carry out attacks within India itself. Organized crime in Mumbai is unique in that almost all of its activities, whether they are contract killings or bombings, are directed from overseas.[5] Further, as Muslims currently dominate the underworld in Mumbai, ties between syndicates in Pakistan and India are strong. This relationship leads to an increase in smuggling by sea and adds to the black market arms that are regularly smuggled from Pakistan into Rajasthan and Gujarat as criminal syndicates are undoubtedly in control of the rampant arms trafficking in India and Pakistan and use the profits to finance their other operations.[6] It is noteworthy that both of these states have a close geographical proximity to Kashmir. This is highly problematic as it has been demonstrated in the past that once weapons are trafficked into India, it is not exceptionally difficult to transfer them to different regions within the country.

In India, cross-border small arms trafficking is a major concern for the Border Security Force (BSF) and India's other paramilitaries with sizeable seizures being made throughout the 1990s up until recent times with the largest seizures being made on India's border with Pakistan. As such, researchers have concluded that arms trafficking in India is a well-organized criminal activity that occurs by all modes of travel (land, air, sea), and that these events have a direct impact on Indian national security, especially given the low-intensity conflicts (LICs) that India suffers from. A clear illustration of the problem is a February 1996 case in New Delhi in which an Iranian national residing in Pakistan and a Turkish national were arrested in possession of a caravan carrying 361 .30 calibre Chinese-made Norinco pistols, 728 magazines and 3,738 live rounds. The investigation confirmed that this shipment was the second transfer with the first being successfully delivered in 1995. When all was said and done, 22 arrests were made, including three Pakistanis and 17 Indians. The basic fact that these weapons from Pakistan could reach New Delhi by road, which involved avoiding a myriad of law enforcement agencies, is very troubling and demonstrates a clear need to strengthen India's border security. IHK is also particularly vulnerable to cross-border arms trafficking and the BSF regularly seizes AK series rifles, heavy machine guns, pistols and revolvers, rocket launchers, rifles, magazines and ammunition.[7]

The Indo-Pak border is highly susceptible to drug trafficking. In the early 1980s Punjab was wracked by narco-terrorism organized by the Sikh extremist Khalistan movement and massive quantities of arms and narcotics were smuggled across the border. Although the Khalistan movement has greatly weakened (but not disappeared entirely), the narcotics smugglers appear to have remained. In January 2001, the Indian Directorate of Revenue Intelligence, Amritsar (Punjab) Regional Unit seized 17,900 kilograms of Pakistani heroin from a truck and in April the same year, 17,000 kilograms of South Asian heroin was seized in New Delhi.[8] Seizures of this magnitude are usually a reflection of a problem of a much larger scale rather than a decapitating blow to a trafficking syndicate. The instance of the 17,900 kilogram seizure of Pakistani heroin in Punjab is troubling in that not only does Punjab border IHK, it also shows the sheer size of cargo that can be smuggled into India. Heroin is not difficult to conceal and neither are small arms and if 17,900 kilograms of heroin can enter India, so can a similar sized shipment of light weapons.

Similar to other subversive organizations in South Asia, syndicates like D-Company have begun to blur the line between strictly profit-seeking criminal activities and ideologically driven acts of terrorism though D-Company is the only syndicate known to attack its own country. Recent attacks in South Asia demonstrate that 'criminal networks and terrorist groups may be deeply intertwined in ways that go well beyond fleeting, tactical alliances of convenience'.[9] Terrorist groups in South Asia now appear to be dependent upon criminal syndicates for the provision of arms and munitions to enable them to engage in attacks and continue insurgencies. Further, the relationship between the two groups is businesslike, with militant groups being permitted to use the smuggling routes of the syndicates while the criminal groups receive weapons and explosives training and are allowed safe passage though militant-held territory.[10] Such partnerships also help to ensure operational security and to avoid overdependence on one particular state sponsor. As such, students of terrorism in South Asia must recognize that organized crime and terrorism are no longer mutually exclusive categories and that most distinctions are artificial.

D-Company: size, scale and scope

Dawood Ibrahim Kaskar was born in Ratnagiri, on the Konkan coast of Mumbai, in 1955. He was one of ten children born to Ibrahim Kaskar, a police constable. Dawood started off as a small-time smuggler but began to rise in the late 1970s and early 1980s following the imposition of the 1975 emergency order in Mumbai that was designed to crack down on mainstream organized criminal syndicates. Ibrahim's rise led to a conflict with a Pashtun gang from Afghanistan lead by Karim Lala and this clash of interests resulted in the killing of Ibrahim's brother Sabir in 1981. In response, Ibrahim had Amirzada Pathan (a chief of Lala's gang) killed in court as he was being led to the witness box. Shortly after, in 1984 (although this year is disputed) Ibrahim fled to Dubai, where he had established a strong relationship with those involved in gold smuggling.[11]

Ibrahim flourished in Dubai and was in charge of a wide range of operations prior to the 1993 Mumbai Blasts and his subsequent move to Pakistan. However, Ibrahim is still able to manage his criminal network in India while residing overseas and is in possession of considerable money and influence. He also maintains networks with smaller groups in addition to his own group in order to continue to function within Mumbai.[12] Further, following the 1993 Mumbai Blasts, Ibrahim now has extremists under his command and has established strong bases not only in Dubai and Karachi, but also in Kathmandu and Hong Kong.[13] As such, Ibrahim would have to have at least an understanding with the Triads in order to operate in Hong Kong. Although many of D-Company's illicit activities in China's Special Administrative Region are likely financial and demonstrate the syndicate's continued prioritization of profit-generating activities, it would be naïve to discount cooperation in other areas such as weapons and narcotics trafficking. The Triads are active in both activities and have extensive connections in Mainland China, thus providing them with access to a wide variety of illicit material. Hong Kong, like Dubai and Karachi, is a major financial centre whose port regulation practices are questionable. Corruption is rife in China and would be a very attractive area for D-Company to engage in trafficking activity. Also, following 9/11 Ibrahim is believed to have moved some of his operations from the UAE to Saudi Arabia after the UAE began to increasingly extradite wanted persons to India and signed an extradition treaty with the United States.[14] Many of the Kashmir-based terrorist groups receive substantial funding from Saudi Arabian Wahhabis. In addition to the UAE and Pakistan, Saudi Arabia would provide another source of revenue generation which Ibrahim could then in turn use to directly finance the insurgency in IHK or to provide insurgents with weapons.

Within India, Ibrahim is the head of the 'Supari Commerce', or contract killings, and his syndicate has operations in many Indian cities such as New Delhi, Goa, Bangalore, Hyderabad, Ahmedabad and several cities in Uttar Pradesh, all of which are involved in the business of organized crime the vast majority of the time though this infrastructure is occasionally used to either facilitate or actually carry out terrorist activity. However, D-Company's Indian headquarters remains in Mumbai although the organization is believed to have fractionalized somewhat within India. Within D-Company, there are specific individuals who specialize in arms and weaponry. These individuals not only acquire arms and ammunition through contacts with terrorists, smugglers and arms traffickers, but, as was demonstrated by the 1993 Mumbai bombings, also possess expertise in clandestine storage. While these services have been developed with the objective of strengthening the syndicate's ability to carry out crimes, they are also ideal for LeT's mission in IHK. As it is a proscribed outfit in Pakistan, weaponry from the Pakistani military establishment would not be quite as readily available as it once was (but likely still available, given the autonomy of ISI). Further, due to India's 600,000–700,000 strong military presence in the state, arms smuggling operations would need to be highly sophisticated and superbly networked. While other Indian criminal syndicates have the ability to engage in smaller scale transnational arms trafficking, none aside from D-Company have the demonstrated ability to consistently smuggle into Kashmir on a large scale nor are other syndicates willing to assist Pakistan-based terrorist groups in attacking their own country, India. In these regards, D-Company is truly unique and in a dubious class of its own. In addition, as the current conflict in IHK has been declared a LIC, secure weapons storage is a necessity for LeT in order to wage irregular warfare against Indian forces and to ensure that they are adequately armed in the event of a flare-up in hostilities, thus demonstrating the dual use nature of this skill. Many of the arms caches that are discovered by Indian security forces in IHK include substantial portions of Chinese-made pistols, automatic rifles, grenades and landmines.

Ibrahim's estimated net worth is US$430 million and his syndicate has between 4,000 and 5,000 members, half of whom are believed to hail from Mumbai. Ibrahim was designated as an international terrorist by the United States for allowing Al-Qaeda to use his smuggling routes to evacuate fighters from Afghanistan and for cooperating with terrorist groups such as LeT.[15] Ibrahim and Chota Shakeel have even been accused of meeting Osama bin Laden outside of Kabul in August 1999.[16] When Deputy Prime Minister L.K. Advani visited Washington DC in June 2003, he told US leaders that 'Dawood Ibrahim has the same resonance in India as Osama bin Laden has in the U.S.'.[17] Further, during a visit by high-ranking US Treasury officials to Pakistan in September 2003, Islamabad was presented with strong evidence regarding Ibrahim's involvement with terror networks such as Al-Qaeda and LeT and it has been said that the man in charge of Ibrahim's narcotics network, Pashtun drug lord Ibrahim Khan, was aligned to Mahullah Dadullah, who was a close associate of Taliban commander Mullah Omar. There is also evidence that demonstrates that Ibrahim has directly financed LeT by channelling funds through front charities established by LeT and that these funds were used to carry out attacks in Gujarat.[18] Despite D-Company's involvement with groups like LeT and the Afghan Taliban, the syndicate's primary goal is purely financial and profit-focused but is not opposed to also involving itself in terrorist activity. This helps to solidify its ties with LeT, maintain its image as being a defender of Indian Muslims, and to ensure that the D-Company leadership continues to become increasingly more difficult to evict from Pakistan in the future as it is viewed as a strategic asset by some in Pakistan's security establishment. All of this is beneficial for D-Company's long-term business interests.

D-Company previously boasted membership from both the Hindu and Muslim community and did not demonstrate any interest in sectarian or terrorist activity. However the 1992 anti-Muslim riots in Mumbai initiated the fractionalization of the group and the 1993 Mumbai Blasts resulted in a split along religious lines although some Hindu criminals do still support Ibrahim. In 1994, Chota Rajan, a former high-ranking Hindu member of D-Company, left for Kuala Lumpur and took much of D-Company's Hindu leadership with him. In response, Ibrahim sent a hit squad to kill Rajan while Rajan dispatched contract killers to Karachi to eliminate Ibrahim. However, following an attack on Rajan in Bangkok, he has gone into hiding. As a result, Ibrahim's Muslim gang has become much stronger than the Hindu gangs. Another reason given for this occurrence is that D-Company is supplied weapons by Pakistan and do not have to purchase them, while Hindu gangs, namely the Chota Rajan gang, do.[19]

Rampant corruption in India, namely in the form of support from law enforcement, has allowed D-Company to establish a strong, secure foothold not only in Mumbai, but throughout India. Ibrahim is a key actor in the Indian and international drug trade and in addition to his trafficking network, he also has other legitimate business ventures in the developed and developing world.[20] For example, Tiger Memon, the main accused in the 1993 Mumbai Blasts, is believed to be Ibrahim's partner in the real estate, stock and finance business in Karachi.[21] Further, as trade liberalized and many 300 per cent tariffs were removed, D-Company began to search for new, more lucrative items and found them not only in narcotics, but also in small arms. The drug trade in India grew largely as a result of geopolitical occurrences in Pakistan, Afghanistan and Iran and transformed India into a major transit point for narcotics, especially heroin. India's border areas remain porous (especially the Indo-Pak border) and domestic heroin reaches Mumbai from Madhya Pradesh, Rajasthan and Uttar Pradesh via trucks, trains or other vehicles. However, Pakistan still serves as the largest provider of heroin to Mumbai.[22]

It is well known amongst law enforcement, intelligence agencies and academia that narco-traffickers very rarely exclusively deal in narcotics and that supply routes are often used for other products, specifically small arms. Small arms, like narcotics, are relatively inconspicuous, light, difficult to trace and not difficult to conceal. The Pakistani connection to Mumbai heroin is noteworthy. Based upon geographic considerations, much of the heroin trafficked from Pakistan comes through Karachi. D-Company is the largest syndicate in both Karachi and Mumbai and exerts control over the primary smuggling routes as part of their extensive network that involves politicians and law enforcement on both sides of the border and ISI. Traffic travels in both directions on these routes and products that pass along these lines adjust to meet market demands. However, once again, while D-Company allows LeT to use these networks to carry out terrorist activities within India (D-Company itself also occasionally uses the networks for terrorist acts), the primary function of them is profit generation thus demonstrating the new dynamic of Shelley's model and her definition of symbiotic relationship.

Small arms are synonymous with narcotics when discussing illicit trade practices in general. However, it is even more so the case regarding Mumbai and Karachi in that there exists a LIC in IHK that claims roughly three lives per day (mostly by small arms fire), a criminal leader that has assumed the dual role of criminal and terrorist (Ibrahim) although the latter assumes more of a secondary role, and a network that has demonstrated that it will attack Indian state interests and has forged relations with Pakistan-backed LeT. Once weapons reach their destination city, they can be trafficked into IHK either through the various lawless regions of Pakistan or through underdeveloped and corruption-wracked states in India. Operations would be financed by either Ibrahim or ISI and would be highly sophisticated as Ibrahim has previously demonstrated his ability to smuggle weapons into and through India during times of heightened security. Many bribes could be offered and legitimate threats of violent reprisals for lack of cooperation made. When discussing the drug trade in India, especially when it involves Ibrahim, it is important to view the business as multifaceted rather than as a monolith.

Unlike many other Western terrorist/organized crime groups, D-Company does not operate under a strictly bureaucratic, hierarchal structure. D-Company is transnational in character and, within India, receives its orders from overseas leadership. D-Company is likely made up of several semi-autonomous cells that are headed by trusted senior members that report to Ibrahim in Pakistan. *Bhais* (dons), *Taporis* (foot soldiers) and *Netas* (corrupt politicians) form the backbone of the syndicate. Without these three integral components, Ibrahim would not be able to run his operations in any of his locations, including Mumbai. The organization of D-Company is fairly decentralized with semi-autonomous cells operating in countries of interest, usually where there is a large Sunni Muslim and/or South Asian community. Although D-Company is indeed global, its primary areas of operation are Mumbai, Karachi and Dubai. Further, each cell adjusts to meet the needs of the market it finds itself in and also forms partnerships with other state and non-state actors in the area. For example, the D-Company cell in Dubai specializes in smuggling and counterfeit currency given Dubai's vast ports and its reputation for being the epicentre of both legitimate and illegitimate business in the Middle East. In addition, D-Company's Mumbai franchise excels in illegal construction/demolition (amongst other things) to fill the gap left by Mumbai's slow and hopelessly backlogged judicial system.

There has been little research done on the overall structure of D-Company. Nonetheless, after reviewing the literature and reasoning through basic organizational dynamics, it is possible to design a coherent model. Ibrahim, the undisputed Bhai, is largely believed to be located in Karachi under ISI protection along with some of his most senior leadership, such as Tiger Memon, given the fact that they are now international fugitives. Nonetheless, D-Company, through ingenuity and informal methods of operation, has managed to continue to enjoy an appreciable amount of success and profit despite being forced to shift bases on two occasions and coming under increased international pressure due to its involvement with terrorist groups.

In Mumbai, D-Company appears to be headed by a Regional Commander who oversees operations, receives orders directly from Ibrahim or one of his trusted aides, and coordinates with other cells. Underneath this regional commander are several Lieutenants who carry information to lower-ranking members and are also trusted to exercise discretion in matters regarding the cell. Each one of these Lieutenants has a specialty given their geographic location. For example, Lieutenants that operate in Mumbai's business district appear to focus their activities on economic crimes such as extortion and bribery while those in areas near Mumbai's ports tend to deal in weapons and narcotics trafficking in addition to various other forms of smuggling. In the case of Abu Salem, he was trusted with extorting money from builders in the city and from Bollywood personalities. However, it is important to note that these Lieutenants are not limited solely to the activities that occur in their operating area and often act independently. Further, there are several graduated levels that Lieutenants can attain. This is once again demonstrated by Abu Salem, who was a third- or fourth-rung Lieutenant in charge of gun-running and providing weapons to D-Company hitmen until his involvement in the daylight killing of Bollywood producer Gulshan Kumar in 1997 spring-boarded him into the higher ranks of the syndicate.[23] Underneath these Lieutenants are the Taporis, who carry out orders and other day-to-day activities of the cell and are the most in number. The Taporis tend to be young entry-level members who are keen to demonstrate their self-worth and to move up the chain. Even within the Tapori sub-section, there is some form of social stratification and a degree of free choice exhibited in their behaviour. They are also the most likely candidates to be tasked with providing logistical support for Pakistan-based terrorists.

Due to D-Company's fractionalization within India, cells have been able to act with more independence from Ibrahim. The fundamental difference between D-Company cells and Western-style subversive groups is the informal ties between members. Relationships within D-Company are held together not by a rigid command and control structure, but by mutual interests and/or fear of reprisal for insubordination. The motto seems to be 'do what you want on the side, and even become rich if you can, but remember who you work for'.

There are two additional positions that play a vital role in D-Company in Mumbai. One is the role of recruiter, a position occupied by one who has been with the syndicate long enough to be trusted and to be familiar with the inner workings of the group. This individual's job is to search the Mumbai area for promising talent that are willing to take risks and commit to D-Company for the long-term. The second role is the liaison between D-Company, the Netas, customs/immigration officials, other small criminal syndicates and the police. Without intentional omissions or the overt complicity of these actors, D-Company would not be able to function. This position tends to be assumed by a senior Lieutenant if not the Regional Commander himself. The primary responsibilities of the liaison are to gauge which districts and areas of Mumbai are safe to operate in, to ensure that prosecutions of key members do not occur, to block potentially harmful legislation and to ensure that D-Company maintains its operational security. Lastly, it is not unreasonable to assume that D-Company has several accountants and lawyers at its disposal, either as full-time members or on a contractual basis. It is important to note that all of this complexity and dedication of resource is to safeguard and ensure the continued functioning of D-Company's profit-generating activities, not its terrorist infrastructure.

The organizational structure of the Dubai cell is likely very similar to that of Mumbai with the exception being that the members in Dubai are fewer in number and in addition to having developed relations with Dubai's state actors, D-Company Dubai has also developed a strategic partnership with ISI. John notes that Ibrahim's network in Dubai is often utilized by ISI as a secure conduit for illegal arms purchases and drug sales.[24] Nonetheless, this is not to say that D-Company Mumbai has not developed a relationship with

ISI as the Mumbai Blasts did indeed demonstrate the working partnership between the two. Further, LeT, one of ISI's non-state weapons of choice in their low-intensity conflict against India (which has now grown beyond ISI control), operates throughout the entire country and would not be able to do so without utilizing D-Company resources such as contacts, smuggling routes and tactical knowledge.

Karachi serves as the de facto headquarters of D-Company at present despite most of its current leadership being Indian. There is no Regional Commander in Karachi and leadership is assumed by Ibrahim himself. Surrounding Ibrahim are several of his longest serving and most trusted aides, such as Tiger Memon and Chota Shakeel, in addition to his other Lieutenants. Much like in Mumbai and Dubai, Ibrahim has likely divided Karachi into districts while making sure that the skills of his Lieutenants match their area of operation and that they utilize their *Goondas* (Urdu version of Taporis) accordingly. Lieutenants are also given a significant degree of freedom to engage in other ventures. This helps to ensure that D-Company's activities remained diversified and profitable while the distribution of power makes D-Company less susceptible to a decapitating strike. One common theme amongst all three cells is an emphasis on smuggling and trafficking activities given the highly strategic ports that are located in each city. However in Karachi, unlike in Mumbai and Dubai, D-Company has a patron in ISI and has had to adjust some of their activities accordingly. For example, prior to D-Company's coerced move to Pakistan, there is no evidence of collaboration with Al-Qaeda, LeT or any other extremist group. D-Company's refuge in Pakistan has come with a price although Ibrahim continues to refuse to fully commit his organization to terrorist activity or even to a point where it could alter D-Company's basic modus operandi.

Ibrahim's aides serve several functions. First, they provide advice regarding critical areas such as finances, adapting to market needs and improving operating methods. Tiger Memon even serves as Ibrahim's partner in D-Company's real estate, stock and finance business in Karachi. Second, his aides carry out some of the high-level tasks that Ibrahim himself does not have the time for or is physically unable to do. The Mumbai Blasts are a clear illustration of the latter service. Although the attacks were planned in Dubai, Tiger Memon did the majority of the legwork such as recruiting operatives, choosing sites and conducting surveillance of potential targets. Memon is believed to have been chosen to perform these tasks as he was less conspicuous than Ibrahim and was able to enter India. He was also not under the same time constraints as Ibrahim. Today, despite the fact that the missions have changed, the mode of operation has not. Ibrahim's terrorist designation has placed him in the international spotlight along with Pakistan, who insists that they are not hosting Ibrahim despite overwhelming evidence to the contrary. As such, Ibrahim must periodically move to avoid detection by Indian intelligence, the media or other hostile parties. Due to Ibrahim's preoccupation with security, he has likely come to rely on his aides much more than he had anticipated.

D-Company Karachi's liaison department conducts different activities than its counterparts. Although they do engage police, customs/immigration officials and politicians, most of their work centres on D-Company's partnership with ISI and LeT. Lele addresses the link between Ibrahim and LeT by claiming that the ISI was instrumental in bridging the gap between them and that LeT is the most active terrorist network in India. Lele describes that relationship as 'one excels in hardcore terrorist operations, while the other provides administrative and technical support'.[25] D-Company Karachi does not have to be nearly as concerned about the authorities as its counterparts do in Mumbai and Dubai due to their protected status within ISI. However, in order to maintain that status and to continue to avoid justice, D-Company must make their relationship with LeT a priority and assist ISI in furthering Pakistan's state interests.

Figures 1 and 2 at the end of this chapter seek to provide a clearer picture of the two organizational structures of D-Company's major cells. These models were initially put forward in an article in *Terrorism and Political Violence* in July 2008 by this author and Stewart Lee.

The Khalistan movement in Punjab: laying the Groundwork for D-Company in Kashmir?

The roots of the Khalistan movement can be traced back to the tensions between Sikh Punjabis and a minority religious sect in the late 1970s. The conflict led to a strengthening of the Sikh identity in Punjab and greatly harmed relations with the Hindu community. Many Sikhs looked to the Akali Dal Party and then Prime Minister Indira Gandhi to address their various grievances. However, Gandhi chose to side with the Hindu population and as a result, many Sikhs across Punjab began to seek a separate state, Khalistan, and engaged in attempts to remove Hindus from Punjab. Hostilities greatly escalated after the 1984 Operation Bluestar raid in which Indian troops stormed the Golden Temple in Amritsar, killing worshipers and well as terrorists and unearthing a massive arms cache. Following the raid, Indira Gandhi was assassinated by her Sikh bodyguards that same year. However, as a result of effective law enforcement, the Khalistan movement ran out of steam in the late 1980s/early 1990s although remnants do exist, especially in diaspora communities.[26] Nonetheless, smuggling routes and ominous precedents were established that would prove to complicate the situation in IHK.

The vast majority of assault rifles seized in Punjab during the insurgency were Chinese types 56, 56.1 and 56.2. Chinese stick grenades and mines, which included anti-personnel Claymore mines and anti-tank mines, were also seized from Punjabi terrorists. Further, sizeable amounts of Chinese M3 submachine guns, RPGs (some of which had night vision and anti-personnel and anti-tank ammunition) and General Purpose Machine Guns (GPMGs) were confiscated by security forces in Punjab. Although all of these weapons have Chinese origins, they are believed to have come from Pakistan.[27] These seizures demonstrate that Pakistan has a history of and possesses expertise in smuggling third party arms (Chinese) into conflict zones in northwest India. This particular instance is of special significance to IHK as both Punjab and IHK not only share a border with each other, but also with Pakistan.

Even though a wide range of weapons made their way into Punjab, the signature weapon used by Sikh militants was the AK-56, a portion of which were provided ISI. Some of these weapons were likely initially purchased by the CIA as part of their Afghan arms pipeline.[28] However, much like the situation prior to the 1993 Mumbai Blasts, ISI would have needed to utilize the smuggling routes of criminal syndicates in order to transfer weapons into Punjab. It is possible that the underworld relationships and smuggling routes that developed during the insurgency in Punjab laid the groundwork for the massive smuggling operation that was required to conduct the attacks on Mumbai in 1993.

Sikh terrorists were spotted openly surveying the gun shops in Dara Adam Khel in the NWFP on the invitation of Pakistan-based Jamaat-e-Islami through the International Sikh Youth Federation.[29] There were also reports that Pakistan was sending Sikh terrorists to training camps in Afghanistan and then transferring them back to Punjab and that a member of the Punjab Assembly, who was a high-ranking member of the drug mafia, sealed a US$357,000 arms deal between Pakistani arms dealers and Sikh insurgents.[30] The arms deal demonstrates that Pakistan has historically been willing to use criminal syndicates to further state interests although it was not able to secure a local partner until D-Company relocated its senior leadership in Pakistan itself. In addition, there is speculation that ISI and the Pakistan Rangers utilize narcotics smugglers in the Rahimyar Khan region during sandstorms to smuggle arms into hotspots in northern India.[31]

In 1988, India erected a double-layered fence along Punjab's border with Pakistan in order to stem the flow of weapons.[32] This tactic, although criticized by some, did slow the flow of materiel to Sikh fighters in a fairly effective manner. However, it seems that the Indian authorities underestimated the adaptive capacities of the arms traffickers on the other side of the border. The fence did not eliminate many of the smuggling routes, but instead forced them to alter their direction. Some of the new supply lines began to flow into IHK, which led many to believe that the Khalistanis and Kashmiris had formed an alliance, commonly referred to as K2, in an attempt to undermine the Indian Union.[33] Although the Khalistanis no longer pose a major security threat to New Delhi, the Kashmiri terrorist groups indeed remain a pressing issue and the cutting of their complex system of supply lines remains a top priority, something which has become much more complicated now that D-Company, an Indian criminal syndicate, is involved.

1993: Ibrahim crosses the line

There are few events in recent history that have had a greater impact on the collective consciousness of the Indian people than the 12 March 1993 series of explosions that rocked Mumbai, resulting in the death and maiming of over 1,000 in addition to millions of dollars worth of damage. The motivations for the attack included avenging the deaths of Muslims that lost their lives in the riots following the Babri Masjid incident in 1992, sparking communal riots which would have resulted in the deaths of many Hindus as the Muslim communities had become armed, crippling India's economic reforms, and to discourage investment.[34] During the attacks, ten powerful RDX bombs exploded all over the city (three more in the city centre did not go off) that targeted important structures such as the Air India building, the Mumbai Stock Exchange, the Centaur Hotel and the headquarters of Shiv Sena.[35] At least seven of the bombs were car bombs. Also, RDX is not available within India and, as it is a plastic explosive, does not show up on X-rays or metal detectors. The car bombs operated on timers and were so precisely placed that the bombs did not even leave a significant crater in the ground. This would have required the expertise of at least ten electronics specialists with enough nerve and expertise to handle explosives, thus demonstrating the nature of the types of individuals that Ibrahim has at his disposal.[36]

In early 1993, three ships left Dubai bound for Karachi and 30 kilometres off of the Pakistani coast, the ships were loaded with enough RDX and small arms to fight a war.[37] The RDX was eventually traced back to an Austrian firm and the consignment was arranged by a Pakistani national who was previously employed at the company.[38] The small arms were likely provided from a combination of Pakistan's illicit gun markets and its own stockpiles, although some of the materiel could have been procured within India itself. This occurrence highlights the fact that Ibrahim is not only capable of trafficking within ports, but also has the rare capability to engage in smuggling on the high seas. To be able to conduct an operation 30 kilometres off of the Pakistani coastline, which would require the avoidance of various navies, coast guards, law enforcement and/or intelligence agencies, is a testimony to the strength of Ibrahim not only as a criminal, but as an active supporter of terrorist groups like LeT.

After the delivery, one ship travelled to the Raigad district of Mumbai while the other two travelled to Gujarat.[39] Customs officials were bribed and once the weaponry was in India, various syndicates smuggled them into Mumbai via trucks. Much of the RDX was packed into boots of cars in garages owned by Tiger Memon. The whole operation was planned in Dubai during a meeting with Ibrahim and those present swore an oath of secrecy on the Koran.[40] Memon was the chief architect of the plan and reportedly chose the sites, recruited local operatives and organized the transportation of explosives while his brother Yakub, who is a chartered accountant, is accused of being the primary financer.[41] The Memon family also engaged in large monetary transactions in order to finance the attacks and fled to Dubai and then to Karachi shortly after the attack (the failure of the UAE police to locate them is suspect). Other suspects fled India via Nepal, where Ibrahim has investments and significant influence.[42] However, Yakub eventually returned to India and surrendered in 1994 and was convicted of involvement in the blasts alongside his siblings Yusuf, Isa and Rubina.[43]

Some newspapers in India suggested that there was a link between ISI, Sikh terrorists and those who carried out the Mumbai Blasts. According to their reports, police interrogations revealed a list of ISI operatives in India and Pakistan and also revealed that Bittu, a former member of the All India Sikh Students' Federation and Lahore-area resident, served as the middleman between the Memons and the ISI.[44] If accurate, this demonstrates that Ibrahim could have ties to Sikh terrorists and may have supplied weapons to Punjab, IHK's neighbour, although this would be difficult to verify. It has also surfaced that the operatives involved in the 1993 blasts, some of which were street criminals from Ibrahim's syndicate, were first sent to Dubai, where they were granted transit visas by the authorities. They were then sent to Pakistan with new identities and false passports and received training on how to use the AK-56, hand grenades, rocket launchers and RDX.[45] Lastly, D-Company has been accused of providing ISI agents with safe houses and assisted them in clandestinely entering and exiting India.[46]

There have been accusations that even several Bollywood figures were involved in the attacks. Well-known actor Sanjay Dutt was arrested under the Terrorist and Disruptive Activities Act (TADA), admitted to illegally possessing an AK-56 and a 9-millimetre pistol (for which he was sentenced to six years in prison), and also provided critical information that linked then Dubai-based Ibrahim to the Mumbai Blasts.[47] Further, two famous film producers, Hanif Kadawla and Sameer Hingora, were also arrested in connection with the blasts in addition to Kamal Raj, an employee at Coca-Cola. Hingora was later convicted of conspiracy for supplying three AK-56 rifles, magazines and ammunition, and hand grenades to Sanjay Dutt's residence. These events are a clear indication that despite living in exile, Ibrahim and his network within India still extends far and wide. It is also noteworthy that criminal proceeds are often laundered through the 'legitimate' financing of Bollywood films.[48]

In the investigation that followed the attacks, 1,034 kilograms of RDX was seized in a Mumbai warehouse with another 2,380 kilograms being discovered in a nearby creek. Also discovered were 459 grenades, which were manufactured in Pakistan, along with 63 AK-56 rifles, ten 9-millimetre Tokarer pistols, 13 9-millimetre magazines, 1,100 electronic detonators, 230 AK-56 magazines and 38,917 AK-56 rounds.[49] In total, 3,876 kilograms of explosives, including at least 2,720 kilograms of RDX, were seized in Maharashtra. Only 300 kilograms were used during the attacks.[50] Mehta describes the weapons seized: 'These were not weapons for an underworld skirmish. These were armaments for civil war.'[51]

The discovery of these yet to be used weapons demonstrate that Pakistan and Ibrahim have a relationship that allows them to traffic the amount of weaponry necessary to wage a sustained LIC like the one in IHK. Even more troubling is the fact that Tiger Memon is believed to have smuggled in at least 7,000 kilograms of RDX into India, thus suggesting that large amounts of RDX still remain unaccounted for.[52] In addition, following the Mumbai Blasts, the Lebanese Coast Guard intercepted an India-bound ship laden with explosives.[53] Although this event cannot be said to be undoubtedly related to the Mumbai incident as there exist other conflicts in the region, such as the recently extinguished civil war in Sri Lanka, analysts cannot rule out the possibility that these weapons were designed to be used in retaliation for the anti-Muslim riots of 1992. Another 1993 seizure following the attacks on Mumbai was a large consignment of AK-47 rifles and explosives that were discovered in Ahmedabad, Gujarat that were traced back to Kashmiri terrorists and were bound for gangs in Muslim-dominated areas of Gujarat and Maharashtra.[54] The latter is possibly one of the first signs of cooperation between Ibrahim and Kashmiri terrorist groups. Ibrahim has long been the undisputed kingpin of the Muslim underworld, especially in Mumbai, the capital of Maharashtra. This failed weapons transfer very possibly involved his overt support as it is difficult to see how these weapons could enter these areas without using D-Company's dominant infrastructure. As LeT was officially founded in 1994, this event could have been one of the first instances of inter-group cooperation that laid the groundwork for the relationship between Ibrahim and LeT.

In summary, the attacks on Mumbai demonstrated many of Ibrahim's capabilities:

- The delivery of arms, ammunitions and explosives was conducted mostly by sea and were trafficked through India on land. This involved comprehensive, well-planned prior arrangements. Knowledge of the territory, major state and non-state actors and the general public would have been necessary.
- The landing required the complicity of customs and other government agencies for the delivery, clearance, transfer and transport of the consignments.
- Without the cooperation of immigration authorities, those involved in the operation would not have been able to enter India.
- In order to obtain safe passage through checkpoints, all transit points, trafficking routes, and to ensure secure storage and delivery, liaison with local police officials was essential.
- Terrorists involved in the attacks were housed, transported and communicated with one another within India without being detected.
- Average citizens such as shopkeepers and taxi drivers were used to conduct surveillance of the intended targets.[55]

If Ibrahim were able to smuggle massive amounts of weapons into India's financial capital during a time of especially heightened security following the riots in Mumbai, he could very well use many of these same abilities to support Muslim terrorists in IHK. India's justice system remains hopelessly inefficient and law enforcement as a whole remains highly vulnerable to corruption. Even if the tactics of law enforcement have improved following the attacks, D-Company has evolved along with them. Much like Ibrahim came to the 'aid' of Muslims in Mumbai in 1993, he is likely doing the same in IHK as D-Company is the only group (criminal or terrorist) in the whole of South Asia that is capable of carrying out these types of activities systematically and on such a large scale and is willing to attack its own country.

The key fact that Pakistan supplied the weaponry used in Mumbai blasts illustrates the nature of the partnership that Ibrahim has with ISI. In this particular instance, Ibrahim allowed ISI to use his smuggling routes and local contacts to land massive weapons hauls in India. Ibrahim was well aware that these weapons would be used against his own country, yet he assisted ISI's effort as he was enraged at the violence committed against Muslims in Mumbai in 1992 and early 1993 and was keen to bolster his image as a true defender of Indian Muslims. Although it is unlikely that Ibrahim is of a complete anti-India stance, he will still work with groups such as LeT to supply arms to areas of India where he feels Muslims are suffering at the hands of the Hindu majority. IHK is the most glaring example. The predominantly Muslim region is racked by an insurgency that kills roughly three people per day while fake encounter killings of Muslims by Indian security forces are not uncommon. There have also been allegations of rape and torture of Muslims lodged against India's military and paramilitary units. Further, the state's economy is in a shambles and lacks vital infrastructure and institutions, resulting in many Kashmiris living in poverty. ISI and Ibrahim have a shared interest but with slightly differing motivations. ISI, though it does claim to protect Muslims, mostly seeks to arm and fund terrorist groups in IHK in order to wrestle the entire territory from the Indian Union. Conversely, while prioritizing profit, Ibrahim likely seeks to demonstrate to the Hindu majority of India that the persecution of Muslims will not be tolerated. This was his primary motivation for his involvement in the Mumbai Blasts. Nonetheless, these two actors form a dangerous partnership that is capable of inflicting massive damage and greatly complicating diplomacy. However, Ibrahim is unlikely to cooperate with many of ISI's other subversive activities within India, as Ibrahim is well known to have affection for his home, especially Mumbai. Although Ibrahim currently relies on ISI for his refuge in Karachi, this does not necessarily imply that their relationship is entirely subservient. Ibrahim has a wide range of resources at his disposal, some of which ISI could not do without. This trend is now accelerating thus greatly weakening ISI's leverage over both D-Company and LeT.

Ibrahim, Chinese weapons and IHK

There are three major sources of weapons for Kashmiri terrorists: Pakistan; the open market, namely the NWFP markets of Dara Adam Khel, Landi Kotal and Miram Shah; and the Indian security forces themselves. Some have also suggested that arms may leak into IHK through the border with China around the Aksai Chin region.[56] Pakistan-sourced weaponry that is not attained through the markets is likely acquired through the smuggling activity of ISI. Further, terrorists pilfer Indian stockpiles and there have even been cases where terrorists have received small arms from corrupt Indian security personnel.[57] However, the majority of the weaponry in the possession of Kashmiri terrorists either comes from the NWFP or ISI, both of which have sizeable amounts of Chinese weaponry, especially the AK-56, as it was the 'staple item of the Afghan arms pipeline'.[58] China and Pakistan have cooperated in ballistic missile procurement in addition to WMD technologies, sometimes clandestinely. Given the desire to cooperate at a 'high level' such as ballistic missile technology, 'low level' cooperation in areas such as small arms transfers likely occurs as well, especially given the fact that Chinese small-arms-producing companies exist in Pakistan. Also, China uses Pakistan as a counterweight to India and views Kashmir as a vital inhibitor of Indian growth and development.

Weapons are trafficked into IHK from Lahore, Karachi and the area in and around Muzaffarabad via couriers that are familiar with the mountainous geography and charge their own smuggling rates. Many of these couriers' prices increase as demand increases, thus causing the price of small arms to rise substantially.[59] Ibrahim's presence and control of the smuggling activities at Karachi's ports cannot be ignored. Although weapons do indeed reach IHK through the mountains from Lahore and Muzaffarabad, Karachi is Pakistan's commercial and economic hub. As was demonstrated by the Mumbai Blasts, Ibrahim is capable of moving massive quantities of small arms from Karachi into northern India for use in areas where he and/or Pakistan feel Muslims are being persecuted. Although it would be an overstatement to claim that Ibrahim is the sole culprit in the small arms trafficking scheme, he is the key actor given the extensive logistical capabilities of his syndicate and his desire to maintain his Robin Hood-type image amongst segments of India's Muslim population, especially in Mumbai.

Some of the weapons that are transferred to Kashmiri terrorists pass through the western regions of the disputed state, possibly via the Haji Pir Pass and the Tosha Pass. These routes form an arc around the main road which leads from the Pakistani border to Baramula and eventually to Srinagar. Once in Srinagar, weapons are often dispersed within IHK through an extensive network of interconnected swamps that are overgrown with vegetation and linked together by various small channels. Given the geography, it is fairly easy for smugglers to penetrate IHK undetected by Indian security forces, many of whom are not native to the area and are unaccustomed to the lake system.[60] Indian authorities in IHK claim that between 1988 and mid-1993, nearly 8,000 AK series rifles, 455 rocket launchers and 8,030 grenades were recovered. In addition, Indian security forces seized more than 10,000 AK series rifles, 465 machine guns and hundreds of mines and explosives in the 1990–4 time period alone.[61] Further, Kalashnikovs, anti-aircraft missiles, anti-tank mines, small arms and grenades have been seized in nearby Jodphur, Rajastan and components of similar weapons have been seized in Surat, a coastal city in Gujarat.[62] These seizures are a strong demonstration of the types of weaponry that can be transferred along Ibrahim's routes.

The introduction of Chinese small arms into Pakistan can be traced back to the Soviet invasion of Afghanistan in 1979 and the apprehension of the United States to initially be seen directly supplying the Afghan militias. As such, the United States purchased large amounts of AK-56s and AK-47s (produced under licence) from the Chinese government and made payments through Swiss bank accounts. During the course of the conflict, the Soviet forces eventually became bogged down as a result of the tactically sound guerrilla methods used by the Afghan militias and signed an agreement to withdraw their forces from Afghanistan in Geneva in 1988. However, following the Geneva accords, US arms supplies to the militias actually increased in order to ensure that the Soviet Union honoured their agreements and left the region. Provisions included Stinger missiles, Milan anti-tank missile systems, Chinese Type 83 mine-clearing rockets, Egyptian and Chinese 122-millimetre artillery rockets, and electronic communications technology.[63] At present, the AK-56 is widely available in the gun markets of the NWFP in addition to Kalashnikovs from other areas such as Germany and Romania and a wide range of other weapons from Egypt and Israel, amongst others. Also, many Soviet AK-47s have been replicated in the NWFP and some even have fraudulent serial numbers. However, as many customers do not want to take the risk of paying the amount required to receive a genuine Soviet AK-47 but instead being given a forged copy, most choose to purchase the AK-56 as they are more widely available and more difficult to reverse engineer.[64]

It appears that although small arms from other nations, such as the former Soviet Union and the United States, do play a role in regional conflicts such as Kashmir, their numbers and prevalence have decreased over time. However, Chinese small arms seem to have filled the void in order to meet the demands of the market. In addition to the AK-56, most of the grenades confiscated in IHK are sourced from China and the Chinese 60-millimetre mortar Type 31 weapon, which has a range of around 1,530 metres, have become prevalent. Further, the first anti-aircraft gun was seized in IHK in August 1997 and a shoulder-fired HY-2 Chinese missile was seized the same year.[65] The seizure of this type of weapon gives strength to the argument that many of the Chinese weapons in IHK were, and still are, supplied by Pakistan and delivered through illegitimate means utilizing the criminal underground, namely D-Company. A weapon such as the HY-2 would have likely been in Pakistan's stockpiles given the high level of defence cooperation between Pakistan and China. Though the possibility that this type of weapon was smuggled through Aksai Chin cannot be ruled out, it is important to note that Aksai Chin is one of China's most remote and desolate regions and is located very close to IHK where 600,000 to 700,000 troops are stationed, some of which are undoubtedly placed on the border given India's sensitivities to boundary issues with its near neighbours, especially China as there have been numerous reports of PLA incursions into what India feels is its territory.

Conclusion

Pakistan looks to D-Company to transport mostly Chinese weapons into IHK much as Islamabad used syndicates to transfer black market nuclear technology on behalf of A.Q. Khan and to smuggle weapons into Punjab. D-Company would not only provide Pakistan with often hard to find specialized knowledge and established yet decentralized criminal infrastructure, but would also provide Islamabad with plausible deniability as accusations of state involvement in organized crime are often difficult to prove. Further, no public or legally binding agreements would have to be made with non-state actors such as Ibrahim nor would D-Company be bound by many of the deterrents that constrain the behaviour of nation states. D-Company would be willing to openly violate laws and take high-risk measures in order to accomplish a task as it already been branded a criminal/terrorist organization and appears to have no issue attacking its own country and supporting terrorist groups backed by India's arch rival, Pakistan. In addition, utilizing these criminal groups to supply third party arms from a nation that is often criticized for irresponsible arms transfers provides Pakistan with even more distance and allows Islamabad to attribute weapons trafficking in IHK to a wide range of other factors aside from their own activity. Such events are likely to continue for the foreseeable future as the conditions across the LOC and within IHK itself remain conducive to armed conflict despite positive statements made at the political level. However, in order to account for India's conventional superiority, Pakistan will continue to rely on irregulars in the form of criminal syndicates and regional terrorist groups that have an established history of working to forward Pakistan's strategic objectives in IHK and throughout India. Similarly, Pakistan will not need to look elsewhere for weaponry given its strong defence ties with China and the high concentration of Chinese weaponry in both the Pakistani armed forces and the nation itself and, as such, small arms such as the AK-56 will continue to filter into IHK, much to the dismay of New Delhi and to those seeking a peaceful and sustainable solution to the Kashmir dispute.

This chapter has sought to highlight more of the 'nuts and bolts' issues regarding the movement of Chinese small arms and light weapons into India and IHK and to demonstrate beyond a reasonable doubt that D-

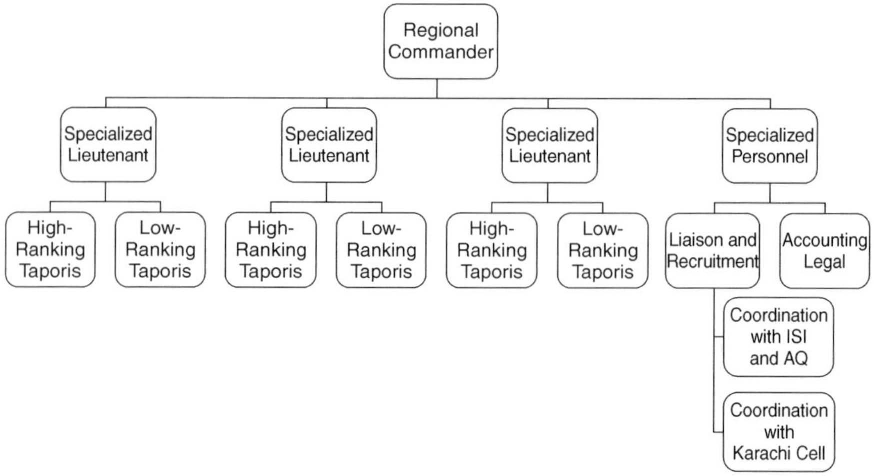

Figure 3.1 D-Company – Bombay and Dubai Cells

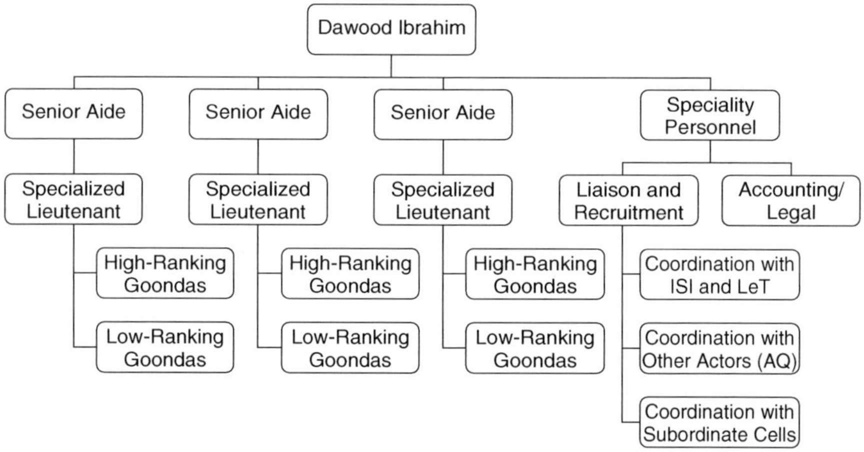

Figure 3.2 D-Company – Karachi Cell

Company is the key actor in this illicit activity. Not only is D-Company the only syndicate in the whole of South Asia that is able to carry out these types of activities on such a large scale, it is the only Indian criminal organization that is willing to support Pakistan and attack its own country. However, as has been demonstrated in this chapter, the primary purpose of the D-Company's organizational complexity and its smuggling networks is profit generation, although they have a dual-use function for occasional terrorist activity. This demonstrates that while D-Company has incorporated terrorism into its modus operandi, something which has had a significant impact on its operations, it is more of a junior partner with LeT in these endeavours and still very much views itself as a profit-oriented criminal syndicate. Continuing on this theoretical point, the next chapter will thoroughly examine the contemporary development of the trilateral nexus between Pakistan, LeT and D-Company and will highlight key decisions made by Islamabad that led it to becoming less and less relevant in this particular equation as LeT shifts its attention from IHK to the whole of India itself with D-Company assistance.

4 Lashkar-i-Taiba

The fallacy of subservient proxies and the future of Islamist terrorism in India[1]

Historical overview

Markaz-Dawa-ul-Irshad (Centre for Preaching; also referred to as MDI) was founded in 1987 to assist the Afghan Mujahedeen against the Soviet Union and to purge Islam in Pakistan of what it viewed as the corrupting influence of Hinduism. ISI and the CIA utilized the Markaz during the Soviet invasion but MDI was abandoned by the CIA after the Soviet withdrawal. However, ISI continued to use the organization to carry out attacks not only in Kashmir, but throughout India.[2] The founder of MDI was Hafiz Saeed, a professor of Islamic Studies at an engineering university in Pakistani Punjab. MDI is associated with the Wahhabi Ahl-e-Hadith orthodox school of thought that even forbids television and pictures. The religious philosophy of the Markaz is Sunni and intensely puritanical and MDI publishes an Urdu magazine, *Al Dawa*, that has a reported circulation of around 80,000.[3]

The Markaz previously had close ties with Saudi Arabia, although differences emerged over MDI's relationship with Osama bin Laden and Riyadh's decision to allow US and other Western troops to be stationed on Saudi soil. Osama bin Laden is reported to have contributed Rs.10 million to the construction of a mosque at MDI's headquarters in Muridke, Pakistan, and is also believed to have built a guesthouse that he himself has stayed in. Further, it has been alleged that bin Laden used to attend the annual gatherings of the Markaz at Muridke but now only addresses them over conference phone from his hideouts in Sudan (former) and the Afghan-Pak border.[4]

LeT was formed slightly after the establishment of its parent organization, MDI, in the late 1980s.[5] LeT's activities began in the provinces of eastern Afghanistan in 1987–8 and focused primarily on engaging Soviet forces although LeT's role was minimal. Nonetheless, ISI felt that LeT had promising potential and began to take steps to shift LeT's focus to Kashmir.[6] By 1994, LeT was the terrorist wing of MDI and unlike other irregular outfits that operated in Kashmir, the majority of LeT's fighters were non-Kashmiris and based in Pakistan. In its early stages, LeT rejected offers of alliance with other indigenous Kashmiri groups in preference of operating independently and was largely ignored by other groups during its initial stages. However,

LeT came to be respected after it began to engage in daring *fidayeen*[7] attacks against Indian security forces.[8] LeT also gained notoriety for its involvement in attacking Indian troops in sync with regular Pakistani forces during the 1999 Kargil conflict by occupying mountain-top positions in upper Drass and Batalik.[9]

Muridke still serves as LeT's headquarters and is largely financed by Middle Eastern and Pakistani donors. This joint complex now consists of a madrassa, hospital, market, residences for 'scholars' and faculty members, a fish farm and agricultural tracts. In addition, some claim that LeT operates around 16 Islamic institutions, 135 secondary schools, an ambulance service, blood banks and several seminaries across Pakistan.[10] LeT also runs a training camp in Bahawalpur (also in Punjab and home to Jaish-e-Mohammed) that has produced fighters that have engaged in terrorist acts throughout India.[11]

LeT was declared a terrorist organization by the United States in October 2001 and froze its assets that fell under US jurisdiction. Pakistan eventually followed suit and seized the group's assets in January 2002.[12] LeT was also banned by Musharraf that same year, largely due to its alleged involvement in the 9/11 attacks, although LeT's involvement in the attack on Indian parliament in late 2001 was the more likely motivator.[13] Prior to this ban, LeT was permitted to operate openly in Pakistan and nearly all shops in the main bazaar of every Pakistani town or city had a Lashkar donation box to assist in funding LeT's operations in Kashmir. LeT/MDI head Hafiz Saeed was also briefly detained in 2002 but was set free after the Lahore High Court ruled that he was being unlawfully held and, upon his release, Saeed declared that it was the duty of every Muslim to wage jihad in Kashmir.[14]

Following this change in Musharraf's strategy, breakaway members of LeT began to attack the Pakistani political establishment and joined other terrorist groups under a loose anti-US banner. As a result of this ban, LeT is believed to have changed its name to Jama'at ud Dawa (Party of the Calling) and continued its activities relatively unabated.[15] As such, the organization is still commonly referred to as LeT despite its official name change and many question whether or not the Zardari regime has the necessary support within the military establishment to fulfil its promises to crack down on the group. Some, such as Jha, goes so far to as to assert that Pakistan-based terrorist activities will continue despite peace negotiations between Pakistan and India at the state level, thus seeming to suggest that Pakistan has created a monster that it can no longer control.[16] Many agree with Jha and claim that Pakistan no longer exerts complete control over LeT and that there have been reports that LeT has a sizeable stockpile of weapons inside Indian-Held Kashmir that will allow them to continue the insurgency for an appreciable period of time.[17]

LeT has fractionalized somewhat as a result of defections over Pakistan's policy of easing tensions with India. These elements feel that Saeed aligned his positions too closely to those of Musharraf and the current government as opposed to continuing to try to force India out of Kashmir.[18] The most notable defection was that of Maulana Zafar Iqbal, a former high-ranking LeT member who left the organization to form Khairun Naas (People's Welfare). Nonetheless, is noteworthy that Khairun Naas has not emerged as a terrorist group thus far and several prominent analysts believe the split was more the result of accusations of nepotism against Saeed.[19] This split caused serious tensions within LeT but most analysts feel that this has not significantly weakened the group's operational capacities.[20] LeT has also experienced friction with other terrorist groups operating in Kashmir, such as Hizbul Mujahedeen, thus causing some to believe that ISI has had to restructure the Pakistan-based United Jehad Council (UJC), a body that oversees many of the activities of the terrorist groups operating in Kashmir.[21]

Although defections from LeT may appear to be a positive on the face, these developments could prove to have negative consequences. As has been demonstrated by other pan-Islamist groups, such as Indonesia-based Jemaah Islamiyah (JI), defectors often form more violent splinter groups that not only cause more damage, but also provide security personnel and policymakers with a whole new list of variables to account for, thus making the dismantling (or at least containment) of a group such as LeT all the more complicated.

Goals

Saeed has stated that Kashmir is the 'gateway to capture India' and that LeT would begin to push for independence of majority-Muslim areas in India such as Gujarat and Hyderabad (Andhra Pradesh).[22] Further, some claim that LeT aims not only to eject India from Kashmir, but also seeks to re-establish Islamic rule over the entire Indian Union.[23] However, others disagree and assert that despite the fact that LeT has advocated extending its 'jihad' from IHK to the rest of India, its goal is to establish two independent homelands for Muslims in southern and northern India.[24] Nonetheless, LeT has forged relationships with other terrorist groups in Afghanistan, Bosnia, the Palestinian territories and Kashmir in order to pool resources, share experience and to improve the effectiveness of their operations.[25] However, these partnerships are a reflection of shared tactical interests rather than a by-product of a larger strategic alignment. Although its infrastructure spans the globe, LeT prioritizes the South Asian theatre regarding its operations and propaganda efforts and only seems to trust D-Company with critical components of its network. Much of this other cooperation is simply information exchange and the sharing of 'best practices' in the use of tactics. Affiliation with iconic struggles such as the Palestinian issue also helps to boost legitimacy amongst potential as well as current donors and aids recruitment efforts within Pakistan.

Many analysts point to the joint venture between LeT and Jaish-e-Mohammed (JeM) in the attack on Indian parliament in December 2001 that brought India and Pakistan to the brink of war as proof positive that there were not massive differences between the Kashmir-centred terrorist groups in terms of their strategic thinking and use of tactics and that many of the differentiations between the groups were artificial. However, such analyses fail to realize that LeT does not view itself as one amongst equals but rather as the premier terrorist group in South Asia, something that is likely driving its current effort to expand its operations throughout India through D-Company infrastructure. Though it recognizes and likely respects the capabilities of JeM and others, the joint attack on parliament was the result of a desire by LeT (and possibly JeM) to share risk in what was likely somewhat of an experiment in the use of fidayeen attacks in a major urban environment and possibly a precursor for the November 2008 Mumbai attacks. Unlike suicide bombing, even though the death of a fidayeen attacker is likely, it is not guaranteed and interrogations of too many LeT cadres could severely damage the group's operational security and its networks in India. The lesson to take away from this episode is that while LeT will partner with like-minded groups to obtain short-term benefits and to enhance its organizational learning, LeT still charts its own path and views such partnerships as a component of its strategy to become the most effective outfit in the subcontinent.

Although there is considerable disagreement regarding LeT's motives aside from ridding Kashmir of Indian rule, two statements from Saeed in 1996 and 1997 to journalists provide substantial insight: 'The jihad in Kashmir would soon spread to entire India. Our Mujahideen would create three Pakistans in India'; 'We feel that Kashmir should be liberated at the earliest. Thereafter, Indian Muslims should be aroused to rise in revolt against the Indian Union so that India gets disintegrated'.[26] These direct quotes clearly illustrate that even though LeT's initial focus was on Kashmir, the organization has developed a more radical regional agenda and is willing to use the Kashmir conflict as a beacon to carry out attacks throughout India. Further, evidence suggests that LeT seeks to establish an Islamic Caliphate of all Muslim-majority states surrounding Pakistan and is believed to have become involved in Chechnya and other parts of Central Asia and have trained other pan-Islamist militant groups such as JI in Pakistan-Held Kashmir and Afghanistan.[27] In addition to India, Saeed considers Israel and the United States as LeT's primary enemies.[28] The controversial B. Raman even alleges that on behalf of the bin Laden-founded International Islamic Front for Jihad Against the Crusaders and the Jewish People (IIF), LeT issued a fatwa claiming that it was the duty of all Muslims to kill the Pope.[29] It is also noteworthy that LeT has links to Al-Qaeda, as was demonstrated by the March 2002 arrest of senior Al-Qaeda lieutenant Abu Zubaydah in a LeT safe house in Faisalabad, Pakistan. This arrest gave rise to the belief that LeT assists in the movements of Al-Qaeda fighters within Pakistan.[30] All of this demonstrates that Pakistan's initial belief that it could use proxies to wage an asymmetric conflict with limited objectives against an adversary

(India) was clearly misguided. More than two decades later, as opposed to remaining deeply committed to Pakistan and even more obedient to its limited objectives, as Islamabad undoubtedly intended, LeT now threatens Pakistan's own security with its activities throughout South Asia and runs counter to Pakistan's own declared policies thus jeopardizing its already tenuous relationship with India as well as the United States, UK, other Western powers, and even its long-time ally China. In regards to the latter, Beijing interprets the rising unrest in its Muslim-majority Xinjiang province as a result of happenings in South and Central Asia.

LeT's recent involvement in the November 2008 attacks in Mumbai represents a considerable shift in the organization's strategic thought. Although some of the gunmen were undoubtedly Pakistani, sustained attacks on such symbolic targets could not have occurred without Indian assets, some of which (based on historical precedent and current knowledge) likely came from D-Company. Further, although the majority of victims were Indians, the terrorists also deliberately targeted foreigners, namely British and American citizens as well as Israelis. These practices are new to LeT and suggest an increasing ideological overlap with more prominent transnational terrorist groups such as Al-Qaeda. The timing of the attacks also cannot be ignored as they occurred during the first sustained Pakistani offensive against Al-Qaeda and both the Afghan and Pakistani Taliban in the tribal areas. It can be reasonably argued that the primary intention of this attack was to re-ignite hostilities between India and Pakistan thus forcing Pakistan to re-deploy a large portion of its troops from the tribal areas to its eastern border with India. As such, the possibility of tactical cooperation between LeT and other regional antagonists, such as Afghan/Pakistani Taliban as well as Al-Qaeda, cannot be ruled out. However, when it comes to long-term strategic partnerships, available evidence clearly suggests that LeT only trusts D-Company (despite the latter's overt preference for profit-generating organized criminal activity) and its Pakistani state backers though they are fading in influence.

LeT enters Kashmir

Under the banner of LeT, foreign terrorists were first introduced into Kashmir in 1993 and were dispersed within the mountainous regions. In this same year, the Islami Inqalbi Mahaz camp in Poonch district was established near the Line of Control (LOC) with the help of ISI and Pakistani military officers and by 1994 LeT was ready to undertake major operations throughout the Kashmir Valley. At first, local terrorist groups were wary of LeT as they were mostly foreign and much more fundamentalist. Although this suspicion has subsided somewhat, it has not entirely evaporated as some indigenous groups question whether a Pakistani-dominated LeT represents the interests of the Kashmiri people or Islamabad's foreign policy objectives.

LeT's first mission was in October 1994 when a group of 50–60 militants ambushed an army convoy and abducted and eventually executed five army personnel, including two officers. Since 1994, LeT has engaged in numerous attacks on not only Indian security forces in Kashmir, but also on Muslim and non-Muslim civilians. Further, fidayeen attacks such as the 27 December 1999 mission on the Indian Special Operations Group (SOG) headquarters have become a LeT trademark.[31]

Even though LeT was in possession of considerable resources in the early 1990s, their successful establishment in Kashmir would not have been possible without ISI assistance. The construction of Islami Inqalbi Mahaz, near the heavily fortified LOC, would have required transport capabilities, smuggling expertise and local contacts, all of which would have required a significant logistics capacity, something that LeT unlikely had in their possession. Bedlington, a former CIA official, supports this view and claims that ISI was intricately involved in LeT's initial development.[32]

Although ISI was heavily involved in the early years of LeT, the outfit clearly does not view itself as accountable to Pakistan any longer. Its involvement in the Mumbai attacks is testimony to this as they occurred at a very inopportune moment for Pakistan. At present, Pakistan is suffering from an economic crisis, surging inflation, a poorly performing stock market and considerable internal instability as a result of a myriad of terrorist and insurgent groups and an overall lack of law and order. Rising tensions with India and the possibility of war would exacerbate all of these difficulties and strengthen the position of extremist groups in the country. None of this is in Pakistan's interest and if LeT was overly concerned about maintaining favour with Pakistan, its leadership would not engage in such a reckless operation, thus clearly demonstrating the fluidity and shifting nature of this trilateral nexus away from Islamabad (which used to be the key component that exerted control over the other two nodes).

Recruitment

LeT recruits and trains many more terrorists than it actually needs to fight in Kashmir at a given time, thus reducing its vulnerability to a massive strike and ensuring that the organization maintains an ample supply of reserves.[33] LeT is also believed to be in possession of thousands of weapons including thousands of Chinese hand grenades and an unknown number of Chinese pistols.[34] Most of LeT's recruits come from madrassas in Pakistan and even a few within India.[35] Although some may find it hard to believe that LeT actually recruits Indian nationals to carry out attacks against their own country, the 2 April 2007 arrest of an ISI agent in Hyderabad is a clear demonstration that LeT does not view the Indian Union as inaccessible. The agent was detained for recruiting youth of behalf of LeT and JeM to engage in terrorist activity in Hyderabad and Gujarat.[36] It is highly unlikely that a Pakistani ISI agent would be able to simply arrive in India and move through the country unnoticed without a sophisticated logistical network created and maintained by Indians. Once again, based on historical precedent and knowledge from previous ISI and LeT operations within India, the only known network that has the necessary capabilities (and is willing to allow Pakistan to use them) is that of D-Company, although its primary function is profit generation through illicit activity.

The Student Islamic Movement of India (SIMI) was suspected of involvement in the July 2006 Mumbai train bombings (commonly referred to as the 7/7 bombings). It is alleged that they worked alongside Pakistan-based LeT operatives and assisted them in illegally entering India. This homegrown terrorist group has gained power and influence over recent years and does not show signs of weakening. Singh states that LeT experienced an increase in the recruiting of SIMI activists following the anti-Muslim riots in Mumbai in the 1990s and in Gujarat in 2002.[37] However, Marwah believes that even though some Indian Muslims have begun to take a more anti-India stance, they have done so to increase pressure on New Delhi to give them more influence in the political system, but not necessarily because of Islamic extremist tendencies.[38] Marwah's point is debatable. The fact that LeT now has Indian operatives based in New Delhi, Mumbai and other major Indian cities and is able to recruit Indian citizens to carry out attacks within India demonstrates that there exists some degree of sympathy towards their radical ideology, although the exact numbers are unknown.

Evidence has recently came to light that LeT has recruited up to 2,000 mostly Punjabi men aged between 18 and 25 for operations in Iraq and that LeT hopes to send suicide bombers overland to Iraq through the porous Pakistan–Iran border.[39] If accurate, this development is a clear demonstration of the increasing independence that LeT is exhibiting in their decision-making as it seeks to expand its scope of operations and possibly extend its influence outside of the subcontinent. Further, by dispatching fighters to Middle Eastern conflict zones such as Iraq, LeT would be attempting to forge links with like-minded terrorist outfits, a move that would enhance LeT's operational capabilities and diversify their financial support base, thus further lessening its dependence on Islamabad and guaranteeing its continued existence in the medium term. However, it is of note that suicide bombings have not yet been used by LeT. Also, expect LeT to continue to prioritize South Asia, and India in particular, while viewing the Middle East as a potential source of expert knowledge and funds.

LeT's India-centric recruitment efforts were not likely foreseen by many in Pakistan aside from the extremist elements within the government that were involved in the gradual evolution of the group. The initial decision to nurture and gradually introduce LeT into Kashmir was based on the premise that it would remain there at Islamabad's behest to carry out limited objectives vis-à-vis India but would not make any ill-advised moves that would escalate tensions to an unacceptable level. For nearly two decades this analysis appeared to hold true until several international events and at least an official policy reversal by Pakistan regarding its support for irregulars prompted a dramatic revision in LeT's strategic thinking and caused it to morph from a subservient proxy strictly following directives and careful not to harm Pakistani interests to a group that is now overtly hostile to the civilian leadership in Islamabad and now makes most of its own decisions emboldened by its recent tactical successes and its access to the D-Company network. This lesson should not be lost in several capitals, namely Damascus and Tehran, and it must be recognized that when it comes to state sponsorship for terrorism or insurgency, no two actors have identical interests and long-established ties do not mean that they are permanent or not subject to a review or even an outright reversal by either party. However, by this time the non-state actor has often developed an intimate knowledge of the society, economy and governance structure of its former patron thus allowing them to target with increased lethality and effectiveness.

Activities and operating structure of LeT

LeT is one of the most dangerous groups operating in Kashmir and throughout India and even though most of its ranks are filled with fighters from Pakistan, LeT still has militants from places such as the Central Asian Republics and a variety of other nations.[40] Its membership is not believed to be much more than 500 core members, thus demonstrating its efficiency in moving fighters, planning and executing attacks, and utilizing scarce human resources.[41] In addition to fidayeen attacks, LeT engages in guerrilla-style 'hit and run' tactics that have targeted Indian civilians, politicians and security forces as well as police stations, hotels, airports, border outposts and public transportation.[42]

LeT's cadres are divided into districts and, at the field level, LeT is organized in a militaristic fashion with a Chief Commander, Provisional Commander, District Commander, Battalion Commander, and so on. The group also has a policy-making body that comprises of an Amir (Chief), Naib Amir (Deputy Chief), and various other strategists that are organized in a hierarchal fashion. LeT has training camps and recruitment offices throughout Pakistan and Pakistan-Held Kashmir in places such as Muzaffarabad, Lahore, Peshawar, Islamabad, Rawalpindi, Multan, Quetta, Gujranwala, Sialkot, Gilgit, etc.[43] However, LeT's largest Pakistan-based camp is believed to be in Muzaffarabad and their most active training centres are believed to be in Pakistan-Held Kashmir.[44] Further, in 2005 John claimed that within Pakistan-Held Kashmir, LeT runs 24 forward operating camps along the LOC.[45] LeT has also established charitable organizations that reward the families of 'martyrs' whose sons have died in Kashmir.[46]

Some believe that LeT has an arms training centre in Kunar province in Afghanistan that can train up to 600 terrorists at one time.[47] However, others dispute this on the grounds that US Special Forces have recently established a base in the province, the area is extremely hostile to outsiders, and that LeT would not be welcome due to the fact that they receive funds from Wahhabis in Saudi Arabia. As such, they claim that if LeT even has camps in the area, they are mobile ones capable of training a handful of fighters at a time before having to move to another location. In addition, they believe that any alleged LeT fighters in Afghanistan are breakaway members as LeT remains focused on Kashmir and the Indian Union.[48]

Nonetheless, there have also been allegations that, according to Afghan media, LeT has been recruiting Afghan refugees to take up arms against Karzai's government in Kabul and has begun to collect donations in Jalozai on behalf of the Taliban.[49] Further, LeT is reported to be active in Nuristan, an isolated, dangerous and warlord-ruled area of northeastern Afghanistan and has fighters stationed there. Due to high levels of violence and random attacks, Nuristan has a very small amount of foreigners, thus allowing warlords, terrorists and criminals alike to travel and operate freely. The intertribal violence combined with a general sense of lawlessness even deters state officials and has allowed LeT to gain a strong foothold in the region and to develop vested interests in ensuring that the current situation in Nuristan prevails. Nuristan serves as a major supply line for insurgent groups operating in the region and is home to Gulbuddin Hekmatyar's at-times pro-Pakistan Hezb-i-Islami.[50] This overlap in operating areas between LeT and Hezb-i-Islami is problematic for Kashmir for a number of reasons. First, it provides both organizations with the opportunity for information exchange and joint training that would in turn enhance LeT's tactics in Kashmir as Hezb-i-Islami is an experienced, battle-hardened group whose leader has been engaging foreign and domestic forces since the Soviet invasion. Second, it would allow LeT to expand its network base through Hekmatyar's extensive regional and global contacts. Lastly, there have been allegations in the past that Islamabad has used Hizb-i-Islami to stage attacks in Kashmir and if these accusations are true, the fighters likely came from Nuristan. If Nuristan-based groups cooperated with LeT to engage Indian security forces in Kashmir in the future, it could further complicate diplomacy between Islamabad and New Delhi as both would have to account for a third regional party (Afghanistan) whose leadership has been openly hostile to Pakistan. Further, unlike in the past, it is possible that through LeT and its links with D-Company, Hezb-i-Islami could access the whole of India instead of only Kashmir.

In addition to operations in India, Pakistan and Afghanistan, LeT is believed to have underground cells in the UK, France, Australia, the United States, and possibly Italy.[51] These overseas cells likely serve predominantly fundraising purposes and solicit the Pakistani diaspora and other sympathetic Muslim groups, although much of LeT's critical financing comes from D-Company through its involvement in organized crime and its obligation to assist LeT in exchange for continued safe haven in Pakistan. However, given LeT's supposed involvement in the 2004 Madrid train bombings and its links with Al-Qaeda, it would be naïve to assume that LeT is not willing to carry out attacks on Western soil. Further, the June 2004 arrest of LeT operative Danish Ahmed in Basra by British forces demonstrates that the group is at least seeking to become active in the Iraqi insurgency. At the time of his arrest, Ahmed claimed that over 2,000 fighters had committed to LeT-led operations against US troops in Iraq. LeT's Urdu weekly, *Gawza* (Assault on the Unbelievers), often calls upon young Muslims to fight in Iraq.[52]

LeT's cells in the West will spell trouble for any Pakistani efforts to reign in the organization as the Pakistani diaspora, some of whom have become very financially successful overseas while still harbouring extremist tendencies, could fill the void left by Islamabad by providing pounds, euros and dollars through the vast hawala system in the Gulf and South Asia. Any such move would serve to undercut the actions taken by the Pakistani government and would keep LeT afloat. In addition, as LeT has made inroads in several European nations, it will likely expand to other wealthy European nations with sizeable Muslim populations as any individual holding a valid visa or passport from an EU nation is granted freedom of movement throughout the entire bloc thus allowing them to take advantage of Europe's extensive and highly integrated financial and transportation infrastructure. Also, similarly to what has been seen in Europe regarding Liberation Tigers of Tamil Eelam (LTTE), low awareness levels as well as a lack of research on LTTE has assisted the group's efforts and has given it more operating space than it would otherwise enjoy.

LeT in India

As LeT has been active in Kashmir and throughout India for an appreciable period of time, the group has been implicated in a long list of attacks. A comprehensive (but not exhaustive) list follows.

- LeT carried out Hindu massacres in January 1996, January 1997, une 1997 and April, June and August 1998.[53]
- LeT was involved in the slaughter of at least 35 Sikh civilians in Chattisinghpura during President Clinton's March 2000 visit to the region.[54] One LeT militant, 18-year-old Suhail Malik, who was involved in the attacks was quoted as saying, 'The Koran teaches us not to kill innocents. (But) if Lashkar e Taiyba told us to kill these people (Sikhs), then it was the right thing to do. I have no regrets'.[55]
- In 2000, LeT attempted to assassinate Shiv Sena head Bal Thakery, a Mumbai-based hardline Hindu nationalist leader.[56]
- LeT attacked the Indian Army barracks at Red Fort in Delhi in 2000.[57]
- LeT's involvement in an armed raid on India's parliament in December 2001 nearly brought India and Pakistan to all-out war.[58] India has accused ISI of providing the support to LeT that enabled them to carry out the attack.[59]

- In 2001, LeT claimed responsibility for an attack on Srinigar airport that killed five Indians and six militants and an attack on a police station in the same city that killed eight officers and wounded several others.[60]
- LeT is accused of an attack on two Hindu temples in Indian-administered Kashmir in 2002.[61]
- A 14 May 2002 LeT attack on an Indian Army base in Kaluchak killed 36.[62]
- In September 2003, it was revealed that LeT was planning to bomb the US embassy in Delhi.[63]
- LeT was blamed for the 2005 Diwali bombings in New Delhi that killed over 60 people. LeT denied involvement.[64]
- LeT allegedly carried out an attack on the Indian Institute of Science in Bangalore in December 2005 which resulted in one death.
- LeT was involved in an attack in Varanasi in March 2006.
- In June 2006, three LeT operatives were killed while attempting to infiltrate the headquarters of Rashtriya Swayamsevak Sangh (RSS), a right-wing nationalist group, in Nagpur, Maharashtra.
- LeT is accused by the Mumbai police of having carried out the 7/11 serial bombings that killed at least 200 in 2006.[65] India also claims that the preparations were made by ISI but were executed by LeT operatives and that SIMI was a participating party as well. India believes that all 11 LeT operatives were Pakistanis and entered India in small groups from Pakistan, Bangladesh and Nepal.[66]
- LeT is believed to be involved in the bombs that exploded outside of a mosque in Malegaon a few weeks after the 7/7 blasts.[67] However, recent investigations suggest that these actions may have been carried out by Hindu extremists.
- The CIA reported that LeT had been directed by a foreign organization to assassinate the Dalai Lama. As a result, security around the Tibetan leader-in-exile had to be tightened.[68]
- LeT has widely been accused of the November 2008 attacks in Mumbai.

These attacks demonstrate that LeT often does not differentiate between combatants and civilians and is willing to hit both hard and soft targets. Further, these actions illustrate that not only does LeT attack other religious groups, such as Hindus and Sikhs, but it also does not seem to have many reservations about placing Muslims in harm's way either. Many LeT operatives are young, fanatic, and have access to a criminal underground infrastructure that allows them to function throughout the whole of India, not merely Kashmir. However, this D-Company network is primarily for generating profit through criminal activity and Ibrahim is not likely to cease this practice and shift the focus of his network to solely engaging in terrorist activities. This runs counter to many views that D-Company is well on its way to becoming a full-blown terrorist outfit thus fitting Shelley's traditional definition of symbiosis perfectly. However, these analysts have not studied the behaviour of D-Company over an extended period of time nor have they properly examined the events that led to D-Company's cooperation with LeT in the first place. D-Company is very much pursuing a twin-track strategy with priority being given to criminal activity while still assigning importance to its secondary task of assisting (and occasionally actively cooperating with) LeT to carry out terrorist attacks throughout India and to nurture the nascent IM, something which will decrease Islamabad's influence in this equation even further. This network is driven and maintained by profit considerations, not Islamic extremism, though its influence is poised to grow.

Several recent high-profile arrests and interrogations over the 7/7 bombings have shed light onto LeT's modes of operation within India. For one, Pakistan-based LeT commander Azam Cheema (still at large) has been determined to have been responsible for transferring RDX (a powerful non-commercial explosive) and Pakistan-based terrorists to assemble the bombs. Further, LeT Mumbai head Faisal Shaikh was arrested for receiving arms training in Pakistan, organizing funding for the 7/7 attacks via the illegal hawala system, and also for planting the bomb that exploded in the Jogeshwari railway station. In addition, Asif Khan Bashir Khan was taken into custody over his involvement in housing Pakistani terrorists that crossed over the Indo-Bangla border and for securing bomb-making materiel and assisting in bomb-making.[69] Trafficking Pakistani terrorists into India through Bangladesh would have required cooperation with ISI and Bangladesh-based Harakat-ul-Jihad-i-Islami Bangladesh (HUJI-B), a group that has been largely cultivated by Pakistan but is now Bangladesh-centric, has close ties to Jamaat-e-Islami, and is involved in planning attacks on Indian interests and in committing acts of economic sabotage such as the circulation of counterfeit currency in an attempt to undermine the strength of the Indian rupee.

Majid Mohammed Shafi, a Kolkata native, is accused of smuggling RDX and Pakistani terrorists across the Indian border with Bangladesh, thus demonstrating that LeT has a network within the Union that consists of Indian-born terrorists. Sajid Margub Ansari, an Indian SIMI activist who ran a mobile phone repair shop, was arrested for providing timer-related electric circuitry and other devices. Further, Ehteshaam Siddiqui, a fellow Mumbai-based SIMI operative, was detained for harbouring terrorists, conducting surveillance on local trains along with several other SIMI fighters, and assisting in the assembling of bombs.[70] These particular arrests are testimony to the fact that, in addition to having Indian natives at their disposal, LeT also liaises with Indian-based subversive groups such as the outlawed SIMI though these relationships are not as critical as those with D-Company.[71]

Kamal Ansari, who hails from the Madhubani district in Uttar Pradesh, received arms training in Pakistan and was tasked with bringing in Pakistani terrorists via Nepal.[72] Once again, these operations would not be possible without ISI/D-Company assistance as these smuggling operations would have to be well-planned and adequately resourced. Although the Indo-Nepal border has historically been porous, efforts would have had to have been made in order for the terrorists to avoid detection. Provisions likely included fake travel documents, substantial sums of currency, 'clean' phones, etc. It is noteworthy that Dawood Ibrahim's D-Company has a significant presence in Nepal and that this particular nation served as an exit point for some of his operatives that absconded following their involvement in the 1993 Mumbai Blasts. ISI is also active in Nepal, as was demonstrated by the 1 August 2007 arrest of Abdul Wahib, a Pakistani national and ISI agent who was detained in Kathmandu with US$252,000 of counterfeit Indian currency.[73] Although ISI's influence is waning (something that it did not intend), it is apparent that Ibrahim does not have an issue with pairing with ISI to launch attacks on his native country in areas where he feels Muslims are suffering at the hands of the Hindu majority. The fact that one of the 7/7 bombs was placed in Jogeshwari, an area that is notorious for sometimes-brutal communal violence, is a clear indication that the main motivation for the attacks was ideological. Although the 1993 attacks on Mumbai were conducted mostly by D-Company and ISI operatives, the 7/11 bombings involved the relatively new LeT, a group that has formed a strategic alliance with Ibrahim and D-Company, a partnership that has developed largely as a result of Ibrahim's refuge in Pakistan. Ironically, Pakistan's fostering of ties between LeT and a transnational criminal syndicate has further lessened Islamabad's leverage and the likelihood that LeT will follow orders as D-Company provides LeT with further opportunities to obtain and maintain financial independence.

On 13 July 2007, India's Anti-Terrorist Squad (ATS) of the Pune police arrested LeT operative Mohammed Bilal. Bilal had been living in Pune for seven months while studying at a city college and working at a private firm.[74] The actions of Bilal highlight a harsh reality in that even though India has made some strides in strengthening border security and intelligence capacities, sleeper operatives such as Bilal are still able to infiltrate and violate Indian sovereignty. Further, despite the fact that the ATS treated this arrest as a major success, it is unclear as to whether they were successful in dismantling the cell that Bilal had undoubtedly established or worked within while a resident of Pune.

Another troubling development for New Delhi is the recent arrests of three LeT operatives in the capital that originate from Manipur. The terrorists were in possession of two kilograms of RDX, two detonators and a hand grenade, and were the first LeT operatives hailing from any northeastern state with intent to attack New Delhi. Singh believes that this demonstrates how vulnerable India's northeastern regions are to jihadi groups.[75] Bhat furthers Singh's concerns and states that with LeT support, Meitei Pangal (Manipuri Muslims) could grow in strength and even challenge already established anti-centre Meitei insurgent groups, thus leading to further instability in the already-impoverished state.[76] There have also been reports that LeT, along with HUJI-B and Jama'atul Mujahedeen Bangladesh (JMB), has made inroads in Assam, the northeast's most populous and strategically important state. These groups are alleged to have forged partnerships with the United Liberation Front of Assam (ULFA) and have established several bases within Assam's Dhubri district which runs along India's border with Bangladesh. The modus operandi of groups in the northeast is to attack government forces and economic installations in the petroleum sector in addition to other soft targets, such as marketplaces.[77] These aims could be very problematic given Assam's large oil and natural gas reserves that are much needed by a resource-hungry and expanding Indian economy. Instability in the northeast also deprives India of a vital economic corridor to the markets of Southeast Asia and ensures that the region remains underdeveloped and plagued by instability.

Recent trends in arrests suggest that initially Kashmir-centred terrorist groups are beginning to target major Indian cities with LeT becoming the most dangerous and persistent. Further, LeT has begun to smuggle its fighters into India by sea as was highlighted by the 10 March 2007 arrests of LeT operatives in the Rajauri district of IHK. Subsequent interrogations revealed that eight of the terrorists had entered India via a boat that set off from Karachi. In addition, a 3 January 2007 Indian Intelligence Bureau report claims that a sizeable amount of LeT cadres are trained to handle large boats and in other navigational skills, to lay land mines and explosives, and in various types of surveillance methods with the aim of all of these activities increasing LeT's abilities to enter India though its coastal regions and/or island territories.[78] Some of these skills were put to use to enter Mumbai for the most recent attacks but the routes and methods that they used were hardly new or innovative. Rather, the routes that the Pakistan-based terrorists used to enter India are likely the same routes that have been used to smuggle materiel and possibly even other terrorists for years and were developed and are controlled by D-Company. It is important to note that many of the Pakistan-based terrorists who were involved in the November 2008 Mumbai attacks thought that they were going to be able to re-board their vessels and sail back to Pakistan once they had completed their operation.

Many of the vessels that are used to violate India's sea borders and to move fighters into its territory are undoubtedly sourced from Karachi, a city well-known for its vast and unregulated ports that provide an ideal environment for organized criminal syndicates to operate and for elements in ISI to engage in some of their more nefarious activities. The potential role of D-Company in this relatively new LeT endeavour cannot be ignored. As was demonstrated by the 1993 Mumbai Blasts, Ibrahim not only has control over much of the smuggling activity that occurs in Karachi, but also has the rare ability to engage in smuggling on the high seas. If D-Company was able to smuggle enough small arms and light weapons to fight a small war into

Mumbai during a time of heightened security following the anti-Muslim riots of 1992 and early 1993, the syndicate would not be hard pressed to smuggle a select group of terrorists on smaller, more inconspicuous ships, some of which may be nothing more than small fishing boats. ISI could not only utilize the expertise and local contacts of D-Company, but could also use the plausible deniability as state involvement in organized criminal activity is notoriously difficult to prove. Further, the fact that this cooperation occurs between two non-state actors that Pakistan does not claim to support makes the chances of independent verification even less likely. Nonetheless, while Pakistan may escape outright detection in these activities, Islamabad is inadvertently pushing itself further and further out of the picture while still being held politically responsible for LeT's activities. It appears that Pakistan erroneously believed that it could govern LeT activities in Kashmir and throughout India through an intermediary, which in this case is D-Company, as Ibrahim and his senior leadership reside in Pakistan. However, Pakistan once again failed to grasp the actual dynamics of this trilateral nexus as it seemed to view D-Company almost as a type of beggar that needed shelter and would therefore never act without consulting Islamabad, especially when it came to LeT and operations in India. Pakistan viewed itself as the dominant actor in this network despite its many weaknesses and internal contradictions though D-Company and LeT clearly are of a different opinion and appear to be betting on the fact that they are simply too indispensable for Pakistan at this point in time. At present, their strategic thinking appears sound.

Funding

LeT collects donations from the overseas Pakistani community in the Persian Gulf and the United Kingdom, Islamic NGOs, Pakistani/Kashmiri businesspeople, and through its parent organization, the now-banned Jamaat-ud-Dawa.[79] The terrorist group also counts on donations from sympathetic Saudis, Kuwaitis and Islamist-leaning ISI personnel who operate at cross-purposes to the civilian government's declared policy.[80] In addition, LeT maintains relations with religious/terrorist groups across the globe ranging from the Philippines to the Middle East and Chechnya by means of the Jamaat-ud-Dawa network. Although most of LeT's monetary assets were previously deposited in mainstream financial institutions, many of these deposits were withdrawn and invested in 'legitimate' ventures such as commodity trading, real estate and manufacturing in order to avoid seizures following Musharraf's crackdown on Pakistan-based terrorist groups.[81] This black money has likely been funnelled through numerous intermediaries and a substantial portion may have even left Pakistan via the underground hawala system. Either as a result of a lack of political will or enforcement capacity, Pakistan's measures to cut terrorist financing remain woefully inadequate.

The October 2005 earthquake provided LeT with an opportunity to once again openly raise funds in Pakistan by soliciting donations towards 'official' construction work. Since the natural disaster, many LeT offices have been re-opened and its members have been given a primary role in construction projects.[82] The presence of terrorists in LeT's camps in Pakistan-Held Kashmir made it possible for them to engage in early rescue missions during the earthquake's aftermath; operations that they sought to use to cultivate a strong local support base.[83] Further, the arrest of Pakistan-based LeT operative Ejaz Ahmad Bhat in Srinigar just five days after the earthquake suggest that LeT strategists sought to capitalize on the goodwill that was generated through relief operations and to recruit new younger members.[84] Also troubling are the allegations that the transfer of millions of pounds from the UK to a Pakistani charity engaging in 'earthquake relief' was actually used in plot to blow up two US-bound airplanes. According to Pakistani officials, a large portion of the funds sent from Britain were siphoned off and used to prepare the attacks and out of the US$10 million that was originally sent, much of which was likely sent to Jamaat-ud-Dawa, less than half was used in relief operations.[85]

The July 2006 arrest of Faisal Shaikh by the ATS shed light onto LeT's underground fundraising network within India as he is suspected of serving as the outfit's Mumbai-based fundraiser who acquired funds from Pakistan and the Middle East via the hawala system.[86] This occurrence is highly problematic for Indian security planners in that if strong cross-border links exist between hawala dealers, the cutting of terrorist financing within India will prove very difficult. Hawala is an informal banking system that is built upon trust and seasoned relationships between actors and even if arrests are made, given the close personal ties within the network, interrogations often do not yield desired results. In some instances in South Asia, those involved in transnational hawala banking are even related. Further, the fact that this particular arrest was made in Mumbai, India's financial and organized crime epicentre, is significant. Although Sheik likely did channel funds from Pakistan and the Middle East to LeT, it would be reasonable to assume that he collected funds from within India as well. Mumbai is not a stranger to communal strife and as many Indian Muslims reap the monetary benefits of India's (and especially Mumbai's) economic boom, a small but powerful minority will continue to have more money to donate towards what they perceive as a just cause. Also, D-Company thrives on both sides of the border, especially in Karachi and Mumbai, and is widely believed to largely have a monopoly over illegal hawala transactions. Given this reality, along with D-Company's partnership with LeT and the syndicate's past experience in utilizing their Mumbai network to provide funding and weaponry for the 1993 Mumbai Blasts, it is a fair and reasonable assumption that Dawood Ibrahim and Faisal Shaikh enjoyed at least a working relationship and that Sheikh used Ibrahim's criminal network as a facilitator for terrorist activity.

In addition to soliciting donations from charities, NGOs and overseas Pakistanis, LeT has branched out and diversified its sources of funding, thus making its financial pipeline less vulnerable to a decapitating strike. Harvard's Jessica Stern claims that LeT has begun to raise funds on the Internet and has acquired so much capital (mostly from Saudi Arabian Wahhabis) that it is actually planning to open its own bank. Some mid-level LeT commanders earn Rs.15,000 a month (seven times more than the average Pakistani) and some top leaders often earn more. Once such leader provided Stern a glimpse of his mansion that was staffed by servants and filled with expensive furniture.[87] LeT is also funded by the same networks of 'legitimate' commercial enterprises that covertly fund Al-Qaeda and although the exact amount of funding available to LeT is unknown, it has been reported that the organization was able to raise roughly US$4 million in the UK in 2001 alone.[88] LeT has even generated revenue through the selling of as many as 1.2 million hides of animals that were sacrificed during Eid, a Muslim festival.[89]

Aside from a few arrests/seizures and reports issued by various arms of the Indian government, there exists little research regarding LeT involvement in drug trafficking for fundraising purposes. However, given LeT's areas of operation, strategic and ideologically based alliances (namely with D-Company, which has already captured a large portion of the market), and the need to secure capital from a balanced range of sources, LeT is likely involved in the trade. Given the huge profit margins that narcotics trafficking can yield, it would allow LeT to act more independently as it would not have as many reservations about undertaking actions that may result in a loss of state funding or donations from other parties. It would also reduce LeT's chances of being held hostage to Islamabad's agenda. Kunnar and Nuristan serve as ideal exit points for Afghan poppies as strong ethnic and linguistic links on both sides of the Afghan/Pak border greatly facilitate smuggling. Further, as the arm of Kabul does not reach Nuristan, traffickers can operate with impunity and not only funnel narcotics eastward towards Pakistan, India and China, but also into Tajikistan and several other Central Asian nations and from there onto the lucrative markets in Russia and the West. As Afghanistan now supplies roughly 92 per cent of the world's opium poppies and as production is predicted to continue to rise, strong, multi-dimensional regional networks have been established (or simply re-established in some cases) in order to fully capitalize on this development. These networks combined with massive profit potential would prove too much for LeT to resist, especially after their official 2002 proscription.

The US Drug Enforcement Administration (DEA) believes that some Afghan heroin (70 per cent of which is either consumed in or transits through Pakistan) is smuggled out of Pakistan through vessels leaving the coastal areas.[90] As Ibrahim enjoys a near-stranglehold on smuggling activities in Karachi and has deep links in Afghanistan, D-Company profits from these activities. Although most of the profits obtained from smuggling Afghan heroin go towards personal enrichment, others go to LeT to support its operations in Kashmir and throughout India. By involving LeT in heroin smuggling, D-Company has provided LeT with an excellent opportunity for international networking as Afghan heroin serves a wide range of markets both in Asia and Europe. These transnational trafficking networks often survive political upheaval and crackdowns and would dramatically increase LeT's chances of survival even if it were abandoned by Pakistan entirely, which is unlikely. LeT could also use the nations that host its trafficking associates to hide fighters wanted by law enforcement or intelligence agencies. Clearly, by encouraging D-Company and LeT to forge ties, Pakistan made a grave strategic error by accelerating an already-worrying trend of increasing independence in LeT's decision-making while Pakistan is still held responsible for the group's behaviour given its past control over the outfit. Put simply, LeT's ties with D-Company have greatly assisted in the development of the former as an even greater security and diplomatic nightmare for Pakistan although Islamabad is yet to realize this grave error.

LeT and D-Company – the crime–terror nexus in Kashmir

In South Asia, a variety of criminal syndicates and terrorist groups have collaborated in international operations and syndicates seem to have adopted ideological or religious modi operandi that motivate their activities, not merely cover them. Traditional symbiotic relationships have developed with terrorist groups dependent upon organized crime for the provision of weaponry and munitions in order to carry out attacks and continue insurgencies. In order for these transfers to take place, trafficking routes have to be carefully cultivated by the syndicates, who in turn require weapons training and safe passage through militant-held territory.[91]

Dawood Ibrahim, a Sunni Muslim, was branded by the United States as an international terrorist in October 2003 for allowing Al-Qaeda to use his smuggling routes to escape from Afghanistan and for working with LeT. Further, Ibrahim and his top Lieutenant, Tiger Memon, were the key architects of the multiple bomb blasts that ripped through Mumbai on 12 March 1993 that targeted the Mumbai Stock Exchange, Air India building, Shiv Sena headquarters, the gold market and the Plaza Cinema, all while avoiding areas with a predominantly Muslim population. These attacks were believed to be in response to the destruction of the Babri Masjid, a historic mosque in the Indian state of Uttar Pradesh, on 6 December 1992 and the subsequent anti-Muslim riots that followed. The blasts were designed to increase Ibrahim's support in the Muslim community by avenging the Hindu violence against Muslims. Also, D-Company's ability to smuggle in tons of explosives and enormous amounts of firepower and to recruit and train operatives in Pakistan demonstrates that the syndicate is capable of engaging in terrorist activity on top of its other profit-driven activities although it clearly prioritizes the latter.[92]

Ibrahim's motivation to maintain his image as the protector of the Indian Muslim minority from the repression of the Hindu majority led him to become involved in the Kashmir dispute. Aside from Palestine, Chechnya and the Balkans, Kashmir is a major grievance in the Islamic world and the primary issue in South Asia. Ibrahim, through his involvement in the 1993 attacks on Mumbai (his birthplace), has made it apparent that neither he nor his syndicate has an issue with attacking their own country. D-Company has well-established smuggling routes in the region, access to materiel, a partnership with LeT and a dependence on ISI for refuge in Pakistan. Although LeT has a wide support base that spans several continents, Ibrahim is the most probable source of weaponry given D-Company's geographic proximity to the operations of LeT and the syndicate's proven ability to clandestinely transfer enough weaponry to fight a small war on short notice. This is accentuated by the fact that in Pakistan, there already exists a close relationship between organized criminal syndicates, narcotics, money laundering, terrorist activity and small arms trafficking.[93]

Ibrahim is believed to have resided in Pakistan since 1993 and now owns malls, luxury homes and shipping and trucking lines that smuggle arms and heroin into India.[94] However, in exchange for his refuge in Pakistan, a percentage of D-Company's profits were diverted to ISI-supported Islamic terrorist groups such as LeT. Evidence demonstrates that these links were formed in late 1993 or early 1994. Photographs of Tiger Memon posing with leaders of the Jammu and Kashmir Islamic Front (JKIF) at an ISI safe house in Muzaffarabad surfaced and served as the first proof of the involvement of mafia money in Kashmir.[95] Tanvir Ahmad Ansari, a practitioner of Unani medicine and LeT operative suspected of involvement in the 7/11 Mumbai serial bombings in 2006, was tasked with strengthening relations between LeT and D-Company. Motivations for this cultivation were both tactical and strategic as LeT's partner in the Islamic Front for Jihad, Al-Qaeda, expressed a desire to expand their operations in East Africa and were willing to offer cash for D-Company's networks. Ibrahim accepted Al-Qaeda's offer (remember the profit motive) and Anees Ibrahim, Dawood's younger brother, made sizeable investments in the shipping industries of East Africa and the UAE to underwrite D-Company's narcotics trafficking activities.[96] The arrest of Syed Abdul Karim, a top LeT operative, in Mombassa, Kenya, is another demonstration of the link between LeT and D-Company as Karim was utilizing the well-established D-Company infrastructure in East Africa to avoid arrest. Ibrahim has strong relations with several wealthy traders in Mombassa, many of whom are of South Asian descent.[97] These occurrences have led some to believe that Ibrahim is the 'point man' for Al-Qaeda and that although Ibrahim is not an ISI agent, he is indeed an accomplice to their subversive activities.[98] However, Ibrahim does not likely believe that he is the 'point man' for anyone, especially a terrorist group, as he views the activity as a secondary concern behind making money and safeguarding key business interests. While D-Company's cooperation with Al-Qaeda helped to earn Ibrahim his international terrorist designation, these links likely have their roots in the smuggling of Afghan heroin, something that Al-Qaeda has been deeply involved in. Yet again, the profit motive is clear though, given the nature of South Asia, it has brought Ibrahim into contact with numerous terrorist/insurgent groups. While this has affected his thoughts and actions, it has not altered his fundamental core as a mafia boss and hardened criminal.

LeT, which is estimated to be responsible for 60 per cent of terrorist-based killings in India, has been able to establish cells in several parts of the world as a result of assistance received from elements within ISI and Ibrahim's network within India and in the Gulf. There have been arrests of LeT operatives all over the world, including seven arrested by the FBI during Musharraf's June 2003 visit to the United States. Even though the information was repressed in order to avoid embarrassing Musharraf, the operatives from Washington and Philadelphia were eventually charged with 'stockpiling weapons and conspiring to wage jihad against India in support of terrorists in Kashmir'.[99] Further, US authorities claim that there are still two wanted suspects related to these arrests that are residing in Saudi Arabia.[100] D-Company has shifted some of its assets to Saudi Arabia fearing a crackdown from UAE authorities and if LeT operatives are indeed hiding in the Sunni kingdom, they are possibly doing so with Ibrahim's knowledge and assistance. Saudi money is also a primary financer of LeT's activities in Pakistan and Kashmir. As D-Company has established infrastructure in Saudi Arabia and as Riyadh's efforts to stem the outward flow of terrorists from its territory have fallen short, traffic may increase as Saudi Arabia will continue to serve as a major transit point for money and fighters for conflicts in Middle Eastern hot spots such as Iraq and the Palestinian territories and also for problem zones in the Indian subcontinent. Although it is important not to adopt an alarmist stance over the potential of Saudi Arabia's enhanced role in Kashmir, it would be prudent for analysts and security personnel to monitor the situation closely.

In 2002, Ibrahim was accused of helping to finance several LeT attacks in Gujarat.[101] Despite the fact that Gujarat has had its own share of communal violence, its proximity to Kashmir cannot be ruled out and if Ibrahim is willing to assist in attacks in a more low-profile area in northern India such as Gujarat, D-Company is involved in LeT's activities in Kashmir as well. The anti-Muslim violence witnessed in Gujarat is not a fraction of what has been seen in Kashmir and if incidents such as Godhra in 2002 are viewed by D-Company and LeT as sufficient justification for violent reprisals, there is no question that Kashmir qualifies to be on the receiving end of this crime–terror nexus. In addition, although investigations are ongoing, D-Company involvement in the November 2008 attacks in Mumbai is a real possibility given the syndicate's extensive resources in the city. If there was indeed any D-Company assistance, it likely took the form of logistical support. D-Company is active on both sides of the border and has both Indian and Pakistani membership with this same characteristic being witnessed in LeT.

LeT and ISI – a cost-effective proxy war

ISI was founded in 1948 by a British army officer, Major General R. Hawthorne, who was serving as the Deputy Chief of Staff in the Pakistan Army at the time. However, Field Marshal Ayub Khan, the former President of Pakistan in the 1950s, greatly expanded the role of ISI in defending Pakistani interests, keeping tabs on opposition politicians and sustaining military rule in Pakistan. Today, ISI is charged with the collection of foreign and domestic intelligence and coordination of the intelligence activities of Pakistan's three military branches. It is also responsible for surveillance over its own citizens, foreigners, the media, political parties, foreign diplomats in Pakistan and overseas Pakistani diplomats. In addition, ISI intercepts communications and conducts covert offensive operations. Not only is ISI believed to not be accountable to the leadership of the army, the president, or the prime minister, ISI is also accused of involvement in narcotics trafficking, financial crimes and other forms of corruption. Drug money was reported to have funded the Afghan war and is believed to be currently financing Pakistan's proxy operations in Kashmir and India's northeast. ISI has roughly 10,000 officers and staff members, although this figure does not include informants and assets.[102]

ISI is sometimes referred to as Pakistan's 'secret army' or 'invisible government' and has been linked to political assassinations and the smuggling of nuclear and missile components. In addition, Bedi claims that ISI openly backs the Taliban and has dominated Pakistan's domestic, nuclear and foreign policies (specifically towards Afghanistan and India) for over 20 years.[103] At present, ISI is divided between moderates and Taliban/jihadist sympathizers, thus greatly complicating its role as a NATO ally in operations against terrorist and insurgent groups in Afghanistan and Pakistan's tribal regions.[104] Further, both Pakistani officials and analysts admit that Islamic extremism is too deeply entrenched in the Pakistani military establishment to make concessions on Kashmir as elements within the army and ISI have taken control of the conflict and have begun to believe that victory is attainable if they continue to push. Lieutenant General Assad Durrani, a former ISI chief, has declared that no border has ever been drawn without blood being spilled.[105] However, it should also be noted that Pakistan's continued involvement is not simply driven by extremism, but rather by a range of other strategic calculations. Most critically, Pakistan's main rivers originate in the Indian portion of Kashmir.[106] Further, if India can demonstrate that it is capable of governing a Muslim-majority region, it undermines Pakistan's fundamental reason for existence: the need for a homeland for South Asia's Muslims.

Several quotes from Hamid Gul, an outspoken and highly controversial retired general and former ISI director, possibly provides some firsthand insight into ISI ideology regarding Kashmir:

> Who is Pervez Musharaf to say we should stop Jihad, when the Koran says it and when the United Nations Charter backs it up? Musharaf says: 'Stop the jihad, do this, that and the other.' No, no, no. He cannot. There is a clear-cut Koranic injunction.
>
> Armed resistance, of the oppressed people, of the persecuted people, of the enslaved people – that jihad has the UN sanction.[107]

It is hard to imagine that this sense of ideological and political legitimacy at the top of an organization such as ISI has not trickled down to middle and lower ranking officers. This open contradiction of Musharraf's statements and Pakistan's official Kashmir policy is a clear indication of the boldness of ISI, which is often referred to as a 'state within a state' that sometimes makes its own decisions and is not accountable to the political leadership or civil society. It is said that Pakistan is governed by the 'Three As': Army, Allah and America. As Washington refuses to chide Pakistan's use of irregulars in Kashmir and continues to provide Islamabad with billions of dollars worth of aid and weaponry, extremists in ISI and its Kashmir-based patrons likely feel that they are on the right side of all three. Further, the lack of US pressure on this issue likely inadvertently sends the message that Washington simply is not interested in dealing with the Kashmir issue and that violence is the only method to reverse this view.

The deployment of a few thousand terrorists by ISI has proven to be cost-effective (provided that they remained in Kashmir, which is clearly no longer the case) as they have managed to pin down nearly one-third of the Indian Army and have enabled Islamabad to degrade India's conventional superiority and thereby restrict India's capacity to engage in conflicts elsewhere.[108] The Pakistani military is also determined to obtain revenge against India for encouraging separatism in the former East Pakistan in 1971 and although there have been rifts between the Generals and the Pakistani government, elements within ISI still provide assistance to LeT.[109] Khan has even gone as far to say that LeT's evolution to becoming a major Pakistani group operating in Kashmir is largely attributed to Saeed's close ties to ISI and the Pakistani military.[110]

ISI is believed to run some of LeT's training camps and is accused of having been the terrorist group's primary financer and supporter although this situation is fast changing. Based upon these facts, some find it highly ironic that the ISI was entrusted to investigate LeT's role in the failed plot to simultaneously blow up as many as ten airplanes on transatlantic routes.[111] ISI is estimated to be running around 256 modules across India and is pushing LeT to become the most dynamic terrorist group that operates in IHK, New Delhi, Mumbai, Bangalore, Hyderabad, Varanasi and Kolkata, while unintentionally factoring itself out of the equation in the process.[112] Lieutenant General Mahmood Ahmed, the then Director General of ISI, was reported to have attended an April 2001 LeT-sponsored conference in Muridke that saw a resolution passed which charged its India-based cadres to capture and destroy Hindu temples and place the flag of Islam on top of their ruins.[113]

Many terrorist groups, including LeT, operate freely in Pakistan-Held Kashmir and the area has become a safe haven for many foreign fighters who have fled Afghanistan. Also, terrorists that have trained at ISI-run camps in Afghanistan are increasingly returning to Kashmir, where many of them have their roots, as some camps that used to be based in the disputed region were moved to Afghanistan by ISI in order to ensure their continued operation. While ISI and the Pakistani Army selectively pursue Al-Qaeda operatives within Pakistan's tribal areas, many of the training grounds that house Kashmir-based terrorists remain largely untouched.[114] This development indicates that ISI seeks to keep them as a reservist force in the event of increased tensions with India and has not abandoned their support as Pakistan has pledged to do numerous times. However, ISI has made a critical error in viewing groups such as LeT and D-Company as static organizations that will not develop independently or stray from their initial focus. Ironically, the longer ISI assists LeT in its operations in Kashmir and within the Indian Union though D-Company infrastructure, the less influence it will have over the organization in the future. At present state, future efforts, no matter how sincere, to shut down LeT will inevitably result in failure as the group will have become multinational with a wide variety of state and non-state sponsors and sources of funding (though D-Company will be the primary backer) and will have fighters and other resources dispersed throughout several areas, namely India.

Pakistan will not likely cease support to groups such as LeT until there is a formal resolution to the Kashmir dispute.[115] However, the resolution of the Kashmir conflict in the short to medium term is an unlikely prospect for a number of reasons. First, India has ruled out the possibility of withdrawing troops entirely and has refused seemingly less risky options such as reducing troop numbers or removing them from certain areas, such as the Siachen glacier. New Delhi has even declined Islamabad's offer to validate troop positions. Further, the recent drop in the number of infiltrations across the LOC and overall militant activity in Kashmir are more of a reflection of ISI focusing its attention elsewhere, such as tribal regions along the Afghan-Pak border, rather than a permanent strategic shift or loss of interest. Third, a series of erroneous decisions on the behalf of President Musharraf (for example, the decision to sack Pakistan's independent-minded Chief Justice only to see him reinstated) combined with internal unrest following the raid of Lal Masjid and the looming threat of a unilateral US military strike against Al-Qaeda leadership in the tribal regions placed Musharraf in an embattled state. As a result, he did not have the support within the army or ISI to push through any significant change in Pakistan's approach to Kashmir despite official offerings of demilitarization, joint management, etc. As such, Pakistan's support for LeT will continue to serve as a destabilizing factor in the region and as a major irritant to bilateral diplomacy between New Delhi and Islamabad. It will also play a critical role in ensuring that an enabling environment for this trilateral nexus continues to thrive in IHK, an occurrence that will result in Islamabad unintentionally seeing itself sidelined as IHK is used as a harbinger by LeT to spread throughout India with increased speed and lethality while also nurturing IM. This will largely occur through D-Company's criminal infrastructure with the profit motive remaining predominant. This is the polar opposite of what Pakistan's earlier strategists intended but Islamabad still appears oblivious.

The future of Islamist terrorism in India

Indian security forces have been witnessing a disturbing trend in the 'indigenization' of several Pakistan and Bangladesh-based militant groups that are believed to have led to the formation of the Indian Mujahedeen (IM). IM is believed to have a substantial number of Indian nationals within its ranks and its recent attacks were likely carried out by Indians, something that runs counter to the conventional wisdom that terrorist attacks in India are invariably carried out by foreigners, usually Pakistanis. Much of this reformation likely involves extremist elements within the ISI who have the goal of establishing native cells that mostly operate autonomously but will still occasionally take directives from abroad. These cells will likely be highly difficult to detect as they are small, consist of Indians with firsthand knowledge of the country who do not appear foreign in any way, and any ruling party in New Delhi will have difficulty enacting tougher legislation to combat the problem for fear of losing the Muslim vote. India is also at a disadvantage as its intelligence services lack Muslim personnel and have become too dependent upon technology at the expense of human intelligence. Lastly, India needs to acknowledge that many Muslims are treated as second-class citizens in the country and have suffered from selective justice and discrimination for decades and that this does wonders for the recruitment efforts of groups such as IM.

Although ISI, LeT and others have assets in India, D-Company's network is far more extensive. As elements within ISI further their agenda of developing and spinning off terrorist groups within India while the civilian leadership pledges to crack down on these same organizations, they will come to rely more heavily on D-Company infrastructure in ventures such as ensuring the safe entry and exit of foreign terrorists and the provision of safe houses, clean phones, weapons, explosives and other related materiel. They will also need D-Company operatives to reconnoiter targets and manage its relationships with corrupt officials within India. Through D-Company, extremists in ISI may be able to establish even greater distance between themselves and the myriad of terrorist groups, namely LeT, that jeopardize Indian stability although this comes at a serious cost with regards to control over operations and escalation. D-Company also benefits from this partnership as it allows them to assist in avenging the deaths of Muslims in areas such as Gujarat, the scene of a serial bombing in July 2008. D-Company had long sought to carry out an operation in Gujarat following the massacres of over 1,000 Muslims by Hindu mobs in 2002 and its participation was likely.

November 2008 Mumbai attacks

The Mumbai attacks displayed a level of advanced planning that shows a considerable evolution in jihadist groups in South Asia. There were multiple targets within an urban environment and highly trained and armed terrorists organized into small teams and targeted Americans, Britons and Jews, as well as Indians, with the major final showdown occurring in hotels, a favourite target of Al-Qaeda.[116] The masterminds of these attacks were sophisticated in their strategic thinking and the operation was able to capture and hold international attention while seeking to exacerbate communal tensions. They also aimed to provoke a crisis between India and Pakistan thereby prompting Pakistan to shift troops from FATA and the NWFP to its frontier with India. This would have taken pressure off the Taliban, Al-Qaeda and other groups operating along the Afghan frontier. After these attacks, the Mumbai attackers further burnished their terrorist credentials and now rival Al-Qaeda in reputation. This operation also foreshadows a continuing terrorist campaign in India.[117] However, an attack of this magnitude required a safe haven from where they could plan, train and communicate without fear of disruption. Given the heightened sense of security in India, such a safe haven is unlikely to be established in the country. As such, any future spectaculars on Indian soil are likely to originate from overseas in the short- to medium-term but will use in-country assets to carry them out. The fact that India's Maoists have been unable to execute any kind of operation that approximates the 2008 Mumbai attacks is a case in point.

All of the facilities attacked were soft targets and at no point during the attack did the terrorists attempt to overcome armed guards. The terrorists attacked predominantly unguarded targets and even in places where they could expect security forces, reconnaissance informed them that those forces could be easily overcome as they were only lightly armed.[118] Terrorist groups will continue to focus on soft targets in India that offer high body counts and have iconic value. Nationally and internationally recognized venues that offer ease of access, certainty of tactical success and the ability to kill in large quantities will likely guide future target selection. Further, as public surface transportation offers terrorists easily accessible, dense populations in confined environments, it will likely remain the most common form of attack.[119]

Some observers claim that the Mumbai attackers felt that they were somehow going to get out alive. This view has been strengthened by reports that this belief was shared by the sole surviving terrorist.[120] If accurate, this is problematic for India as the quality of future fidayeen-style terrorists is likely to be higher than standard suicide bombers. If the chance of survival is present, no matter how slim, these types of attacks can potentially attract highly motivated terrorists keen to engage in extended operations that are guaranteed to gain international media attention due to their shock value. Participation in a fidayeen attack can bring prestige to the individual as well as the group as it is considered a more courageous act by many within the larger jihadi community.

The two-man team that stormed the Trident-Oberoi Hotel called the news media claiming that seven terrorists were in the building and demanded that India release all 'mujahedeen' in Indian prisons in exchange for the release of hostages.[121] A key question here is whether this was a primary objective of the operation or if it was something more spontaneous. It is of note that India has released terrorists in exchange for hostages in the past with the most notable release being JeM's Masood Azhar in 1999. Though this demand appeared to be hastily arranged and possibly generated on the spot, the release of imprisoned comrades could become a driver behind future operations. Such events would hardly be unprecedented in India as the Maoists have engaged in successful jailbreaks freeing hundreds of their members.

The dispersal of the attackers into separate teams indicates an effort to reduce operational risk. Once the attack commenced, the failure or elimination of any single team would not have put the other teams out of action. This type of operation, where attackers assault and penetrate deep into the target and try to kill as many as possible, has been a LeT hallmark against Indian forces in Kashmir.[122] Fortunately for India, this capability is beyond IM at this point in time as it is still somewhat of a disjointed organization in the consolidation stage. However, IM can develop it with a safe haven, in Pakistan or otherwise, in time. The recent scaling up of IM's campaign demonstrates clear intent to take their operations to the next level and if regular contact with groups like LeT are maintained through D-Company, more destructive attacks with multiple sophisticated objectives are a real possibility. In addition, Indian security forces have made the startling discovery of at least six training camps within India itself.[123]

According to the testimony of the surviving terrorist, the goal of the operation was to kill as many people as possible. However, when compared to the 2006 Mumbai train attack or the 1993 Mumbai bombings, casualties in the 2008 operation were lower as bombs were not the primary weapon. Indiscriminate bombings, namely those in London and Madrid, have been criticized in jihadi circles as being contrary to the Islamic code of warfare. As such, it is likely that by relying on shooters, this 2008 attack would appear to be more selective even though the majority of victims were still civilian. This perception of selectivity was further underscored by the terrorists' search for Americans and Britons and the killings at the Jewish Chabad Centre. It also enabled the attackers to engage the police and soldiers in what could be portrayed as a heroic last stand. Security could have been another factor in that, based on the patterns of previous attacks, Indian authorities were focused on truck bombs at hotels while rail security focused on trying to keep bombs off trains as opposed to armed assailants out of the actual train stations.[124] Following the most recent attacks, LeT is anticipating another round of target hardening in India and Mumbai in particular and will have to innovate if it wants to maintain its position within the South Asian terrorist community. As LeT thinking evolves, it will seek to carry out attacks that have chain reaction-type effects that remain long after the attack itself, alter behaviour and ensure that a sense of fear remains, something that will require the expertise of an in-country partner such as D-Company. Although LeT is a distinctive outfit in its own right, it is likely in tune to international best practices and is aware that one of the most effective ways to weaken a regime and damage a nation's long-term development is through consistently hitting economic targets. Key drivers of the Indian economy, namely IT, financial services and steel manufacturing, should be viewed as potential high-value targets. Despite the horrific human losses that were inflicted by LeT gunmen in Mumbai, the permanent damage to India's economy was minimal and it did not take Mumbai long to return to its normal state. Similar events were witnessed following the train bombings in 2006. Given LeT's proven ability to learn and evolve as an organization, this lesson it not likely lost on them. However, IM is not able to carry out this level of operations though its LeT patrons are keen to see them develop the capability. As such, the onus for carrying out mass casualty attacks in India will remain on LeT and D-Company's logistical support network for the time being.

Terrorists have proven themselves capable of analysing current security measures, devising new tactics to circumvent them, and to do the unexpected. The terrorists also demonstrated that even with simple tactics and low-tech weapons they are still able to produce vastly disproportionate results. Further, the success of the Mumbai attackers in paralysing a large city and commanding the attention of the world's news media for nearly three days will encourage similar operations in the future. Terrorists will continue to effectively embed themselves among civilians, taking hostages and using them as human shields to impede responders and maximize collateral casualties.[125]

Terrorist attacks are intended to cause fear but also to inspire other terrorist constituencies and attract recruits. By succeeding, which in this case means humiliating the Indian security services, causing large-scale death and destruction, and garnering international media coverage, terrorists hope to attract both Pakistani and Indian recruits to their cause.[126] A critical factor will be the overall response of Indian Muslim 'fence-sitters' who are disillusioned with contemporary India and their place in society but have not yet resorted to taking up arms. Given the legitimacy that many Pakistanis assign to the Kashmir dispute, LeT is not likely to experience recruitment difficulties in the near future but if the group is to achieve its objectives in India, it will need more capable domestic recruits, obtained through D-Company. This is a variable that has yet to be worked out and if LeT begins to consistently hit economic targets in India (or prompts a more capable IM to do so),

D-Company, which already prioritizes profit and illicit business interests, may degrade its involvement though it will not be able to walk away from LeT entirely. While ties between these two groups are strong, LeT must be careful not to damage D-Company's bottom line and the criminal infrastructure that LeT is dependent upon to maintain its prestige and to escalate its campaign in India.

Two alleged Indian LeT operatives, Fahim Ansari and Sabauddin Ahmed, were arrested and accused of scouting for the attacks.[127] Indian nationals are also believed to have possibly helped with the pre-positioning of supplies. According to one account, Indian commandos discovered a backpack at the Taj Hotel containing seven loaded AK-47 magazines, 400 spare rounds, four hand grenades and various documents that may have been placed beforehand.[128] New Delhi claims that all of the Mumbai attackers were members of LeT, received advanced military training in Pakistan and arrived in India by boat. Although met with initial scepticism by some, these claims seem to have been validated. However, it should be noted that in order to carry out an attack of such scale, considerable reconnaissance was required on these symbolic targets, something that would have taken months or even longer and could not have happened without in-country assets. In addition, although the devastating effectiveness of this operation was due to its lack of many interconnected moving parts, it was still a substantial logistical exercise, especially regarding target location. The Taj, Oberoi, Chhatrapati Shivaji rail station and maybe even the Leopold Café were not difficult to identify, but the deliberate targeting of Nariman House and the Jewish centre inside likely could not have occurred without local knowledge.

This is not to suggest that the operation was not mostly a LeT venture, but much like the serial bombings in Mumbai in 1993, such an ambitious plan could not have been completely developed outside of India and only by Pakistanis. As stated earlier, LeT, D-Company and their Pakistani handlers have been pursuing a policy of indigenization of terrorism in India, meaning that as LeT cells expand throughout the country, they obtain more Indian cadres and link up with like-minded groups such as the Student Islamic Movement of India. Indian authorities believe that this is how IM was formed along with segments of other groups based in Bangladesh. However, without the native component, the Indian Mujahedeen would have difficulty functioning.

So why are Indian Muslims now willing to be involved in attacks that kill their fellow citizens on a massive scale and try to damage their own economy by hitting hotels and other commercial sites like bazaars? There are many analysts who attribute this to pervasive and systematic discrimination against Muslims in Indian society. They claim that Muslims die earlier, are less healthy and do not have the same access to education as their Hindu counterparts. However such disparities are also witnessed in minority communities in many countries, including the United States, although they do not resort to taking up arms against their own country.

A major contributing factor to the resort to Islamist terrorism in India is the selective nature of Indian justice when it comes to prosecuting acts of communal violence. For example, India relentlessly pushes for the extradition of Dawood Ibrahim from Pakistan for his involvement in the 1993 Mumbai attacks while many of those who perpetrated or instigated the 2002 Gujarat riots, in which scores of Muslim innocents were killed, have not been brought to justice. Contradictions such as these serve as powerful motivators while evidence is also starting to emerge that some Indian Muslims are beginning to identify with the Kashmir dispute. This is something that could prove disastrous if not addressed.

Many Indians are convinced that LeT is sponsored by the Pakistani government and, as such, India is likely to respond to these types of attacks in a manner that holds Islamabad directly responsible.[129] LeT and their allies are aware of this and will seek to actively exploit the situation in order to reverse any positive momentum in relations between India and Pakistan. If New Delhi believes a state hand is behind LeT spectaculars, its response will be more bellicose thus exacerbating tensions and, ironically, assisting terrorists to achieve their objectives. Further, if India conducted military attacks on suspected terrorist training bases in Pakistan, it would provoke anger and strengthen Pakistani hardliners.[130] It will also increase public sympathy for many of the Kashmir-centred groups, namely LeT, as it would further bolster their image of being on the front line against a hostile India.

Future directions of the Indian Mujahedeen

The fundamental difference between the attacks by Islamists in Kashmir and the more recent attacks in India is that while the previous operations were carried out by foreigners or 'hardcore' locals, recent attacks involved individuals and cells from a broader section of India's Muslim population. The growing popularity of the anti-Muslim agenda of the Hindu nationalists is causing greater communal polarization and prompting many Indian Muslims to support the concept of Muslim 'self-defence' more strongly. Recognizing the situation, Pakistan and the ISI are believed to have used D-Company and, to a lesser extent, SIMI to provide the contacts, safe houses and front organizations needed to enable LeT, JeM and Harakat-ul-Jihad-i-Islami Bangladesh (HUJI-B) to become all-India threats. Indian security officials cite the terrorist attacks in Bangalore, Ahmedabad and Surat (25–27 July 2008) as recent examples of this nexus at work.[131] However, these attacks are more reactive in nature and driven by anger and feelings of alienation rather than the desire to achieve complex political objectives. This type of urban terrorism likely does not require much, if any, planning and training outside of India and, if conducted in isolation and not part of a coordinated campaign, the long-term effects are not incredibly severe. However, as demonstrated by the Provisional Irish Republican Army (PIRA), if IM can transform these somewhat isolated attacks into a consistent campaign, they can cause long-lasting damage even if their tactics do not advance considerably. It is possible that this is actually the intention of IM's foreign patrons at present.

In the wake of the Mumbai bombings in 2006, LeT came under intense pressure from the Musharraf regime to scale back its offensive operations against India. As such, Zakiur Rahman Lakhvi and other LeT commanders prodded their Indian counterparts to set up a self-sustaining network in India. On the eve of attacking three court buildings in Uttar Pradesh in November 2007, the group finally named itself the Indian Mujahedeen.[132] IM was still very much a work in progress when LeT had to scale back its assistance rather unexpectedly. This stunted IM's growth and likely caused LeT to modify its expectations for the group. In the early stages, it appears that LeT, with D-Company assistance, aimed to turn IM into their India-based crack force that remained completely obedient. However, once it became clear that these aims were unrealistic, LeT had to improvise and accept an autonomous outfit that takes occasional directives from LeT and its allies outside of India. Though this helps to hide foreign involvement, it also greatly lessens the amount of command and control that can be exerted over IM by LeT.

Key leaders of IM escaped a nationwide police hunt which led to the arrest of over 80 of its operatives in six states in 2008. Police services across India claim that they have credible intelligence that IM is planning further strikes and dozens of Indian jihadists have received training in Pakistan.[133] Even if these reports are accurate, recent attacks by IM were not particularly sophisticated and did not require many specialized skills. Though importing certain components such as bomb-making skills and financial assistance are real possibilities, it is critical that India does not overemphasize the importance of Pakistan and Bangladesh with regards to IM. Even without foreign assistance, IM can still carry out attacks though not at the level of LeT.

Kashmir – expanding the conflict theatre

Faced with India's conventional superiority, Pakistan believed that its interests were favoured by a military equation that saw the largest number of Indian troops diverted away from a possible Indian strike force aimed at Pakistan towards internal security operations. Islamabad also believed that it could calibrate and control this policy, an assessment that generally held until the Afghan jihad ended with the fall of Najibullah's communist regime in Kabul in April 1992. Although Islamabad's policy remained constant, several other external factors made IHK an increasingly volatile flashpoint. First, the victory over the USSR inspired Kashmiri terrorists to believe that New Delhi could also be beaten. Second, a moderate number of Pakistani and Indian Kashmiris received training and combat experience in Afghanistan during the war against the Soviets and believed that they were ready to fight Indian forces. Third, Islamist NGOs from the Arabian Peninsula looked for post-Afghan causes to support and Kashmiri separatists figured prominently. Lastly, after Al-Qaeda's formation in 1988, it took a strong interest in the Kashmiri terrorists and began to assist them after the Soviet withdrawal. Each of these factors lessened Islamabad's ability to effectively regulate the violence in Kashmir and thereby limit chances of a military confrontation with India. Even if Islamabad tightened the screws, assistance came from other sources.[134] Now, another driver has been added to the equation with the introduction of D-Company and its criminal network within India itself.

Pakistan's covert operations alone would not have posed a threat to Indian security and stability but rising anti-Hindu sentiments among India's 150 million-strong Muslim community have complemented Pakistani operations and enhanced the threat posed to India's communal harmony and economy, something that increases the likelihood of an unintended India–Pakistan war. Nonetheless, this situation was still manageable but with the rise of Hindu nationalism and cultural chauvinism, or Hindutva, the situation has become more severe and created breathing space for D-Company and its self-crafted image. The rapid growth of the BJP and the simultaneous expansion of the Mumbai-based Shiv Sena (Army of Shiva) began to challenge the secular credentials of the Indian state in a manner that was openly anti-Muslim. By the late 1990s Hindu nationalist leaders were pushing for the imposition of domestic policies, namely in the area of counter-terrorism, that widened the Hindu–Muslim communal divide and created a permissive environment for the development of anti-Hindu Islamist terrorism in India. Further, since the US-led invasion of Afghanistan in 2001, Pakistan has continued its covert operations in Kashmir and, as a response to Indian moves in Afghanistan, aims to create an insurgent/terrorist capability across India to attack the booming economy.[135]

After lying low for a few months following the November 2008 Mumbai carnage and the subsequent crackdown on its Pakistan-based camps and leadership, LeT began scaling its operations back up in IHK. LeT fighters engaged Indian regulars of 1 Para and 6 Battalion Rashtriya Rifles (a counter-terrorism paramilitary unit created in 1990 for use in Kashmir) in a five-day firefight beginning on 20 March 2009 in the Shamasbari forest range of Kupwara district near the LoC. LeT claimed responsibility for the ambush on an army patrol and the following encounter in which 17 terrorists and eight soldiers (including a major) were killed. The Indian Army attributed its losses to the technical sophistication of the insurgents and their use of GPS systems in the densely forested region. India claims that it has also recovered snow gear, advanced maps, satellite phones, rations and medical supplies.[136] This equipment points to continued involvement of elements within Pakistan's security forces. Following the admission of involvement in LeT by the sole surviving Mumbai terrorist, the group's image suffered tremendously throughout Pakistan as well as Kashmir as it risked pulling the decades-old dispute into the greater 'war on terror' framework, something that would allow India to become even more inflexible regarding negotiations on the issue. LeT appears keenly aware that its core source of legitimacy stems from its fight against Indian security forces in Kashmir and that this cannot be compromised. Wisely, LeT waited for the regional security environment to settle somewhat before re-engaging the Kashmir theatre. These actions sought to clearly communicate to New Delhi and the Kashmiris that LeT remains resolutely focused on Kashmir while also attempting to signal to ordinary Pakistanis and their allies in the security forces that LeT is still a reliable partner that seeks to forward Pakistani objectives vis-à-vis India. By continuing to fight in Kashmir, LeT makes it more difficult and politically unpopular to crack down on its activities in Pakistan despite the fact that its other actions in India and elsewhere clearly undermine Pakistani security.

After recently overhauling its infrastructure in IHK, LeT has vowed to continue its operations against security forces and vital installations in the state. Further, unconfirmed reports state that LeT has opened up more camps in Muzzafarabad, Mirpur and Kotli for the fresh recruitment and training of new fighters and has replaced the commanders that were taken into Pakistani custody. As such, many have raised questions regarding how LeT was able to bounce back so quickly even after Pakistan's so-called crack-down following the Mumbai attacks.[137] Reports about training camps are often exaggerated and nearly impossible to verify. However, until Pakistan's border dispute with India as well as Afghanistan is resolved, Islamabad is not likely to drop its support for irregulars as Pakistan has come to view many of them as an insurance policy against what Islamabad assesses to be hostile neighbours. Unless these fundamental issues are addressed, Pakistan is likely to continue on this ultimately self-destructing path much to the detriment of regional and international security.

Veteran Kashmiri guerilla commander Ilyas Kashmir is overseeing the development of the new 'neo-Taliban' strategy in Afghanistan which seeks to complement the traditional guerilla war of the Kandahari clan in south-western Afghanistan and suicide operations in and around Kabul and in southeastern Afghanistan. These neo-Taliban also intend to spread chaos throughout Pakistan and India through kidnappings, high profile attacks and other asymmetric tactics. After this, they intend to go to a step further by actively engaging security forces once military operations are diverted by the chaos that has been caused. The Arab and former Kashmiri fighters that form the bulk of the neo-Taliban have been fighting under the command and strategy of the Taliban in Afghanistan but have now formed into a separate entity.[138] Given the background of this group and the nature of terrorism in the region, this outfit likely has links to Kashmir and can shift back to that theatre if it becomes disenchanted in Afghanistan or if the conflict ends. In the event that this group returns to Kashmir and greater India, it will be even more capable after spending years engaging American and NATO forces in Afghanistan and, through D-Company, will have the ability to move throughout the whole of India for the first time.

The Mehsud tribe is believed to provide base camps for these fighters and also raises money. It is estimated that between November 2008 and April 2009 alone, TTP's network in Karachi generated at least 250 million rupees (US$3.1 million) through various operations including extorting fuel contractors for coalition troops in Afghanistan and ransom money from kidnappings and threats. These proceeds have been used to open up new guerilla training camps in both Pakistan and Afghanistan.[139] TTP has links with mainstream LeT so these fighters in Afghanistan can hardly be viewed as insulated from the Kashmir insurgency. TTP also uses LeT and other infrastructure of the Punjabi-dominated groups to attack in settled areas of Pakistan such as Lahore and Islamabad. This will inevitably have an impact on India and with additional safe havens to plan and train, another spectacular by LeT or a related group on Indian territory cannot be ruled out. Pakistan's Punjabi militants are the most highly trained and have become battled-hardened after years of fighting in India and IHK. In such an event, there is no guarantee that American diplomacy could prevent a major conventional war.

It is believed that the March 2009 attacks on a police academy in Lahore were carried out by terrorists who have been associated with LeT and Harakat-ul-Jihad-i-Islami Pakistan (HUJI-P). Security sources claims that the group travelled to Lahore from a terrorist camp in the North Waziristan town of Razmak. After killing a number of cadets and taking many others hostage, the lead terrorists are reported to have slipped away leaving behind a few men to keep the shootout with security forces going for eight hours. The fugitives most likely then travelled to cities in southern Punjab, namely Multan. Intelligence agencies maintain that some of the terrorists came from Punjab and spoke Urdu, Punjabi and Seraiki even though FATA-based TTP claimed responsibility for the attack.[140] These attacks and the attack on the Sri Lankan cricket team in Lahore represent some dangerous muscle-flexing by Pakistan's 'original' jihadis, mostly Punjabis trained by the military in the 1990s as the first line of defence for the country, especially in Kashmir. These terrorists remained neutral after the US invasion of Afghanistan in 2001 and only joined the Taliban's fight against foreign forces in Afghanistan in 2004 through the provision of training and logistics. However, they did not involve themselves in the hostilities in the tribal areas.[141] This has now clearly changed thus rendering any distinctions between terrorists even more indisputably obsolete and demonstrates that Pakistan's outfits, including its supposed allies like LeT, have made a strategic decision to escalate their campaigns in the country even if it pushes Pakistan to the brink.

LeT's parent outfit, Jamaat-ud-Dawa (JuD), is considered to be the best organized Islamic charity in South Asia with a social network unmatched by other Islamic groups or militant outfits. By responding to social and economic ills under the platform of Islamic social justice, groups like JuD have done extremely well in meeting the population's expectations in times of crises or natural disasters and win their loyalty as a result. Through these provisions of social services, JuD is able to connect in a way that the Pakistani state cannot. This puts pressure on the state and also prevents external actors from exploiting the local population to steer them away from the Islamists' camp. In doing so, JuD and by extension LeT are able to expand their organization through social networking. This allows them to maintain a level of independence and qualify as legitimate authorities to a population that increasingly perceives the civilian government as corrupt and weak in the face of Western demands.[142] This is a major impediment to shutting down LeT infrastructure as it could create a massive vacuum that would likely be filled by another non-state actor. By thinking strategically, LeT and JuD have taken steps to ensure that any effort to uproot them will be most painful for society and the government.

LeT seems to have a heightened awareness of the power of emotions and a need to continue to engage in surprising moves to maintain its elevated status. LeT/JuD also seek to appeal to a global audience despite being a local group, something that has prompted comparisons with Al-Qaeda. It also attracts members from outside of Pakistan and has infrastructure in Central Asia and the Arab world.[143] This likely has much to do with LeT's inflated ambitions but it still cannot afford to shift its primary focus from Kashmir and India, for which it needs its long-time partner, D-Company. For this, LeT has to maintain its infrastructure in IHK, carry out innovative spectaculars in India and continue to nurture IM.

Assam: the next front?

The 30 October 2008 Assam blasts claimed 85 lives and injured nearly 500. Sophisticated weaponry and unknown smuggling networks were used to carry out these attacks as opposed to the relatively crude locally assembled explosives used elsewhere in India such as New Delhi, Mumbai, Hyderabad and Varanasi. The bombs used in Assam have raised concerns over the region's porous borders as well as links between local separatist groups, especially from Bangladesh and Myanmar. Security experts say that the car and motorcycle bombs that were often laden with over 80 kilograms of RDX (rapid detonating explosive) were well beyond the capability of domestic separatist outfits such as the United Liberation Front of Assam (ULFA) or the National Democratic Front of Bodoland (NDFB).[144] Prior to the bombings, there had been brutal anti-Bengali/Muslim riots and communal tensions were high.

India's Home Ministry believes that HUJI-B was involved in the Assam bombings and that the group maintains close ties with IM. In Assam, HUJI-B is believed to utilize its close connections with illegal immigrants from Bangladesh for new recruits, safe houses and logistical support, and reports suggest that the Indian government has identified 46 points along the border with Bangladesh that are being used as exit and entry points by HUJI-B.[145] Bangladesh is facing a major yet little publicized national security challenge from terrorist groups. Unfortunately, a common perception exists amongst the greater counter-terrorism community that Bangladeshi terrorist groups do not have significant linkages with groups outside the country and therefore do not pose a challenge to international security. Put simply, the common viewpoint is that these groups are waging an internal struggle and are not linked to global terrorism.

Potential radicalization of security personnel in Bangladesh?

While investigations are still underway into the Bangladesh Rifles (BDR – a paramilitary border security force) mutiny that took place in February 2009, there have been allegations made by several quarters, including the minister responsible for coordinating the investigations, about a possible involvement by Bangladesh-based Jamaat-ul Mujahedeen Bangladesh (JMB) and other terrorist organizations. If the suspicion proves to be true, this would have serious implications for the national security of Bangladesh as well as India. Many of the bodies of the Bangladeshi Army officers that were killed in the mutiny were mutilated in a very barbaric, brutal fashion. Does this point towards a possible radicalization of certain members of the security forces? If that is the case, then it would raise serious concerns and would require Bangladeshi authorities to have a hard look at the internal oversight procedures of the security apparatus. It is also of note that over 1,800 BDR personnel still have not returned for duty and are dispersed throughout the country. Despite the Operation Rebel Hunt which has been launched, some of these deserters are not likely to be located. Potentially radicalized paramilitary and regular soldiers are problematic for a number of reasons. First, they tend to be much better trained in combat techniques and the use of weaponry. Second, as they have previously served in the armed forces or paramilitaries, they have knowledge of the layout of various facilities and the strengths and weaknesses of the security forces. Lastly, their actions can serve a powerful motivator for many 'fence-sitters' who are also disillusioned with their positions as well as with society at large and extremist ex-soldiers may even have a line of communication open with still-serving personnel. These soldiers not only constitute a large group of well-trained men, but they also possibly have a significant portion of the weapons and ammunition that was looted from BDR during the mutiny.[146]

Now equipped with the necessary resources, Bangladesh and India have to contend with the possibility of the ranks of existing groups mushrooming or witnessing a dangerous proliferation of self-starter groups, either of which will have knock-on effects in India, especially in nearby areas where there is communal tension and a conducive environment like Assam. Further, IM is not likely to have remained idle while massive amounts of weapons flowed out of BDR headquarters and Bangladesh's border defences were also down. As such, IM's biggest operational upgrade may come from Bangladesh instead of Pakistan but will require access to a sophisticated underground network that is capable of picking up and distributing these stray weapons. In the case of India, the only group that possesses such a network is D-Company and, given its involvement with LeT and IM, it is clearly the most likely candidate.

Bangladesh–Afghanistan connection

A fact that is often ignored is that the senior leadership of Bangladeshi terrorist outfits such as JMB and HUJI-B took an active part in the Afghan rebellion against the Soviet Union. The leaders of HUJI-B saw action in Paktia province in Afghanistan during the war and it was during this time that they came into close contact with individuals who later went on to assume important leadership positions in terrorist groups across the South Asian region and beyond. For around a decade these individuals fought side by side against a common enemy, imbued and enthused with the same ideology. The relationships formed on the battlefields of Khost, Kandahar, Helmand and Paktia did not fade following the Soviet withdrawal nor are they likely to disappear in the future. In addition to JMB and HUJI-B, the senior leadership of the vast majority of Islamist terrorist groups in South Asia still includes individuals who fought in the Afghan rebellion. Therefore, there is a very real possibility that Bangladeshi terrorist leaders are able to leverage the long-term relationships that they have forged with their comrades in arms from South Asia and possibly the Middle East and can translate this into a strong collaborative operational relationship between their groups.[147] The bonds that were initially formed in Afghanistan are more than likely to have been further cemented over the years as they continue to engage in activities that are driven by the same ideological reasoning. As such, it is vital that this phenomenon is examined and that the transnational linkages of Bangladeshi terror groups are adequately understood if counter-terrorism policies, strategies and tactics are to be effective.

Different enemies, common justifications

A concept that frequently appears in the strategic communications put forward by South Asian terrorist groups is the comparison of everything that they stand against with *Taghoot* or the force of evil. Referring to some select verses in the Koran and interpreting it to suit their requirements, these groups try to portray their enemies as alongside the forces of evil.[148] The same reasoning is used by JMB, LeT, JeM and a number of other Islamist terror organizations across the region. The forces that these groups claim to fight against are diverse. While JMB is fighting Dhaka to establish a puritanical Islamic state in Bangladesh, LeT and JeM are fighting against the Indian state using Kashmir as their main justification. However, while the targets are different, the ideological justifications are usually the same. They also share an almost pathological disdain for the West (and the United States in particular) as well as India. When JMB sends a message, while the Bangladeshi state and society remains the main enemy, the West and the United States are also lambasted. Further, HUJI-B is imbued with the same extremist Deobandi ideology which inspires JeM and other groups, thus posing a clear threat to India.

The threat from Bangladeshi groups

Amongst the counter-terrorism community, while Indian and Pakistani terror groups get a lot of attention, the groups operating in Bangladesh are often believed to be substantially weaker and operating mainly with local motivations. However, certain events over the past few years point towards a different direction. Three particular incidents will be highlighted to illustrate this point. In 2003, three JMB members were apprehended by Bangladeshi police and found to be carrying uranium. Police and sources at Bangladesh's Atomic Energy Commission later remarked that they possessed enough uranium to manufacture a dirty bomb.[149] To this day it is not clearly established why those JMB terrorists were carrying such fissile material and it is still unknown whether they were planning an operation in Bangladesh or acting as couriers for one of their regional partners. Whatever the mission may have been, the consequences of its success would have been cataclysmic.

Second, JMB carried out near simultaneous terrorist attacks on 17 August 2005 when it detonated a total of 463 bombs over a span of 50 minutes in 63 out of 64 district towns in Bangladesh.[150] This was by no means a simple feat as an operation of that nature required superb organization, planning and coordination to achieve the desired results, skills that likely came from external sources. Furthermore, each attack site was also left with a leaflet carrying the key messages of the group. The motivations may have been local but it is unlikely that without support of either a tactical or logistical nature from an international partner, such an operation could have been mounted. JMB's 2005 attacks represented a massive leapfrog in capabilities that caught many terrorism experts and Dhaka off guard. It was accepted as a fact in Dhaka that JMB was not a serious threat and could be effectively dismantled by arresting a few key leaders. JMB's rapid evolution holds critical lessons for India as IM's 'terrorist cycle' is several years behind JMB and New Delhi has the rare luxury of being able to observe the successes and failures of Bangladesh's efforts to deal with emerging terrorist groups.

Third, there is now an elaborate structure of financing that is used by Bangladeshi terror groups. Recent research has shown that both HUJI-B and JMB extensively use the large Bangladeshi expatriate population for fundraising and are known to have received funds from Europe and the Middle East.[151] In addition, a HUJI-B terrorist apprehended in 2008 admitted during interrogation that he had undertaken several visits to countries in Southeast Asia. It is also important to note that one of the key masterminds of the deadly bomb attack on 21 August 2004 on the Awami League political rally (where the incumbent Bangladeshi Prime Minister was seriously wounded), Maulana Tajuddin, is currently in South Africa according to various reports. It is believed that South African organizations have been used for raising funds and, as such, it is clear that JMB and HUJI-B have spread and their linkages transcend well beyond Bangladesh's immediate vicinity.[152]

The international community must note with caution the potential fissures and divisions that exist within Bangladeshi society and the impact that they can have on India as well as the trilateral nexus between Pakistan, LeT and D-Company. Bangladesh has evolved into a secular society where culture and religion cohabit in the same space without having any contradiction or collision. The terrorist and extremist groups operating in Bangladesh find this to be disdainful and these groups will continually try to resist the forces in favour of preserving the secular liberal nature of the state where people practise their respective faiths while there is no room for sectarianism or communalism. What remains to be seen is how long this battle will last and who will ultimately emerge as the triumphant force. In the aftermath of the mutiny of the BDR in Bangladesh, it is critically important to examine the kind of fissures that terror groups can create within the security forces of Bangladesh while bearing in mind that HUJI-B tried to stage a coup in connivance with some members of the Pakistan Army in 1995. The attempt was meant to topple the elected government and install an Islamist regime but the coup was averted due to early intelligence reports.[153] Given the historical, operational and administrative links that exist between HUJI in Pakistan (HUJI-P) and HUJI-B, this is something that needs to be taken into account.

Links to groups in India

Many analysts as well as Indian security officials believe that HUJI-B actively works with the banned Student Islamic Movement of India, is a component of IM as part of its design to expand its support base and to destabilize India, and was possibly involved in the November 2008 Mumbai attacks. HUJI-B poses a very serious threat to Indian security not only because of its links to other transnational terrorist groups that are antagonistic towards New Delhi and have a proven ability to carry out large-scale attacks, but also because many of its cadres do not arouse suspicion as they speak a language (Bangla) and are of an ethnic background (Bengali) that is also prominent in India. This is compounded by the porous nature of the poorly policed Indo-Bangladesh border and the lack of an extradition treaty between the two countries. As such, future efforts to prevent infiltration will prove most difficult even if sufficient political will is available, something that is debatable.

Like most of India's smaller South Asian neighbours, there is considerable apprehension in Bangladesh regarding New Delhi's ambitions in the subcontinent as well its perceived interference in Bangladesh's internal affairs. However, at the same time it is not in Bangladesh's interest to have a hostile relationship with its giant neighbour and, as such, any leadership in Dhaka must toe a fine line by maintaining at least a stable relationship with India while not appearing to be too close to New Delhi. Failure to do so risks jeopardizing their domestic as well as international legitimacy and regime security.

Following the most recent election in late 2008, Sheikh Hasina returned to power. Largely perceived to be pro-India, it has been widely anticipated that her administration will seek to crack down on groups that threaten regional stability, such JMB and HUJI-B, but also several insurgent groups in India's northeast that New Delhi believes have taken refuge in Bangladesh. Much of Hasina's credibility in India will rest upon the extent to which she can effectively reign in these groups and, given her previous failures, her half-life with the Indians is not incredibly generous. This fact is not lost on her Islamist adversaries who recognize that carrying out attacks in India has a multiplier effect in that it increases the group's profile, enhances its credentials as an international terrorist outfit and also actively undercuts any potential for improvement in Indo-Bangladesh ties, something that could put a major dent in their activities. It can also provoke irrational responses by India and strengthen hard-liners in New Delhi thus creating an environment that is even more conducive for terrorist activity in both countries. If HUJI-B or JMB were to carry out an attack in India, it would have multiple objectives and sophisticated political aims. However, if these groups wanted to use violence effectively in order to achieve the maximum political impact, it would need a local partner that is more in tune to the political, social and economic situation on the ground and who understands the critical human geography. D-Company and IM would fill this need while also benefiting from the increased prestige that would accompany improved capabilities and IM's affiliation with more established terrorist groups, something that could greatly enhance IM's recruitment efforts within India. However, once again this would be a case of Islamist terrorism using primarily profit-generating criminal infrastructure.

Links to groups in Pakistan

HUJI-B was initially an offshoot of Harakat-ul-Jihad-i-Islami Pakistan (HUJI-P), a Pakistan-based, Kashmir-centred group that had strong links with the Pakistani security apparatus and, until recently, was the stronger half. Traditionally, HUJI-B has taken much of its training and arms supply from Muzaffarabad in PHK as a component of its partnership with HUJI-P but this has now changed and it has become the role of HUJI-B to maintain relevance by continuing to carry out attacks in Bangladesh and India. Nonetheless, HUJI-B still maintains some of its most critical Pakistani links and interrogations of captured militants have revealed that the group has recently enjoyed trainers from Pakistan-based LeT and JeM.[154] However, as the international spotlight shines brightly on Pakistan, HUJI-B has shifted many of its training and logistical operations into Bangladesh itself, although information sharing still likely continues.

Jalaluddin Haqqani's network has existed in Pakistan since the Soviet era and also extends throughout the Pashtun areas of Afghanistan and into Kabul. Haqqani is arguably the most credible 'mujahedeen' given his personal history and lack of involvement in Afghanistan's brutal civil war. Further, unlike the Tehrik-i-Taliban Pakistan (TTP), the Haqqani network is usually friendly towards Pakistan and often urges other groups to avoid engaging the Pakistani security forces and focus all of their resources on Afghanistan. As such, while still being on the receiving end of many American drone strikes, his network has not been the focal point of military operations by the Pakistan Army. Any cooperation between the Haqqani network and HUJI-B could greatly enhance the latter's operational capabilities through training while also providing HUJI-B with established infrastructure to raise funds and to hide wanted members. It is of note that a considerable amount of Bangladeshis have been arrested while trying to go to Afghanistan in recent years.[155] Nonetheless, none of these enhanced capabilities can be put to use in India if HUJI-B is unable to enter and efficiently move around the country. As is the case with LeT, HUJI-B needs D-Company to scale up its activities in India. However, at this point in time it is unclear if D-Company is willing to extend its services to HUJI-B and take on the risk that would accompany that decision. It is important to note that, unlike LeT, D-Company is not obligated to support HUJI-B.

Haqqani runs an extensive unregulated network of madrassas near the border with Afghanistan. These schools are often blamed for helping to spawn the Taliban movement in Afghanistan in the 1990s and were known to provide thousands of frontline troops during their advances.[156] Most of the madrassas are still operational and have also been the target of American drone attacks, suggesting that they still support insurgents in Afghanistan, both domestic and foreign. Bangladesh also has an unregulated network of thousands of private 'Qaumi' madrassas that develop their own curriculum and are not required to make their sources of funding known to Dhaka.[157] Any further transfer of radical ideology from overseas into Bangladesh's Qaumi madrassas is extremely dangerous as this has been a major driver behind groups such as JMB beginning to look beyond Bangladesh in their strategic planning. Further, while Pakistani groups like the TTP and the Tehreek-e-Nafaz-e-Shariat-e-Mohammadi (TNSM) are still somewhat nationalist in their rhetoric and locally focused, this is not the case with HUJI-B, a group that is increasingly identifying itself with global terrorism and making less of a distinction between the 'far' and 'near' enemy. Increased contacts with other radical madrassa networks in South Asia and access to D-Company's underground network could accelerate this trend. However, it should be noted that, by and large, unregulated Bangladeshi madrassas produce lower-ranking members for HUJI-B and JMB as they do not equip graduates with many practical skills. Nonetheless, these individuals still form the bulk of the membership of these outfits and are the ones who are charged with executing attacks and implementing various strategies and directives.

HUJI-B and JMB have undoubtedly been watching developments in Pakistan's Malakand Division (which houses Swat) with much interest as, like Sufi Mohammed and the TNSM, one of their main complaints with the Bangladeshi state is over the lack of Sharia and the slow, inefficient and corrupt practices that are commonplace in the British-style judiciary. A careful analysis of strategies and tactics used by the TNSM is likely underway and information exchange cannot be ruled out. HUJI-B and JMB also have a latecomer's advantage in that they have been able to witness the successes and failures of previous groups and can avoid many potential pitfalls. As such, expect a deliberate and precise strategy by HUJI-B and JMB that seeks to incorporate many of the lessons learned from other terrorist/insurgent theatres. Already they are attempting to employ their own inkblot strategy by building their support base and cadre strength district by district. Further, these groups seek active participation in the legitimate political process and HUJI-B attempted to run in the elections in late 2008 under the Islamic Democratic Party but was denied permission by the Election Commission. Also, JMB has now split and established a 'mainstream' ideological wing that claims to operate separately from the terrorist outfit and has reconstituted its *Shura*, or key decision-making body.[158] All of these developments point to long-term strategic thinking and the intent to systematically intensify their campaigns in Bangladesh and exert influence in India.

Implications

Just like financial markets, terrorist or insurgent 'markets' influence each other. Successes by terrorist or insurgent outfits in other South Asian theatres will embolden the Bangladeshi groups as well as IM, something that can lead to an increase in recruiting as well as more audacious tactics provided they have consistent access to a strong logistical network. Also, as HUJI-B, JMB and IM are considerably younger and less well known than most of their regional counterparts, they will likely attempt to springboard into the limelight through more violent yet innovative methods of attack and subversion. However, this will require guidance from external sources.

Like the rest of the world's most prolific terrorist groups, Bangladesh's outfits have recognized the power of ideas and increasingly sophisticated propaganda videos have begun to appear that are available in multiple forms in order to reach as many potential recruits as possible. In addition, JMB's information operations (IO) are very effective and place great emphasis on leaflets and on immediately explaining the rationale for their actions in a clear and concise manner. For example, JMB explained the lack of massive casualties during their coordinated bomb blasts in 2005 as being the result of an intentional decision to not cause harm to innocents. Instead, they claimed that the bombs were designed to serve as a demonstration of power and a warning to Dhaka. If IM is to become a long-term factor in India, it will also have to develop a more advanced IO capacity. As JMB is operating in an environment that shares many similarities with India (official secularism, constitutional governance, democratic institutions, etc.) its rationale and justifications for its attacks could provide a useful framework for IM. In addition, the influence of the pan-Islamic Hizbut Tahrir has mushroomed in Bangladesh while the country still faces a critical shortage of iconic moderate Muslim clerics to counter this development and the increased propagation of radical Islamic ideology. Without an effective counterweight, breaking the recruitment cycle of groups such as HUJI-B and JMB will prove most difficult, if not impossible.

Like the Afghan Taliban in the 1990s, TTP, Al-Qaeda and others, JMB and HUJI-B have creatively blended select Islamic themes and socio-economic issues into a simple, easy-to-digest manner that does require much critical thinking. This ensures that their ideology is not solely dependent on Islamic arguments, messages that can be countered by qualified religious leaders, thus enhancing its survivability and long-term viability. These groups have also successfully identified their target audience (semi-educated 18–25-year-old Bangladeshis with limited employment prospects) and are carrying out an aggressive marketing campaign. HUJI-B and JMB have also seen how causing high civilian casualties and not adhering to local traditions can quickly drain the oxygen out of a movement, something that Al-Qaeda in Iraq (AQI) learned the hard way.

Given the close ties between LeT and both of HUJI's chapters in Pakistan and Bangladesh that have been forged over the years in Kashmir and elsewhere, coordination of efforts to enhance IM's capabilities is likely highly desired but requires an in-country enabler. While the world closely analyses Pakistan's every move regarding counter-terrorism, Bangladesh is still considered a non-factor by many. As such, HUJI-B, JMB and LeT may be able to use Bangladeshi territory to aid IM's efforts to carry out consistent low-tech attacks throughout India while leaving spectaculars to LeT for the time being. This is not to play down the threat to India originating from Pakistani soil but several South Asian terrorist groups likely view Bangladesh in the same manner that an investor views an emerging market. Efforts to increase terrorist capacity in India and nearby Bangladesh will be spearheaded by LeT as a component of its strategy to become the most prolific terrorist group in the region. However, none of it will be possible without D-Company on board and, at present, there is no evidence to suggest that this is yet the case.

Concluding thoughts

Although LeT was a key component of Islamabad's regional strategy in the past, the organization is growing beyond Pakistan's control and is beginning to undertake its own independent operations without factoring Islamabad into the equation. LeT does still indeed view Kashmir as a vital issue, but now feels it is the central component of a larger pan-Islamic strategy. Pursuant to this objective, LeT has forged selective tactical partnerships with fellow Pakistani and other regional terrorist groups and, while maintaining its larger strategic partnership with D-Company whose activities undermine Pakistan's own security, has escalated its terrorism campaigns throughout South Asia and increased the risk of an inadvertent war between India and Pakistan. One such group is Al-Qaeda, an organization whose presence on Pakistani soil Islamabad has promised to eradicate. LeT is also believed to have been involved in attempts on the lives of several Pakistani leaders, including General Musharraf and the recent attacks in Mumbai. As such, it appears that LeT no longer feels that it is accountable to its former patron as a whole, but rather to itself and a select few officers in ISI and the Pakistani military (current and/or retired). However, if support for LeT from the Pakistani intelligence and military establishment continues unabated, LeT will become a multinational organization with access to an extensive criminal network in India which allows it to determine its own agenda as it will have a wide range of sponsors, sources of funding, and will have fighters and other vital resources spread throughout several regions. Ironically, Pakistan's decision to encourage/push D-Company into a partnership with LeT is what sparked this trend and a shift in the trilateral nexus. While D-Company was meant to augment LeT's capacities, D Company's Indian network opened up a new door of possibilities over which Pakistan has very little control. Further, as these networks are used primarily for profit-generating activities, they are sufficiently robust and resistant to tactical intervention by the authorities and will not be fading any time soon. In this case, the profit motive very much serves as the key enabler and sustainer for Pakistan-based terrorism in India. This clearly defies the logic used by several state sponsors of terrorism that irregulars can be sustainably used in an asymmetric fashion to achieve limited objectives against a conventionally superior adversary and that such groups will not eventually deviate from the process of not escalating tensions past a certain point. This throws into doubt such claims that ties between groups like Hizballah and Tehran/Damascus are a permanent reality and are not vulnerable to fractionalization.

LeT has not had problems in recruitment as many madrassas in Pakistan remain unsupervised and do not equip graduates with practical skills. Further, communal tension within India has allowed LeT to develop a working relationship with SIMI and to establish IM, assist its operations and guide its development and strategic planning. In addition, these tensions have made it possible for LeT to recruit within India, thus providing it with ideal operatives that speak without foreign accents, are highly familiar with their surroundings and have an extensive network of local contacts. Equally troubling is the fact that LeT has upgraded its activities and has begun to operate throughout India using D-Company infrastructure and will likely target transportation and economic infrastructure and the political establishment as opposed to Indian security forces exclusively. It has also adopted new methods of destabilization such as recruiting from India's troubled northeast and smuggling terrorists into India by sea, a serious infringement on India's sovereignty.

Despite being a proscribed outfit, LeT still enjoys funding from ISI and through donations from a wide range of domestic and overseas sympathizers, including Indian Muslims. Further, after capitalizing on the 2005 earthquake, LeT has been able to re-establish some of its fundraising activities within Pakistan. On top of this, LeT now raises funds on the Internet and has become market-savvy while making 'legitimate' investments in a range of sectors. LeT is also undoubtedly involved in trafficking Afghan heroin, an extremely high-yielding venture given the low overhead costs and high domestic and overseas demand. However, given D-Company's dominance in this market in South Asia, it is almost impossible to imagine a scenario where LeT would be able to do this without utilizing D-Company assets and expertise. All of this has resulted in a diversification of LeT's financial pipeline, thus reducing the possibility of being held hostage to a particular party, decreasing its vulnerability to a decapitating strike, and ensuring its continued existence, even if it is abandoned by Islamabad entirely.

India will continue to face a serious threat from Pakistan-based terrorist groups for the foreseeable future. However, India lacks military options that have strategic-level effects without a significant risk of a military response by Pakistan and neither Indian nor US policy is likely to be able to reduce the terrorist threat substantially in the short- to medium-term. Due to this, other Indian extremists will inevitably find inspiration and instruction from the November 2008 Mumbai attacks. Local radicalization is a major goal of the terrorists and this will remain a major social and political challenge for India.[159] Although LeT spectaculars grab international attention and inspire, their impacts on India and Mumbai in particular are not usually long-lasting thus rendering LeT unable to translate short-term tactical 'victories' into long-term strategic gains on their own from Pakistan. Due to this, LeT will rely more heavily on IM to increase its membership and to engage in low-tech campaign terrorism throughout India if it is to succeed in undermining the Indian economy, disturbing communal relations and dashing any hopes of improving ties between India and Pakistan. However, to do this it will need consistent and sustained access to D-Company's underground criminal network in India. Based on precedent and previous behaviour (and a lack of evidence to suggest that the situation has demonstrably changed), D-Company is likely to grant this access as long as its senior leadership is dependent upon Pakistan for its safe refuge and the activities of LeT and/or IM not to transgress a certain limit where they would jeopardize D-Company's business interests as this is the main driver of the network in the first place.

Although LeT and groups like HUJI-B have high hopes for IM, the group remains relatively primitive in terms of operational capacity and information operations. LeT's rise to prominence has largely followed a more sophisticated understanding of politics and strategic thought thus causing the group to come to view violence as a tool rather than an end in itself. IM's urban terrorism currently appears to be reactive and driven by anger rather than by more complex strategic objectives, something that LeT undoubtedly seeks to change. At present, IM's attacks do not require a safe haven or training in Pakistan as they are relatively simple but if the group intends to evolve then the role of both Pakistan and Bangladesh will become more prominent. However, although LeT would like to see a much more advanced IM, it will still seek to claim the title of South Asia's most effective terrorist group. If this is to occur, LeT will continue to plan major Mumbai-style operations in India while also scaling up attacks in IHK in order to maintain legitimacy. Further, in order for HUJI-B to play a more decisive role in India, like LeT, it will need access to D-Company's network but it is presently unclear whether Ibrahim is willing to take on additional risk without additional commercial benefits.

As many of LeT's cadres are Pakistani and IM is still a somewhat of a disjointed organization, D-Company's logistical network will be critical, especially in major urban centres such as Mumbai. This network can be utilized for recruiting, smuggling weapons and terrorists in and out of India, and providing pre-operation and post-operation services like surveillance, reconnaissance and assisting terrorists in moving through India undetected. Without D-Company's vast cross-border network, LeT is not likely able to achieve its objectives in India and the growth of IM will be inhibited thus limiting it to inconsistent low-tech terrorism which has few lasting effects despite the loss of human life and damage to property. Though investigations are still ongoing and the full story may never be available, as is the case with the 1993 Mumbai blasts, any revelation of D-Company involvement in the 2008 Mumbai attacks should not surprise analysts but they must keep in mind that terrorism is a secondary objective.

India faces a considerable security challenge from Bangladesh with two major terrorist groups that have ties to LeT and other groups in Pakistan and are increasing their capabilities alongside their ambitions and political awareness while the country has been neglected by international counter-terrorism efforts. The bomb blasts in Assam and the BDR mutiny serve as a startling preview of what is to come if current trends are not reversed. Given the porous nature of the Indo-Bangladesh border and the shared ethnicity between the two countries, knock-on effects in India and on IM's capabilities would be nearly unavoidable. Further, in the event that Pakistan actually engages in a meaningful crackdown on terrorist groups operating from its territory, Bangladesh would become IM's most viable option for strategic guidance and material support provided that they were able to access the D-Company network.

No group from Pakistan, Bangladesh or elsewhere could make headway in India unless conditions in select areas were conducive to such activity. Without the Indian component, these groups would remain confined to carrying out occasional large-scale attacks that do not result in political gains and the

IM project could not be successful. This fact is something that New Delhi must continuously emphasize to its civilian population as opposed to focusing a disproportionate amount of attention on foreign groups. As long as the Indian media and political leadership continue to point the finger exclusively towards external forces, many in the security bodies and the general public will look overseas along with them. If a new counter-terrorism body is formed under these misconceptions, there is little to suggest that it will be any more effective than its predecessors. In addition, New Delhi's approach could alienate its regional neighbours, thus unnecessarily undermining any potential for stronger inter-state cooperation. Until New Delhi faces up to this, it will unlikely be able to implement a functioning counter-terrorism strategy and these attacks will tragically continue. This will prove most detrimental to India's internal stability, business climate and the faith of its people in the political leadership and security forces, and could drag South Asia's nuclear-armed rivals into a war.

This chapter has sought to provide a thorough, detailed analysis of both D-Company as well as LeT in order to highlight the very different origins of both groups and to provide critical context regarding how their partnership was forged. Also, it crucially explored the development of the trilateral nexus between Pakistan, LeT and D-Company and shed light on key Pakistani decisions that had the opposite of their intended effect: they actually led to rapidly decreasing Pakistani relevance with regards to LeT's operations throughout India, something that is enabled by D-Company's robust criminal network. Further, this chapter has analysed a rare situation in which one terrorist group (LeT) uses the network of an organized criminal syndicate (D-Company) to establish and eventually spin off another terrorist group (IM) with the profit motive of D-Company underwriting the entire enterprise. In the event that the IM project is successful, it is reasonable to expect D Company to dedicate more of its time and resource towards enabling and cooperating in terrorist activity within India but it will continue to primarily focus on illicit commercial activities, thus remaining firmly outside of Shelley's traditional definition of symbiosis while still exhibiting some of its characteristics.

The following chapter will deal with the reasons for Pakistan's seeming refusal to recognize, let alone act upon, the dangers that are posed by LeT and D-Company's continued safe havens in the country. It will dissect Pakistan's irrational belief that the 'type' of Islamist terrorism advocated and carried out by LeT and enabled by D-Company is distinctly different to that of the Pakistani Taliban, Al-Qaeda and other sectarian groups and therefore does not pose a serious threat to Pakistan itself. It also examines the concept of D-Company being viewed as a strategic asset by some in the Pakistani establishment and analyses the myriad of other internal security issues that Pakistan currently faces. The aim of the following three chapters is to clearly demonstrate the reasons for Ibrahim's continued safe haven in Pakistan despite the obvious threats his syndicate poses to the country and the region.

5 LeT and D-Company in Pakistan

Selective justice, sectarianism and artificial distinctions

Dawood Ibrahim – strategic asset in Karachi but wanted in Mumbai

The *Oxford English Dictionary* defines crime as 'an offence against an individual or the state which is punishable by law'.[1] Similarly, *Merriam-Webster* defines it as 'an act or the commission of an act that is forbidden or the omission of a duty that is commanded by a public law and that makes the offender liable to punishment by that law'.[2] In order to gain a fuller understanding of these definitions with regard to Dawood Ibrahim, they must be applied in both an Indian and Pakistani context.

India is the world's second most populous state and is well known for corruption, selective law enforcement and the infamous nexus between organized criminals and politicians. India's justice system, both civil and criminal, is hopelessly backlogged and the rule of law is not as strong as it is in many other democratic societies. Nonetheless, in India, as is the case with nearly all other nations, murder, smuggling, extortion, weapons and narcotics trafficking, and the destruction of both government and private property are very serious offences, some of which are punishable by death. For example, if Dawood Ibrahim ever faces trial over his involvement in the 1993 Mumbai Blasts, a death sentence is almost guaranteed.

However, despite having legislation that explicitly proscribe these activities, it seems that in India there are special circumstances in which these laws do not apply. Although much attention has been paid by Indian scholars, media, as well as state officials, to the 1993 Mumbai Blasts and D-Company, very little emphasis has been placed upon the barbaric anti-Muslim riots in Mumbai and throughout India that preceded them. The attack on Mumbai sparked a diplomatic flurry marked by Indian diplomats as well as senior government officials exerting heavy pressure on the United States to label Ibrahim an international terrorist and to seize his assets under their jurisdiction. It also strengthened India's lobbying of the international community to label Pakistan a state sponsor of terrorism. Even today, many of India's most wanted were involved in the attacks in 1993 and are mostly believed to be residing in Pakistan while being actively pursued by RAW as well as other Indian intelligence services and law enforcement agencies.

Interestingly, despite this sustained effort to bring these Pakistan-based terrorists to justice for the atrocities that they have committed, there have been very few prosecutions, let alone convictions, of individuals who were involved in the aforementioned anti-Muslim riots in Mumbai in late 1992 and early 1993. The riots killed almost 1,000 people and displaced thousands more with most of the victims being Muslim. The methods in which many were killed were extremely primitive, such as dousing victims with gasoline and setting them on fire, and the rape of Muslim women by Hindu extremists was widespread. Further, a similar situation occurred in Godhra, Gujurat, in 2002 and there have even been accusations of active complicity by senior provincial officials, including the Chief Minister. Nonetheless, very few have ever faced justice for these actions. Why has India not pursued these Hindu terrorists with the same zeal as they have Islamic ones? Hindu terrorists have killed thousands of Indian citizens in recent times but there does not seem to be the same determination by the authorities to apprehend them. In India, the law is clearly subjective and vulnerable to political and other external influences.

Just as India and Pakistan have a shared history, culture and close linguistic ties, Pakistan's society and overall justice system suffers from some of the same defects as India's. Pakistan is consistently rated near the bottom in terms of rule of law, corruption and government transparency, and accusations of state involvement in illicit activities within the subcontinent and the Middle East are endless. Pakistan is also wracked by sectarian and political violence (although the line is blurred at times) but most perpetrators go unpunished. The end result is a civil society that lacks confidence in the abilities of the state security apparatus to provide the protection and stability necessary to live peacefully and to ensure positive social and economic growth.

Despite its wide range of problems, Pakistan does retain a British-style justice system in most parts of the country even though many laws have been adapted to be more in accordance with Islamic principles. Also, much like India, Pakistan has clearly proscribed all of the activities that Ibrahim engages in and has arrested and even killed other non-state actors, such as Balochi rebels and political leaders, for similar offences. As such, it is clear that Islamabad, namely the intelligence and security apparatus, has factored in a variety of other external factors and has decided that these weigh more heavily than the equal application of the law even though D-Company activities actually undermine Pakistan's own security.

Ever since independence in 1947, Pakistan has felt the acute vulnerability of being positioned next to a much larger neighbour. These two nations have engaged in several conflicts and the Kashmir dispute seems deadlocked with neither side possessing the political will nor the domestic support to make meaningful moves towards a lasting settlement. Indo-Pakistan relations have been marked by tension, hostility and active support to subversive elements in the other's territory. However, despite its consistent efforts, it appears that while Pakistan can help to create perennial low-level instability in some parts of India, such as the northeast or IHK, it does not have the ability to cause a fracturing of the Indian Union. However, given Pakistan's geopolitical, economic and social situation, the dissolution of Pakistan is not inconceivable. Because of this reality as well as India's conventional superiority, Pakistan has had to resort to other methods to deter Indian designs, real or perceived. One of these methods is utilizing the resources and expertise of a well-known criminal to wage a low-intensity conflict against New Delhi without engaging Indian forces directly. In this particular case, Pakistan has decided that the forwarding of foreign policy objectives and generating revenue take precedence over the rule of law.[3]

In order to make sense of the rationale behind Pakistan's use of non-state actors, it is necessary to understand the governmental structure of Pakistan itself. The Army has governed over Pakistan for the majority of the nation's existence and has still held considerable power even under civilian administrations, such as that of the late Benazir Bhutto or Nawaz Sharif. As such, security and defence assume top priority and tend to guide foreign policy leading to short-term thinking and actions that would not normally be undertaken by responsible nation states. Also problematic is that there exist extremist elements within the Pakistani Army, several intelligence agencies and retired personnel who share much of the radical ideology with the terrorist groups that they are supposed to be countering and dismantling. Further complicating the matter is that the security apparatus is not subject to any kind of legitimate civilian oversight nor can it be held accountable to the public for many of its actions. As the Army has been given free rein, it has been able to develop and maintain ties with a raft of like-minded non-state actors such as Ibrahim even though these actions will ultimately prove to be self-destructive.

Overview of Pakistan's internal security

> Pakistan's internal threat environment is plagued by a multitude of internal security threats and governance challenges including, inter alia, numerous varieties of terrorism, organized criminal activity, and corruption. Terrorism remains a particularly serious problem with bomb attacks and random killings emerging as a monthly occurrence over the last few years.[4]

Pakistan has a major problem with terrorism as well as organized crime, specifically in the drug trade, and Pakistan is a major transit and consumption point for Afghan opium. The Karachi Mafia is the main criminal group in Pakistan and has become a major smuggler and exporter of light weapons and explosives and is believed to be hiding Dawood Ibrahim. In addition, acts of violence have become nearly everyday occurrences and motivations range from sectarian tensions and family feuds to rivalries amongst criminal groups.[5] The 27 May 2005 suicide bombing at the Bari Imam shrine near the diplomatic quarter in Islamabad that resulted in the deaths of at least 20 Shia worshippers is a clear demonstration of the 'intractable intensity and lethality of Pakistan's sectarian conflict'.[6]

Further complicating the internal security situation is the fact that in Pakistan the line between political/religious and criminal violence has begun to blur and that crimes like kidnapping for ransom, carjacking and armed robbery have soared as these crimes are often committed by people with links to political or religious groups and serve as revenue-generating activities.[7] A major trouble spot for these activities outside of the Federally Administered Tribal Areas (FATA), the Northwest Frontier Province (NWFP) and Balochistan is Karachi, Sindh's largest city and Pakistan's economic hub. The primary source of violence in Karachi is sectarian tension and there have been shootouts between police and suspected Al-Qaeda terrorists, bomb attacks on foreigners, an attempt on the life of former President Musharraf, the murder of US journalist Daniel Pearl and the assassination of Benazir Bhutto.[8] All of these activities have led some to declare that Pakistan lacks a 'comprehensive internal security strategy'.[9]

Musharraf survived at least six assassination attempts during 2002 and the risk of a coup staged by senior military officials who disapproved of his relationship with the West was a possibility.[10] In the event that Musharraf was overthrown, Pakistan's nuclear arsenal of up to 75 warheads could have fallen into the hands of Islamic extremists.[11] However, it is highly unlikely that the United States would have allowed such a situation to occur and many believe that in the event of a coup, US Special Forces would move in to Pakistan and seize Pakistan's strategic assets.[12] Such a move would be highly resented by Pakistani officials as well as the civilian populace and would be viewed as a flagrant violation of Pakistan's sovereignty if a foreign power exerted their control over what some Pakistanis view as their nation's primary deterrent to Indian aggression. There would likely be rioting, reprisal attacks on government targets and US forces, as well as possible attacks on the nuclear sites themselves. Ironically, sending US troops into Pakistan could do more to jeopardize the security of Pakistan's nuclear weapons rather than improve it.

Information exchange between the Pakistani police and the Inter-Services Intelligence (ISI) is very poor as ISI has begun to focus more on the promotion of national interests rather than on domestic concerns.[13] This development is interesting in that it highlights a very important disconnect between two vital government bodies. Further, it demonstrates that ISI is becoming increasingly more independent and less accountable at the same time. This is problematic for any regime in Islamabad as there exists the possibility of the failure to follow orders or directives from the political leadership as well as the possibility that Pakistan's premier intelligence agency may actually operate at cross purposes and against Islamabad's declared interests. This is currently being witnessed in FATA with segments of ISI and the paramilitary Frontier Corps continuing to provide both the Pakistani and Afghan Taliban with arms, funds, intelligence and even medical support despite official policy claiming that Pakistan is allied to the United States and NATO in their fight against these groups.[14] Further, elements within ISI continue to back LeT and D-Company despite the fact that this has prompted them to scale up their operations within India without Islamabad's consent, something which could drag Pakistani into an unwanted and costly war with India.

Pakistan's police force is corrupt and poorly trained and they remain ill-equipped to counter the overall lack of law and order. They are deficient in basic investigative skills such as collecting evidence and following chains of custody while few have access to technical resources. Pakistan has no centralized criminal database and, until fairly recently, no forensic laboratories. In addition, international airports in Pakistan have only just begun to implement a digitized system that tracks those who enter or leave the country and have not yet developed structures enabling the development of a credible terrorist or criminal watch list.[15]

The Karachi police have been unsuccessful in their efforts to effectively police Karachi and the city is now a major exporter of violence and has attracted key international terrorist actors. Al-Qaeda suspects are arrested regularly in Karachi and the city has been accused of harbouring Osama bin Laden and serving as a meeting place and main coordination cell for Al-Qaeda fighters. It is noteworthy that two journalists from al-Jazeera were invited to Karachi to interview two top Al-Qaeda leaders.[16] Also, atrocities based upon religious extremism are commonplace in Karachi such as the murder of the entire staff of the Christian Commission of Justice and Peace in 2002.[17] Also, in June 2004, Jundallah, a shadowy Sunni Islamist group, attempted to assassinate the Pakistan Army Corps Commander in Karachi. Interrogation reports demonstrate that most of Jundallah's members are from provinces north of Sindh but its most senior leaders hail from Karachi. Apparently, this particular operation was meant to target the Corps Commander, the ISI Operations Officer, the Aga Supermarket and Pak Towers –places where foreign diplomats come to shop.[18]

The Burmese slums in Karachi have become a problem spot for the Karachi police as it has been reported that some Burmese are willing to harbour any wanted person and even smuggle them out of the country through sea routes. Further, these Burmese smugglers charge a modest amount (between US$1,000 to US$2,000) to carry out theft, robbery or killings. Afghan and Bengali slums also provide similar problems and are known to offer shelter to terrorist groups in their massive, unregulated ghettos.[19] These issues just add to the long list of seemingly insurmountable challenges that face the Karachi police to exercise control over a city that has a constantly changing population and intersecting interests of a wide range of actors that operate outside of the law.[20]

Sectarian violence: Pakistan's long war

Roots of sectarianism

Shia–Sunni tensions go back even further than the days of Zia to the 1950s, when the leadership of Jamaat-i-Islami (JI) and other like-minded parties began to utilize Islam to engage in exclusionary politics and public riots by politicizing the question, 'Who is a Muslim?'. Today, a member of parliament can comfortably call a Shia an infidel and Sunni extremist Azam Tariq was infamous for his encouragement of anti-Shia violence but still won a seat in the National Assembly several times, most recently in 2000 from his jail cell, and he eventually became an ally of the Pakistan Muslim League – Quaid-i-Azam (PML-Q) before being assassinated.[21]

Sectarian violence in Pakistan is the direct consequence of state policies of Illumination and marginalization of secular democratic forces. Co-option and continued patronage of religious parties by successive military governments has reached a point where religious extremism threatens to erode the very foundations of the state and society. Further, the political use of Islam by the state encourages aggressive competition for official patronage between and within the multiple variations of Shia and Sunni Islam with the clerical elite of major sects and sub-sects striving to build up their political parties, raise militias, expand madrassa networks and, as happened under Musharraf, become part of government.[22]

Pakistan's Sunnis can be divided into four broad categories: Barelvis, Deobandis, Ahle Hadith and revivalist movements like JI. The first three of these sub-sects emerged as religious educational movements in the nineteenth century under British rule in India while JI came into being in the 1940s. The Ahle Hadith is a small, ultra-orthodox sect inspired by Saudi Wahhabism which does not follow any of the four Sunni schools of jurisprudence. What is commonly referred to as Sunni–Shia violence is actually more of a conflict between Shias and Deobandis with the latter receiving support from the Ahle Hadith, the strain of Islam that LeT subscribes to and spreads throughout Pakistan. Both the Deobandis and the Ahle Hadith reject the other more tolerant, pluralist forms of Islam and also dismiss Pakistan's shrine culture as a form of idolatry. They are also against traditional marriage and death rites borrowed from local South Asian cultures. In addition, modernist Islamist movements, of which JI is one of the most prominent, seek to purify Islam and restore it to its pristine form and view traditional multicultural Sunni beliefs and practices as un-Islamic. Groups such as Sipah-e-Sahabba (SSP) and its militant offshoot, Lashkar-e-Jhangvi (LeJ), are exclusively Deobandi although they have not been around nearly as long as LeT. On the other hand, the Athna Ashari sect (The Twelvers) are the dominant group amongst Pakistan's Shia minority community. Smaller variations of the Shia school include the Ismailis (followers of Aga Khan), Daudi Bohras (followers of Syedna Burhanuddin) and their rivals Sulemani Bohras (followers of Masood

Salehbahi). The Shias share a devotion to shrines and saints with the Barelvis as well as other followers of Sufi Islam.[23]

Shia–Sunni conflicts were largely unknown prior to Partition in the areas which now constitute Pakistan due to the influence of *pirs* and *sufis*. Pakistan initially had a secular agenda and despite Mohajir migration to Pakistan from areas in India that were known for having sectarian tensions, clashes were minimal. However, the successful resistance to Zia's Illumination drive and the Iranian revolution empowered Pakistan's Shia. Following the Iran–Iraq war, which was largely viewed in Pakistan as a war between Sunnis and Shias, Iran funnelled large sums of money to Pakistan's Shias and began to aggressively open up cultural centres. Many Shia began to study Persian and received scholarships to study in Iran. Upon their return, some sought to re-create Pakistani society and wanted to rationalize religion, be involved in politics to empower the Shia, and introduced pan-Islamic concepts into Shia mosques.[24]

Today, Pakistan signifies the near inversion of what Muhammed Ali Jinnah stood for. Jinnah's vision of a democratic Pakistan, where religion was to be a personal matter, has been eclipsed by frequent military takeovers and a rising spiral of sectarian violence that is unprecedented in the history of the subcontinent.[25] Also worrisome is the fact that post-9/11, the objectives and goals of sectarian terrorists are closer to those of transnational groups like LeT but the internal enemy is still prioritized, something that has been referred to as a 'two track jihad'.[26] There is another regional dimension to sectarian terrorism in Pakistan as its Sunni sects are anti-Iran while their Shia counterparts are hostile to Saudi Arabia and Wahhabism. The Barelvis are also resentful of Saudi Arabia and its religious practices.[27]

The destructive impact of sectarian violence extends far past body counts or the number of hardcore terrorists in Pakistan. Rather, the real danger that sectarian violence poses to the country is the potential development of a religious culture that underpins the networking of terrorist groups and the mainstream religio-political parties in Pakistan and beyond, thus blurring the boundaries between 'extremist' and 'mainstream' in the Islamist spectrum.[28] However, it should still be noted that Pakistan's Islamists have never been able to do well in electoral politics until the legislative election of 10 October 2002 when they won a significant number of seats in parliament and control of the NWFP. Their strength in recent years is not due to increasing public support but rather can be attributed to covert state patronage and the military's decision to assign them a role in its regional strategy.[29]

There are around 130 million Shias globally and they account for 10 per cent of the world's Muslims. The majority live in the area between Lebanon and Pakistan and constitute a majority population in Iran, Iraq, Bahrain and Azerbaijan. Shias are also the single largest community in Lebanon and make up sizeable minorities in Saudi Arabia, Afghanistan, Pakistan, India, Tajikistan and East Africa. The cultural and religions ties that bind Shia populations from Lebanon to Pakistan are politically relevant once more after two decades of suppression by Sunni regimes. The Shia are again demanding greater rights and their place in the political arena and this is likely to fuel greater Sunni militancy and activism and may well lead to regime changes in the Muslim world.[30]

Modernization changed ties between Shia elites and other communities. In the early process of state formation in Pakistan, landlords and tribal elders represented the Shia community and these *zamindars* cut deals with the Sunni ruling classes. It was through these elite-level bargains that rank-and-file Shias ended up in mostly humble positions in Pakistan in that the zamindars would benefit from their ties to power and in turn were expected to represent and control the Shia community, something which did not happen. The concept of the modern nation state further enticed everyday Shias on the grounds that it was a path forward that was free of the baggage of religious identity and promised a level playing field. As such, many Shias enthusiastically embraced Pakistani nationalism while imagining that Shia–Sunni divisions would not matter. The modern world seemed to hold the promise of ending centuries of prejudice and persecution but this proved illusory as Pakistan became increasingly authoritarian and began to utilize Sunni sectarian biases to shore up governmental authority.[31]

In India and Pakistan, Sunni *ulama* directly challenged Iran's Khomeini and classified his attacks on the House of Saud in the 1980s as *fitna* (illegitimate rebellion). Khomeini's challenge to the Saudi regime was depicted as a Shia rebellion against Sunni authority and, as such, the Saudis become the defenders of Sunnism and the symbol of its resistance against Shia 'usurpers'. Riyadh was driven by its desire to both control its own Shia minority and to thwart Khomeini's challenge to the Islamic legitimacy of Saudi Arabia. In Pakistan, Shia communities became more aggressive and potentially threatening and prompted Zia to place greater emphasis on the Sunni identity of the country and to sanction violence in order to put Shias back into their place. Shia attempts to attain greater power in Pakistan, as well as South Asia, eventually failed and sectarian forces linked to the Pakistani military who were equipped with fatwas from Wahhabi clerics in Saudi Arabia engaged in systematic bombings of Shia mosques and assassinations of Shia community leaders, government officials and religious figures. Such violence continues and in March 2004, 43 Shia were killed in Quetta while commemorating Ashura on the same day that 143 Shia died in Baghdad and Karbala.[32] Due to these types of developments, Nasr feels that the late Benazir Bhutto actually felt the need to downplay her Shia identity:

> Feeling the wind shift in the 1990s, Benazir styled herself a Sunni, but her Iranian mother, her husband from a big Shia landowning family, and her father's name, the name of Ali's twin-bladed sword, make her Shia roots quite visible. In a way, Benazir's self-reinvention as a Sunni tells the tale of how secular nationalism's once solid-seeming promise

> has given way like a rotten plank beneath the feet of contemporary Pakistan's beleaguered Shia minority.[33]

The overthrow of Benazir's father, Zulfiqar Ali Bhutto, by hard-line Sunni generals essentially ended the Pakistani experiment with inclusive Muslim nationalism. Though Shia politicians, generals and business leaders remained, a steady 'Sunnifying' of Pakistan came to make the country look more and more like the Arab world. In many ways Pakistan captures the essence of the political challenges that the Shia have faced and demonstrates that the promise of the modern state has eluded them as secular nationalism has been colonized from within by Sunni hegemony.[34] Nonetheless, the recent wave of Shia empowerment that has followed the US-led invasion of Iraq will inevitably extend beyond Iraq's borders and involve the broader region from Lebanon to Pakistan. The anti-Shia violence that has plagued Iraq has its roots in South Asia and Afghanistan in the 1990s with militant groups linked to the Taliban and Al-Qaeda. It should be noted that bombings in Baghdad, Iskandariya, Karbala, Najaf and other Shia strongholds in Iraq closely resemble attacks in Mashad, Karachi, Quetta and Mazar-i-Sharif since the early 1990s. Further, sectarian Sunni fighters in Iraq are likely to draw upon the ideological and organizational resources of the broader network of Sunni militancy that has developed over the past decade or so and has put down firm roots in the societies and politics of the greater Middle East. This will undoubtedly have an impact on sectarian relations where those resources originate, which in this case is South Asia and Afghanistan and Pakistan in particular.[35]

The role of madrassas

The madrassa and the pulpit have been the most used instrument by sectarian groups and the spread of sectarian movements and terrorism is directly proportional to the size of the clergy-run sector of madrassas and mosques.[36] However, contrary to most analyses, madrassas rarely produce highly lethal terrorists with management capacity as they do not equip graduates with many practical skills. Terrorism requires a relatively sophisticated knowledge about politics and strategy and, in some cases, considerable technical aptitude, none of which is acquired through the rote memorization of the Koran in a madrassa. What some Pakistani madrassas do produce are the bulk of mid-level commanders and foot soldiers that form the majority of the membership of sectarian outfits. Although these individuals rarely make major decisions, they are still tasked with implementing directives from the top. Further, mid-level commanders are vital to the survival of any terrorist organization as they often serve as the go-between for the leadership and the rank-and-file and will also be expected to evolve into leadership positions in the future. Although many of the skills that are necessary for success in terrorism are likely acquired on the job, extremist madrassas play a crucial role in the mental conditioning of terrorists.

The number of madrassa graduates (maulanas) that specialize in religious polemics to promote their own sectarian ideologies has grown exponentially, something which has inevitably raised public consciousness of sectarian differences. In addition, mosque pulpits are used to incite people against religious minorities as well as other Muslim sects with various forms of media widely disseminating sectarian views. As such, controversies over religious syllabuses in schools often take a violent turn. Also, terrorism is simply one component of religious intolerance as terrorists only form a small minority of Pakistani fanatics. Social discrimination, legal bias and cultural repression based on an individual's or a family's sectarian identity is unfortunately commonplace in modern Pakistan and is even institutionalized in some cases. Lastly, Pakistani governments, elected or authoritarian, are usually pressured by religious lobbies to grant concessions or to take decisive action against their sectarian rivals. These demands range from enforcement of their version of Sharia (Islamic law), rival claims over mosques, excommunication of heretics and the removal of officials because of their faith. However, the clergy has generally enjoyed more influence with authoritarian leaders whose lack of legitimacy cause them to be more vulnerable to sectarian demands.[37] For this reason, if nothing else, the success of Pakistan's current experiment with multi-party democracy is an absolute necessity.

Sectarianism in the contemporary period

Even prior to 9/11, Musharraf attempted to crack down on sectarian groups as he viewed them as terrorists and threats to national unity and sacked two of his generals that he deemed to be sympathetic to their cause.[38] Some even believe that the primary motivation for Musharraf offering his nearly unconditional assistance for US military operations in Afghanistan was to enlist US support in quelling regional extremist groups, most of which are based in Pakistan.[39] Nonetheless, despite some efforts and foreign aid, it is widely assumed that the government of Pakistan has failed to prevent or stem sectarian violence despite promises it has made to the international community as well as minority groups in the country.[40] The key reason for this failure is that Islamabad makes an irrational distinction between the threat posed by LeT, the Taliban and Al-Qaeda on the one hand, and the challenges posed by domestic jihadis on the other. However, this distinction is artificial as membership is often integrated and based upon overlapping ideology and a regressive vision for the future of Pakistan. They also tend to attend the same mosques and madrassas and continue to enjoy support from elements within the intelligence services and armed forces. The key difference between domestic terrorist groups like Lashkar-i-Jhangvi and LeT lies not in ideology, but rather in that LeT focuses much of its terrorist actions on the *kafirs* in India (Hindus, Sikhs, Christians and others) through D-Company criminal infrastructure while Lashkar-i-Jhangvi lacks this access. However, as Lashkar-i-Jhangvi is a younger and less established outfit, it has undoubtedly drawn inspiration from LeT and learned valuable lessons with regards to both operations and propaganda from LeT's decades of experience. Given the ideological overlap regarding Islamic schools of thought as well as ideas of what Pakistani society should become, the fallacy that support for LeT does not have negative implications for sectarianism in Pakistan becomes clear. Despite the vast array of terrorist groups in Pakistan, LeT is held in the highest esteem amongst other terrorist outfits as well as everyday Pakistanis with many attempting to make a distinction between the 'mujahedeen' in LeT and the 'anti-nationals' of Lashkar-i-Jhangvi. However, while their targets vary somewhat, their actions are driven by the same ideological reasoning.

Between January 1985 and 31 May 2005, a total of 1,784 Pakistanis were killed and 4,279 injured in 1,866 incidents of sectarian violence across Pakistan.[41] Further, as many as 900 Pakistanis lost their lives in over 650 attacks in 2006, with another 1,500 people seriously injured. Attacks occurred with the greatest frequency in the regions bordering Afghanistan: Balochistan, NWFP and FATA. One of the more spectacular incidents was a suicide attack on 9 February 2006 on a Shia religious procession in Hangu (NWFP) killing over 24 and injuring 50. In the following April, at least 57 were killed in an apparent reprisal attack on a gathering of Sunni (Barelvi) religious leaders in Nishtar Park, Karachi.[42] Although strict measures were taken against sectarian groups by Musharraf, most continue to enjoy free rein. Further, despite several high profile arrests and crackdowns, the organizational infrastructures of these banned groups largely remain intact and continue to be well-funded and armed.[43] Due to this, some analysts feel that banning these organizations is actually counterproductive as not only does it not weaken them, it also forces them underground and makes them even more difficult to trace and dismantle.[44]

Sectarian violence in Pakistan is highly unpredictable and attacks can follow months of calm. Many of the Shia victims are of the Hazara community and as there have been an exceptionally high number of Shia killings in Karachi, many professional Shias have left Pakistan.[45] Also problematic is the fact that the remaining Shias have completely lost faith in the state's ability to provide them with security. Shah identifies the implications: 'If such a visible minority, whether ethnic, religious, or sectarian, loses faith in a state, then the very existence of that state is jeopardized. It comes close to being a "failed state"'.[46] The scale, scope and intensity of the sectarian violence, even though not new to Pakistan, is unprecedented in the nation's history.[47] Further, it will be difficult to clamp down on terrorist groups within Pakistan as they enjoy support within the intelligence agencies, the military, as well as in the bureaucracy. The well-known Indian analyst Chellaney even claims that 'entire echelons of the army and ISI officer corps have developed a Taliban-like mind-set'.[48] Chellaney also feels that the war in Afghanistan is likely to exacerbate sectarian violence in Pakistan.[49] Many agree with Chellaney and claim that sectarian violence became more intense and brutal after many jihadis left Afghanistan and entered Pakistan following the US invasion. Suicide attacks spiked and became common in a nation that largely did not experience such attacks in the pre-9/11 period. Also, the tactic of car bombing was imported into Pakistan post-9/11 and is a trend that is expected to continue.[50] However, Stern, of Harvard, is less sympathetic and singles out the Pakistani government for criticism as she feels that Pakistan's sectarian violence is largely caused by external forces. She writes: 'The impotent Pakistani government has essentially allowed a Sunni Saudi Arabia and a Shia Iran to fight a proxy war on Pakistani soil, with devastating consequences for the Pakistani people.'[51]

In addition to Shias, minority Christians are often targeted by terrorists and told to convert to Islam or face severe consequences.[52] On 17 March 2002, an American diplomat's wife and daughter were killed in a grenade attack on the Protestant International Church in Islamabad's diplomatic enclave. Also, in August 2002, there was a series of attacks on a Christian missionary school at Murree and the chapel of a Christian hospital in Taxila which claimed a total of ten lives. Another 25 September attack on the Karachi offices of the Christian welfare organization Peace and Justice killed seven.[53]

By redirecting Pakistan's internal security services, an increase in Pakistan's sectarian violence may actually ease pressure on Al-Qaeda and allow the group to operate more freely.[54] Also troublesome is the fact that while sectarian violence continues to increase in Pakistan, those implicated in the commission of violent acts are rarely prosecuted and hardly any action has been taken to protect affected communities. There have even been accusations that the Pakistan Rangers, a paramilitary force, have been involved in the kidnapping of Shia activists.[55] If these events continue unabated, an even more entrenched culture of impunity will develop in Pakistan and the little deterrence to acts of violence that presently exists will eventually evaporate.

Sectarianism in Punjab

As 68 per cent of its population lives in rural areas, Punjab is still an agrarian society and, except for some rural pockets in southern Punjab and around industrial towns such as Gujranwala and Faisalabad, militant sectarianism has yet to put down firm roots in the villages. However, urban areas are hard hit by sectarianism and are home to many terrorist groups.[56] There are three groups that are the most active in sectarian violence: the *bazaar* (market) merchants who finance sectarian outfits; the madrassa students who provide manpower for these movements and parties; and the semi-educated unemployed youth in urban centres who act as hired guns.[57]

Southern Punjab, namely the belt that stretches from Jhang to Dera Ghazi Khan, has the highest rate of growth and concentration of madrassas in the province and is also the birthplace of organized sectarian militancy in Pakistan. Jhang district is believed to have a population of around three million, 25 per cent of which are Shia while half of the urban population are migrants from East Punjab (India), many of which are Deobandis. Local Sunnis and Shias have had no history of conflict even though sectarian politics in Jhang can be traced back to the 1960s. Anti-Shia violence was relatively non-existent until Haq Nawaz Jhangvi, the then Vice President of the Jamiat-Ulama-i-Islam (JUI) in Punjab, formed the Sipah-e-Sahaba Pakistan (SSP) in September 1985 and openly began to espouse sectarian militancy.[58] During this time period, Shias in Jhang largely controlled the agriculture and transportation sectors and Sunni businessmen rallied behind Jhangvi to counter growing Shia influence.[59] SSP is now estimated to have a vote bank of between 40,000 to 60,000 in Jhang city as Sunni merchants continue to back the SSP to counter the traditional political dominance of Shia and Sunni *pir* families. The SSP also receives funds from Pakistani expatriates in the Middle East in addition to support from urban youth and madrassas in Pakistan. Nonetheless, the SSP has still failed to make viable inroads into Punjab's rural population that closely adheres to Sufi traditions.[60] However, the situation in rural Punjab is hardly static and as extremist ideology continues to gain traction throughout the country against the backdrop of increasing stress on resources and the economy, these closed communities could be penetrated. This would prove disastrous as violent sectarian concepts could spread like wildfire through tight-knit rural Punjabi family and social structures.

In central Punjab, Arab influence, especially through Saudi charities, has had a major impact on sectarianism. This influence played a key role in the establishment of the Markaz-Dawa-ul-Irshad (MDI), the parent organization of Lashkar-i-Taiba. LeT is so orthodox that some Pakistani terrorists accuse it of actually undermining the insurgency in Kashmir by promoting sectarian divisions amongst the terrorist groups. LeT largely recruits from Gujranwala and surrounding areas with many having some connection with Deobandi and Ahle Hadith madrassas; the same madrassas that supply manpower and ideological justifications for Lashkar-i-Jhangvi. LeT also has considerable influence in central Punjabi villages such as Gondlanwalla, which is now referred to as *Pind Shaheedan* (the village of martyrs) because at least one person from every family has fought or died in the Kashmir insurgency while fighting for LeT. Villagers in the area have even accepted LeT arbitration in disputes.[61] This undermines local democratic governance and helps solidify anti-Shia norms in society thus arguably fuelling further violent anti-Shia responses. In the post-2001 period, sections of LeT are becoming increasingly involved in terrorism within Pakistan itself and possibly played a role in some of the more brazen attacks in Punjab. If unchecked, this unintended blowback from Kashmir will further accelerate sectarianism in Pakistan and could play a role in the cessation of Pakistan as a functional state. In addition, further attacks in India through D-Company infrastructure (provided that they are not perceived by Pakistanis as senseless) will continue to burnish LeT's credentials and increase its ability to influence sectarianism in

Pakistan. This is yet another dynamic that the Pakistani security establishment has failed to recognize and helps to explain why they continue to, at a minimum, tolerate the presence of both D-Company and LeT while fringe elements actively support them at their own peril.

Sectarianism in Sindh

Karachi, Sindh's capital and Pakistan's largest city, suffers from endemic sectarian violence and sniper shootings and terrorist attacks on both Shias and Sunnis are common. Victims have included high-ranking, pro-Taliban Sunni clerics as well as SSP leaders. These attacks are believed to be in retaliation for the killings of Shias in Karachi and elsewhere with strikes and mob violence following most attacks. Karachi only had four madrassas in 1950 and 20 in 1971 with only four being Deobandi and one Shia. Now there are believed to be around 979 in the city with a higher proportion being Deobandi.[62]

Karachi began to witness religious politics not long after Pakistan's inception with the influx of Indian migrants, or Mohajirs, who were represented by their own politico-religious parties, namely JI. In the mid-1980s, the new Mohajir political force, the Muttahida Qaumi Movement (MQM) rose to prominence with military support. The MQM included many JI members and consolidated its position through violence and, by the mid-1990s, Shia–Sunni violence raged throughout Karachi. During this phase, the number of sectarian terrorists grew, aided by the city's madrassa networks.[63] However, some of the tension in Karachi is due to ethnicity rather than religious differences although the latter issue has become exacerbated as of late. Tension is particularly acute between Mohajirs and Pashtuns as the latter are assuming an increasingly prominent role in business, namely the transportation sector. However, attacks by LeJ in the city, several of which have targeted Barelvi functions, demonstrate that religion still plays a major role in the unrest.[64]

Recent years have seen an increasing presence of Pashtuns in Karachi, especially in Banaras. Many have been forced out of FATA and the NWFP and entered Karachi through several northern and southern routes and settled in slum areas or on previously uninhabited land. Afghan slums have been a part of the Karachi reality since the Soviet invasion of Afghanistan but the events now being witnessed suggest new developments. Disaffected Pashtun youths have been seen directing traffic, attacking those dressed in Western clothing and carrying out other Taliban-style activities not only in FATA and the NWFP, but also in several districts of Karachi, most notably the middle-class area of Gulshan-i-Iqbal. Government officials are now predicting major clashes and claim that many of these youths are linked to the TTP and aim to take control over the resources of the city. However, a TTP takeover of Karachi is an extremely remote possibility given its strategic and economic importance to Pakistan. Nonetheless, the TTP and its proxies are able to generate much unrest within Karachi's multi-ethnic and multi-religious society. They are also able to cause significant economic disruption which could allow them to capitalize on the growing popular anger arising from the increasing costs of food and fuel as well as water and electricity shortages that have already caused large-scale demonstrations and even riots in the city. If the TTP is able to consolidate its positions in the city, expect a distinct focus on economic targets as they will seek to further aggravate the tense situation in the country and could spark more clashes. Ports would be the most likely casualty as well as major sources of international trade and foreign currency earnings, namely banks, other financial institutions and the Karachi Stock Exchange (KSE). Sustained attacks on any of these targets could send Karachi, and Pakistan as a whole, into social and economic chaos. This would undoubtedly paralyse Islamabad's abilities to combat Taliban, Al-Qaeda or sectarian activity while simultaneously deflecting public hostility away from Islamic extremist groups and towards the political establishment. Though there are no clear policy prescriptions for bringing stability to Karachi, any strategy will have to start with improving the capacities of the Karachi police force, an organization that is currently unable to control large parts of the city.

Sectarianism in FATA and the NWFP

Pashtun feuds have traditionally centred around land, other natural resources or business disputes.[65] However, three events have changed this and have caused them to increase in intensity: the Afghan war against the USSR; Al-Qaeda's introduction into the region; and the Iraq war. The story of Wahhabism coming along with foreign fighters and the subsequent explosion of madrassas in FATA is well known, as is Al-Qaeda's introduction of more violent tactics, such as suicide bombing, into the region. However, less discussed events like Iran's increased involvement in the early 1990s during the civil war in Afghanistan, which prompted a greater Saudi response, also played a major role. Much like the 1980s, Riyadh utilized the already-established infrastructure in FATA to support the predominantly Sunni Taliban while it battled against rival factions, such as the Shia Hazaras, thus further cementing sectarian tendencies in a region that had recently become awash with weapons. In addition, the removal of Saddam Hussein has led to the only Shia-led Arab state and, along with Iran's increased prevalence in the region, has sparked concerns about an increasingly aggressive Shia movement in the Middle East as well as Pakistan.

Pashtuns in FATA and the NWFP have largely gravitated towards a very puritanical form of Sunni Islam. Even prior to the increased Deobandi influence, the Afghan civil war and the proliferation of madrassas enhanced the strength of the JUI in Pashtun-majority areas. Given that the NWFP also has sizeable Shia populations in Kurram and Orakzai agencies as well as Parachinar and Hangu in Kohat district, the growth of Deobandi extremism has exacerbated sectarian tensions and conflicts. This has even been witnessed in Hindko-speaking areas like Mansehra and Abottabad.[66] However, most analysts make the error of assuming that religion is the primary driver behind increased violence amongst Pashtuns in northwest Pakistan. Tribal feuds are part and parcel of Pashtun society and pre-date the introduction of Islam. *Badla*, or revenge, is a key pillar of *Pashtunwalli* (a code of conduct) and is viewed as an obligation if an individual, family, tribe and/or clan is wronged. As such, the spread of extremist ideology must be viewed within this context.

Sectarianism in FATA and the NWFP is unique in that it can pit entire tribes or villages against each other and as the region already has an ample supply of weaponry, sectarian violence (which also includes Sunni infighting) now often translates into prolonged conflict in which rockets and missiles are used.[67] Unfortunately, this trend appears set to continue and even accelerate as TTP ideology (which is pre-dated by the extremist ideology of LeT) spreads through the tribal regions following repeated destructive yet ultimately ineffective offensives by the Pakistani military and Islamabad's consistent refusal to develop an effective counter-insurgency doctrine that identifies the local populace as the centre of gravity. Also, spikes in violence in Afghanistan which are likely to accompany additional NATO troops will have a knock-on effect in Pakistan as terrorist and extremist madrassa networks will be firing on all cylinders to meet the challenge. Lastly and arguably most importantly, Pakistan's policy of supporting tribal lashkars, or local militias, to fight against the TTP and Al-Qaeda will inevitably lead to more violence which will be driven by the desire for revenge against the pro-government lashkars as well as religious differences that have become even more pronounced. Several de-mobilized lashkar members have already been killed, and in some cases mutilated (something that is extremely offensive in Islam), in their home villages. If and when the Pakistani security forces scale down their presence in FATA and the NWFP, expect a vicious cycle of retribution against former lashkar combatants and similar responses from the tribes that rose up against the TTP and its allies. Two agencies of particular concern are Bajaur and Mohmand.

Hangu, Dera Ismail Khan and Peshawar districts in the NWFP and Kurram and Khyber agencies in FATA were the worst sectarian flashpoints in 2008. Dera Ismail Khan was the hardest hit area and the strength of the SSP and LeJ grew in the city. The SSP was able to win a Provincial Assembly seat in the February 2008 election in Dera Ismail Khan and also won support from the South Waziristan-based Taliban commander, Qari Hussain. Hussain has provided logistics and terrorist training to sectarian Sunni groups and also launched suicide attacks against the Shia population in Dera Ismail Khan, Bannu and the nearby Punjabi city of Bhakkar. Nonetheless, sectarian violence dropped slightly in the province, as well as throughout the whole of Pakistan, in 2008 although the threat still remains acute with 842 deaths and 654 injuries reported. In addition, Mohmand agency witnessed clashes between Salafi and Deobandi Taliban groups and clashes occurred between the Deobandi Lashkar-i-Islam and the Ansarul Islam group in Khyber agency which killed 108.[68]

Initially, the TTP was not interested in participating in sectarian violence. However, LeJ began operating independently, while pretending to be Punjabi Taliban, against the Shia in Kurram agency. Mistaking LeJ for the TTP, Shia fighters began attacking local TTP commanders in the agency and rumours started to circulate that the Shia Hizballah was involved. These events prompted the TTP to reverse its previous policy decision and it now engages in sectarian violence.[69] Further, despite pulling the TTP into an unnecessary conflict in Kurram, LeJ still operates independently in FATA and will continue to gain strength thus posing a greater long-term threat to Pakistan than the TTP or even Al-Qaeda. However, LeJ will remain weaker than LeT but will continue to draw inspiration from LeT's actions in Kashmir and throughout India. Further, given the overlapping nature of both groups, it is not unreasonable to suggest that LeJ may push LeT for access to D-Company's criminal infrastructure as LeJ is well aware that attacks in India can greatly enhance a group's image and recruitment efforts. However, there is no clear evidence at this point in time that suggests that this has happened nor is it clear that D-Company would be willing to grant such access and take on the additional risk without any clear additional benefits for doing so.

Although the levels of sectarian violence are alarming, especially in FATA, many Pashtun terrorists feel that they have a common enemy at present in Islamabad, something that has caused them to temporarily shelve some of their differences. Ironically, if relations with Islamabad improve, many seething tribal disputes are likely to flare up again as these issues, by and large, weigh more heavily than religious differences. For example, intra-Pashtun disputes in North Waziristan, South Waziristan and Bajaur are predominantly tribal-based and are not fully attributable to Shia–Sunni tension. However, these tensions can play a somewhat stronger role in other parts of FATA, such as Kurram agency.

Sectarianism in Balochistan

In 1950, there were only seven madrassas in Balochistan but this figure increased to 1,045 by 2003. Over half are controlled by the Deobandi JUI-F (a faction headed by Fazlur Rehman, who is a fervent supporter of LeT) and tend to be located in mostly Pashtun-majority areas of Quetta, Pishin, Qilla Abdullah, Chagai and Loralai. This increase has contributed to sectarian tensions although it is also attributed to the proxy wars between Iran and Arab states which has involved the Shia Hazara refugees settled in the provincial capital of Quetta and the Pashtun, pro-Taliban Afghan refugee population. In addition, the influx of Afghan refugees upset the demographic balance between the Baloch and Pashtun communities with the former fearing that migration from Afghanistan and other provinces of Pakistan will reduce them to a minority in their own resource-rich homeland.[70] TTP has also established a chapter in Balochistan but does not have links with the ethno-nationalist insurgency there and Pashtun–Baloch relations remain relatively stable.[71] Province-wide sectarian violence is unlikely in Balochistan because Baloch tribal culture is not nearly as immersed in religion. The province is also sparsely populated and while demographics have been disturbed in several urban areas, the same is not true of the whole province. However, Quetta is a worrisome potential flashpoint.

Religious extremism has begun to surface in the province, something that many attribute to regional developments. Balochistan's proximity to Afghanistan and its own sizeable Pashtun population turned the province into a militant hub. Simultaneously, the Iranian revolution encouraged a strong Sunni response in Pakistan and the Baloch–Iran border gained additional strategic importance. Quetta is a Pashtun-majority city and this fact, along with the proliferation of JUI-F-funded Deobandi madrassas along the border with Iran has greatly contributed to this rise in extremism. Further, Al-Qaeda and Taliban groups have recently extended their network in Balochistan, namely Zhob district, and it is of note that a prominent local Taliban commander, Abdullah Mehsud, was killed in July 2007 during an encounter with security forces in this district.[72]

After 9/11, LeJ has dedicated a considerable amount of attention to Balochistan as did SSP, albeit in different manners. SSP, with its well-organized network previously rooted in Punjab, faced a law enforcement crackdown in 2000 and 2001 which prompted many to flee to Balochistan as well as Iran. From these havens, SSP reconstituted its network and developed a new generation of leadership. Conversely, LeJ shifted focus to Balochistan after its training camps in Afghanistan were destroyed while also facing pressure in Punjab and Karachi and the geography and political influence of JUI-F made the province a relatively safe option. SSP, LeJ's patron outfit, also has a sizeable support base in Balochistan despite being banned twice and LeJ was granted an opportunity to establish a permanent presence when tensions began to rise between the ousted Taliban and their extremist allies and the local Shia Hazara community which were supporting the Wahdat-e-Islami, a partner of the Northern Alliance in Afghanistan. The Taliban are also suspicious that local Shias provide US forces with information about their movements. Initially, sectarian attacks by LeJ targeted Shia processions and the terrorists were imported from other provinces. However, LeJ is now believed to have a Baloch cadre and targets Western interests as well as Christians.[73]

LeJ will only be able to gain the necessary political space in areas of intense Shia–Sunni tension, which in this case is Quetta and select areas near the Afghan border. LeJ is highly unlikely to be able to establish infrastructure throughout the whole province as it would find itself bumping heads with an avowedly secular ethno-nationalist insurgent movement that would hardly take kindly to 'foreign' terrorists operating on their land and disturbing communal relations, something that could irreparably damage their insurgency. As such, spikes in sectarian violence are likely to be witnessed in select pockets of the province although this by no means suggests that there is room for complacency.

Lashkar-e-Jhangvi and Sipah-e-Muhammed Pakistan – damaging the fabric of Pakistani society

Sunni terrorism

Sipah-e-Sahaba Pakistan (SSP) is a Sunni organization that engages in terrorist violence mostly against the Shia community in Pakistan. Its current stronghold is in Jhang, Punjab and it wants Pakistan to be declared a Sunni state, to establish Sharia law, and is resolutely opposed to the alliance between Islamabad and Washington; goals which are also all in line with those of LeT.[74] SSP also feels that Pakistan's Shias have too much power and influence and strives to maintain a political role through its representation in Punjab's coalition government as well as through Jamaat-e-Islami (JI) and Jamaat-Ulema-e-Islam (JUI), two major Pakistani Islamist parties.[75] It was formed on 6 September 1985 and, aside from its operations in Jhang, SSP possibly maintains major facilities in the two largest Deobandi madrassas of Punjab-Jamiat-ul-Uloom Eidgah in Bahawalnagar and Dar-ul-Uloom Deoband Faqirwalli in Fort Abbas. However, others claim that nearly all the organizational controls are exercised from regional headquarters located in Jamia Faruqiya, Jia Moosa, Shadora and Lahore while the international units are controlled by the Madrassa Mahmoodiya in Jhang. This seemingly contradictory information is a clear indication of how little is actually known about SSP.[76] However, what is largely accepted is that SSP has influence in all four provinces of Pakistan and is the most powerful sectarian group in the country.[77]

In addition to engaging in hostilities with Shia groups, since the late 1980s SSP and its militant wing, Lashkar-e-Jhangvi (LeJ), have been engaged in a shadow war in major Pakistani cities with Iranian intelligence services and their local Pakistani agents, both Shia and Sunni. There have been reports that LeJ cadres have purchased arms from smugglers in the NWFP and may be preparing for suicide missions within Iran and Shia targets in Pakistan.[78] In the past, SSP has carried out attacks in Iran which have led to retaliatory attacks by elements in Iran, such as the assassination of several SSP leaders.[79] One such attack was a car bomb on a SSP procession in Multan, Punjab, that killed over 40, including SSP leader Maulana Azam Tariq.[80]

SSP was outlawed by Musharraf on 12 January 2002 for its involvement in terrorist activities and more than 1,500 of its members were arrested and over US$120 million have been seized.[81] Immediately following the ban, SSP renamed itself Milat-e-Islami Pakistan (MIP) and the group continues to target Shia and Iranian interests in Pakistan. SSP also continues to receive considerable financial and logistical support from Saudi intelligence, an occurrence that the Pakistani authorities turn a blind eye to largely because Pakistan maintains historical ties with the House of Saud. There have even been reports that the United States and some other Western nations supported SSP to counter growing Shia and Iranian influence in the region. In addition, SSP is now a national and increasingly international group with tens of thousands of supporters and has forged ties with other Deobandi groups both within and outside of Pakistan, namely LeT. Some of SSP's relatively new international offices are believed to be in Saudi Arabia, Bangladesh, Canada and the UK, and there is evidence that LeJ terrorists have undergone training in Afghanistan while fighting alongside the Taliban. This suspicion was bolstered by the 20 December 2004 arrest of LeJ cadre Malik Tahseen by Lahore police for his involvement in securing Afghan bases and for having connections to the Taliban. Tahseen was arrested alongside five associates of Libyan Al-Qaeda operative Abu Al-Faraj, a man who is wanted for masterminding two assassination attempts on Musharraf.[82] Lastly, Stern has claimed that Kashmir-centred Jaish-e-Mohammed (JeM) used SSP personnel during a fundraising drive in early 2000 and that SSP also has ties to other Sunni extremist groups, some of which operate in IHK.[83] Once again, this is a clear indication of the fallacy that there are various and mutually exclusive strains of Islamist terrorism in Pakistan and that Islamabad can pick and choose certain groups to forward state interests without having an impact on the others. By continuing to back LeT and D-Company, Pakistan not only loses control over their activities in India and marginalizes itself, Islamabad also inadvertently plays a key role in the escalation of sectarian terrorist activities at home. Unfortunately, Pakistan continues to miss the contagion effect that LeT and, to a lesser extent, D-Company have on Pakistan's own internal security despite their official focus on Kashmir and India as a whole.

If little is known about SSP, even less is known about its militant wing, LeJ. LeJ is believed to have been founded in 1996 and that this breakaway faction was formed in order to protect the political integrity of SSP and to allow LeJ to function solely as a paramilitary/terrorist organization. LeJ shuns media exposure and attempts to operate as clandestinely as possible, is allied to the Afghan and Pakistani Taliban and the Islamic Movement of Uzbekistan (IMU), has links with Al-Qaeda and is 'undoubtedly the most prolific and callous terrorist organization in Pakistan'.[84] The entire leadership of LeJ consists of Afghan war veterans and the majority of its cadres are drawn from Deobandi Sunni madrassas, much like LeT. The operational structure of LeJ is decentralized and consists of loosely coordinated subunits within Pakistan, particularly in Punjab. These cells are made up of five to eight cadres each and operate independently of each other. LeJ cadres are largely unaware of the number of total members within their organization and are ignorant of the overall structure of operations. At present, LeJ's current strength is estimated to be 300 and has important training centres in

Muridke and Kabirwall. It also had a training camp in Afghanistan located near Kabul (although its current status is unknown) and has fought alongside the Taliban against the Northern Alliance.[85] Following a security crackdown, LeJ relocated to FATA and has undergone a drastic reformation. It is now much closer to Al-Qaeda and uses more lethal tactics, namely suicide bombing.

The relationship between LeJ, the Taliban and Al-Qaeda pre-dates 9/11 as was demonstrated by LeJ's failed assassination attempt on Nawaz Sharif on 3 January 1999. The three LeJ militants arrested in connection with the attack admitted receiving training in Afghanistan while one was a trainer himself in a camp run by Hizbul Mujahedeen (HM), another Kashmir-centred terrorist group. At the same time, the symbiotic relationship between SSP/LeJ and the mainstream religio-political organizations, namely factions of the JUI and its madrassas, suggests that the religiosity and aspirations that sectarianism exemplifies are well-received in sections of the mainstream religious groups as well.[86] LeJ has also carried out church bombings, killed four American oil workers in Karachi in 1997, and is responsible for a bus bombing in March 2002 that killed 15, including 11 French engineers.[87] Aside from Nawaz Sharif, LeJ also attempted to assassinate Musharraf and has begun to target Western interests after the United States toppled the Taliban regime. One such attack was on 14 June 2002 on the US Consulate in Karachi that killed 12.[88] LeJ has worked with Al-Qaeda to plan car bomb attacks and to strike targets within Pakistan and is accused of involvement in the July 2006 train bombings in Mumbai.[89] Further, in September 2002 three chemical labs were found in LeJ safe houses in Karachi even though, according to Pakistani authorities, LeJ was not sophisticated enough to know how to maintain the stores of cyanide and other toxic chemicals found in the labs. Because of this, Pakistani authorities believe that LeJ worked with Al-Qaeda operatives to move Al-Qaeda's chemical stores out of Afghanistan.[90] Al-Qaeda's influence is beginning to be observed more prevalently in LeJ's tactics, especially in their training of female suicide bombers to attack the female quarters of Shia mosques.[91] It is important to note that LeJ is the only sectarian group in Pakistan with links to Al-Qaeda and this is largely due to the fact that, first, while members of other jihadi groups that fought in Afghanistan were able to return home, LeJ members faced arrest in Pakistan. Because of this forced exile, LeJ cadres became involved with the Taliban and their training camps where they interacted with other Al-Qaeda operatives.[92] However, this was not LeJ's first foray into Afghanistan as they had also been involved in the 1980s.

LeJ is one of the most dangerous groups in Pakistan as it has extensive experience in terrorist tactics in both urban and rural environments (like LeT) from its time in Punjab and FATA. LeJ also has members who speak Urdu, Punjabi, Saraiki, Bangla, Balochi and Pashtu and has survived the loss of several leaders due to arrest or killings but was still able to re-organize. Conversely, the TTP is a mostly Pashtun outfit that is dominated by the

Mehsud tribe and has little experience outside of FATA although it has demonstrated its ability to strike in settled areas as of late. However, unlike LeJ, as TTP is a conglomerate of 27 Taliban groups, it is vulnerable to internal disputes and rivalries and has local constituencies to account for. This lack of external baggage allows LeJ to focus its undivided attention on its core missions (which are underpinned by an ideology largely established by LeT) thus posing a greater long-term threat to Pakistan and the region.

Reports have surfaced that LeJ has actually broken into two factions: one that targets Western interests and is closer to Al-Qaeda and another faction that remains dedicated to exclusively attacking Shias in Pakistan. This is a worrying development, especially given LeJ's recent adoption of suicide bombing. It is now believed that LeJ actively recruits suicide bombers from areas where there has been Shia–Sunni violence, namely Dera Ismail Khan. These adjustments have helped LeJ to morph from a Punjabi-only outfit to one that has membership from all over Pakistan, including Balochistan.[93] Terrorism campaigns are clearly escalating not just in Pakistan, but throughout South Asia. Although South Asian groups such as LeJ and LeT may forge ties with more international terrorist groups such as Al-Qaeda, they are unlikely to merge or allow themselves to become franchises like several Arab-dominated groups in the Middle East. Both LeJ and LeT will strive for market share in South Asia while drawing their legitimacy from the regional theatres of Afghanistan, Kashmir and India. Further, LeT will continue to espouse semi-nationalist rhetoric that highlights their continued commitment to securing Pakistan by fighting in Kashmir as well as throughout India (while further inspiring LeJ) even though their actions could pull Pakistan into a war.

Shia terrorism

Like the Sunnis, the Shia community has also developed pressure groups, political parties and religious organizations. The main Shia party is the Tehrik-i-Islami (also referred to by its previous name, Tehrik-i-Jafaria Pakistan, TJP). The Sipah-e-Muhammed Pakistan (SMP) is the Shia terrorist counterpart of LeJ and was established in 1992. Over 70 per cent of those killed in sectarian violence since 1985 have been Twelver Shias as their religious rituals and gatherings are prime targets for terrorist attacks. Though there was previously a zeal for an Iran-style Shia revolution, this has since died down and Shia terrorism and activism can now mostly be classified as a defensive response to Sunni militancy. In addition, Shia political parties tend to support mainstream secular parties as opposed to extremists.[94] The official objectives of TJP are the creation of society based upon Shia Islamic principles, the protection of the social, political and religious rights of the Shias, the furthering of Shia ideals, the coordination of other Shia movements, and to fight 'imperialism'.[95] TJP and SMP are believed to have links with the Iranian clergy and finance themselves through the Shia community in Pakistan and Iran as well as through commercial activity. At present, TJP's stronghold, much like SSP, is in Jhang but, as a result of Sunni pressure, TJP has become less radical and more accommodating than it has in the past. Possibly because of this change, SMP has emerged as a splinter and as the most prominent Shia terrorist group involved in anti-Sunni campaigns.[96]

Although anti-Sunni groups such as SMP do indeed pose a significant internal threat to the Pakistani state, groups such as SSP and its militant wing, LeJ, currently have much more destructive power given their links with several other Deobandi groups such as LeT and both the Afghan and Pakistani Taliban, groups that work counter to Pakistan's declared interests and who have attempted to kill several senior Pakistani officials, including former President Musharraf, and undermine Pakistan's security through their operations in India. However, Iran may increase its assistance to SMP and/or TJP in the future if Tehran feels that Pakistan has allied itself too closely with the United States or allows Washington to use its territory for covert or even overt operations against Iran. Such an event would further escalate sectarian tensions and cause even more instability in Pakistan as Islamabad may use LeJ or other like-minded groups to counter an emboldened TJP with increased Iranian backing.

Sectarian violence in Pakistan has the potential to greatly weaken national unity and to polarize Pakistan's multi-ethnic society, something that could indeed contribute to the failure of Pakistan as a functional state. As such, Pakistan must take strong measures to curb the activities of these groups and not merely enact legislation to proscribe them and execute occasional crackdowns. These groups threaten the primary thread that unites Pakistani society (Islam) and, if not effectively combated, they will continue to grow in size and scope. However, in order for this to occur in a sustainable fashion, Islamabad must go after the key enablers and drivers, which are the Kashmir-centred groups (Pakistan's 'original' jihadis) and LeT in particular as the domestic terrorist groups in Pakistan base their actions upon the same ideological reasoning though they lack LeT's consistent access to India.

What is Jundallah?

Evidence suggests that a new Sunni ethno-religious insurgent movement with separatist ideology has formed. Interestingly, this movement, which calls itself Jundallah, has a sectarian background and claims that it seeks to establish a Sunni Balochistan that consists of Baloch-majority areas of both Pakistan and Iran.[97] Very little reliable information is available on this group but it is often confused with another Iran-focused outfit that has also referred to itself as Jundallah, which has kidnapped and killed scores of Iranian security personnel. It has previously appealed for outside help in its struggle against Tehran and Iran has accused Washington of backing the group.[98] Recently, the group has adopted the title of the People's Resistance Movement of Iran (PRMI) and claims to be a defensive organization that was formed to campaign for freedom and democracy in Iran and to protect the Baloch people as well other religious and ethnic minorities. It also aims to remove the present regime and establish a new system in Iran, which it claims will be based on equality. Further, it vehemently denies links to Al-Qaeda, the Taliban or other extremist networks and claims that it does not work with the United States or the UK.[99] PRMI is believed to be led by Abd el Malik Regi, someone who has fought with the Afghan Taliban and is also a known drug smuggler. Regi, who is now believed to be in Iranian custody at the time of this writing, commanded several hundred guerrilla fighters that staged attacks across the border into Iran against military and intelligence officers, often bringing them back to Pakistan and executing them on camera. PRMI, or Jundullah Iran, took credit for an attack in February 2007 on a bus carrying members of the Iranian Revolutionary Guard.[100] PRMI's claims that it operates in isolation are difficult to accept. Though few doubt the 'two Jundallah' phenomenon, PRMI and the Pan-Baloch Jundallah share too many commonalities in terms of goals and shared grievances to not at least engage in joint ventures and common membership cannot be ruled out. While one chooses to focus on Iran while the other devotes most of its resources to operations in Pakistan, their ultimate goal is the same: either outright independence or a high degree of autonomy for Baloch-majority areas.

Regi occasionally engages in nationalist rhetoric and claims to be a proud Iranian but the actions of his group suggest otherwise. Regardless, the PRMI/Jundallah conundrum poses a major challenge to diplomatic relations between Iran and Pakistan, which have already been frequently strained over each other's activities in Afghanistan. Any sustained spike in activity by the PRMI could result in a massing of Iranian troops on the border if it is believed that the PRMI is operating from a safe haven in Pakistan. This would likely be responded to in kind by Pakistan and, in such a scenario, a wide range of miscalculations and misunderstandings can occur.

Concluding thoughts on sectarianism

Sectarian violence has had a major impact on stability in Pakistan and has resulted in Islamabad having to divert resources that could be used to combat Taliban and Al-Qaeda activity (especially in FATA) towards containing the threat posed by SSP, LeJ, TJP and SMP instead. These sectarian groups have made no secret about their desire to assassinate secular or pro-Western leaders in both Pakistan and Afghanistan and are striving to develop more extensive links with regional terrorist groups centred on Kashmir, India, as well as Afghanistan, some of which are also likely seeking to become active in India through D-Company infrastructure (although current evidence suggests that only LeT has consistent access). Periodic bombings and other acts of religiously motivated violence greatly harm the investment climate in Pakistan as they portray the country as perennially unstable and thus deny Pakistan much-needed foreign investment and hard currency earnings and actually further its dependence on the type of illicit revenue provided by D-Company. This helps to ensure that Pakistan's economy performs well below its potential with occasional descents into a near-crisis state and that the steady supply of recruits for terrorist organizations from Pakistan's countryside and urban slum areas remains uninterrupted.

The formation of the Shia splinter group, SMP, is particularly troubling. As is often observed, splinter groups generally take several years to develop but tend to become much more violent and indiscriminate than their predecessors. They are also much more difficult to detect and neutralize as they are usually highly decentralized and operate in small, mobile, but mutually insulated cells. A resurgent splinter Shia group with training, arms and funding from Iran's al-Quds force or Iranian intelligence could plunge Pakistan into unprecedented communal chaos, especially in sensitive areas of the NWFP, FATA and Pakistan's major cities, namely Karachi, as increased Iranian support would likely be reciprocated by a Saudi Arabia keen to defend Sunni interests.[101] It could also upset the precarious balance in a rural Pakistan that is experiencing declining agricultural efficiency along with increasing food price inflation as a result of years of underinvestment and the recent scrapping of fuel subsidies, and sectarian groups could capitalize upon this unrest. This instability would undoubtedly harm the already strained position of the United States in Pakistan and could lead to a massive backlash against Islamabad's close ties with Washington and the perception (real or perceived) that Pakistan has allowed its territory to be used by the United States to forward its own foreign policy objectives, which in this case would be to contain Iranian influence in South Asia, without concern for the consequences that would come to bear in Pakistan. This unrest, which could be much larger in scale relative to what is being witnessed at present, would further constrain Islamabad's ability to crack down on Taliban and Al-Qaeda elements within Pakistan's borders and to coordinate activities with US and NATO forces. Such an occurrence would not bode well for stability and the state-building project in Afghanistan as cross-border raids by Taliban fighters would increase much as they have following the questionable peace deals they have signed with Islamabad in the past. In addition, sectarian violence in provinces that border Afghanistan, many of which have mixed populations, has the potential to spill over into Afghanistan thus posing another challenge to the Karzai regime, Afghan security forces and the foreign troops in the country.

While this chapter has provided an in-depth analysis of the specifics and key dynamics of sectarian violence in Pakistan, the primary aim was to demonstrate the centrality of LeT despite the fact that it is officially focused on attacking Kashmir and the Indian Union. While LeJ has dedicated much of its time to targeting Shia interests in Pakistan, its actions are underpinned by the same ideological reasoning that was espoused by Hafiz Saeed and LeT. Further, while elements within Pakistan's security and intelligence apparatus continue to support LeT and D-Company based on the flawed conception that their actions enhance Pakistan's security, they also fundamentally fail to realize that every 'successful' LeT operation in India which is enabled through D-Company illicit profit-generating infrastructure (remember the new fold of Shelley's model) emboldens their domestic counterparts who have similar views to LeT but merely lack consistent access to India. They also have not yet come to the realization that any distinctions between these groups is artificial as they frequent the same mosques and madrassas and also share the same recruitment pools while some even have dual membership in LeJ and LeT. Put simply, Pakistan's perception of the current dynamics of Islamist terrorism in the country is the exact inverse of reality.

6 Breakdown of order in FATA

Driven by the Pakistani Taliban and Al-Qaeda but ideologically underwritten by LeT

Recent trends in FATA and the NWFP

Islamist terrorist violence, although it has been on the rise since the US-led invasion, spiked in Pakistan's border regions in mid-2004. During this time period, a suicide bomber killed a senior Pakistani intelligence officer in Kohat, a suicide bomber killed nine people in an attempt to assassinate Pakistan's then-Prime Minister designate, and gunmen killed a police officer in a failed effort to kill the Balochistan Chief Minister. Unfortunately, violence levels in Pakistan's traditionally lawless territories near the Afghan border have risen and there is a strong suspicion that many of the terrorist groups operating in this region are financing their activities through the processing and trafficking of heroin.[1] One particular problem location is in the Khyber agency as the Afridi tribe enjoys a near monopoly over the heroin trade not only in their own area, but throughout Pakistan's tribal areas and northern Afghanistan as well. As such, the NWFP and Central Asia are experiencing a higher level of heroin trafficking than southern Pakistan and Iran. Heroin is easily transported into the NFWP from Afghanistan across Afridi territory and the Khyber Pass, a route that is now commonly referred to as a drug pipeline.[2]

The Talibanization drive that has been launched by militants is 'slowly engulfing the entire western areas of Pakistan bordering Afghanistan'.[3] There is also a belief that Al-Qaeda's command base in Pakistan has been funded by capital flowing from the group's affiliate in Iraq. In 2007, unidentified senior US intelligence officials apparently claimed that there has been a significant increase in the movement of Al-Qaeda operatives and funds from Iraq to Pakistan.[4] Further complicating the matter is the fact that successive Afghan governments have refused to recognize the British-drawn international border and periodically make claims on Pakistan's Pashtun-majority NWFP, FATA and the Pashtun belt in Balochistan. In response, Pakistan has lent covert support to Islamist Pashtun proxies in Afghanistan to both weaken Pashtun nationalism within Pakistan and to exercise influence over its neighbour. Pakistan, much like the British, uses the tribes that straddle the border with Afghanistan to buffer against Afghan influence and to interfere in the affairs of Afghanistan.[5]

FATA overview

FATA is 27,220 square kilometres in size, shares a 600-kilometre border with Afghanistan, and is home to a predominantly Pashtun population of 3.17 million. Since 1947, Pakistan has ruled FATA through a colonial-era administrative and judicial system that is no longer compatible with modern governance. A repressive system combined with a denial of political representation has generated resentment, thus fuelling terrorism. FATA consists of seven semi-autonomous districts – Bajaur, Khyber, Kurram, Mohmand, Orakzai, North Waziristan and South Waziristan. It also includes the tribal areas adjoining the Peshawar, Kohat, Bannu and Dera Ismail Khan districts of the NWFP. These agencies are mostly inhabited by Pashtun tribes with the Durrand Line of 1893, the 2,500-kilometre border drawn by the British colonial rulers of India between Afghanistan and Pakistan, dividing the Pashtuns and separating the areas that now comprise FATA and Afghanistan. FATA remains one of Pakistan's poorest regions with high levels of poverty, unemployment and underdeveloped infrastructure. As FATA is located on the Afghan border, it is a primary transit route and its economy has become dependent upon smuggling and ever since the civil war in Afghanistan there has been a sharp rise in narcotics and weapons trafficking activity.[6] D-Company is intimately involved in this trade and generates millions in illicit revenue, some of which goes to the Pakistani state. D-Company also allowed Al-Qaeda to use its smuggling routes to escape from Afghanistan, leading Ibrahim to be branded as an international terrorist by the United States. Similarly to what is witnessed in India, D-Company allowed its primarily profit-generating criminal networks to be used for the purposes of terrorism. However, their key function must be kept in mind and it is likely that D-Company was obliged to assist Al-Qaeda in order to maintain the strong business relationship and D-Company's consistent access to Afghan heroin. As is the case with LeT, available evidence suggests that D-Company only cooperates with terrorist groups that help to maintain and/or expand crucial business interests. As such, D-Company will remain firmly outside of Shelley's orthodox definition of symbiosis while still possessing some of its characteristics.

FATA's per capita income is half of the already-low national per capita income of US$500 while 60 per cent of the population lives below the national poverty line. Per capita public expenditure is one-third of the national average and social development indicators remain at unacceptably low levels. The overall literacy rate is 17.42 per cent compared to 56 per cent nationally with male literacy being 29 per cent and female literacy only 3 per cent (32.6 per cent is the female national average). Only 41 hospitals are serving nearly 3.2 million people with a person per doctor ratio of 1:6,762 compared to the national 1:1,359. Most locals depend on subsistence agriculture as a result of little industrial development and few jobs. Some accuse Islamabad of deliberately keeping FATA underdeveloped in order to keep the area under firm control.[7] However, FATA remains perennially unstable despite the presence of roughly 80,000 troops in the area and the Pakistani government has not been able to bring stability to FATA.[8] Former Indian intelligence chief B. Raman has even gone so far as to say that if 'you name any jihadi organization in the world, it has a presence in FATA'.[9] One common reason given for this failure by Pakistani security forces to rein in pro-Taliban forces within FATA is that these extremist groups still receive support, both logistical and financial, from sympathetic elements in ISI. Some analysts have claimed that attempting to use ISI to weaken the Afghan Taliban is comparable to asking a father to give up his child.[10]

Since the launch of Operation Enduring Freedom (OEF), there are indisputable indications that foreign terrorists connected to the Afghan and Pakistani Taliban and Al-Qaeda have logistically relocated to FATA within the NWFP as well as Balochistan and are now utilizing these lawless areas to consolidate resources for anti-Western attacks as well as renewed offensives in Afghanistan.[11] Further, Al-Qaeda leaders such as Ayman al-Zawahiri and Osama bin Laden often frequent FATA and the area is also believed to shelter Tohir Yuldashev of the IMU.[12] In addition, due to Musharraf's previous appeasement policy towards the terrorists, parallel Taliban-style policing and court systems have been established in North and South Waziristan and Talibanization is spreading into other FATA agencies and even into the NWFP's settled districts. This recent phenomenon has its roots in the Afghan civil war, a period of time in which several hundred foreign extremists settled and married into local tribes in FATA. However, their movement received a massive boost after the fall of the Taliban regime as fighters were forcibly evicted out of Afghanistan. Many local militants and tribesmen have received significant financial assistance from displaced Taliban in return for shelter and logistical support.[13]

Tehrik-i-Taliban Pakistan: the consequences of a short-sighted Afghan policy

Historical overview

The Tehrik-i-Taliban Pakistan (TTP) was officially formed in December 2007 and brought 27 Taliban groups under one umbrella organization. This merger was driven by a common desire to pursue the Talibanization of Pakistan while conducting defensive operations against the Pakistani security forces in FATA and the NWFP. The conglomerate was initially headed by Baitullah Mehsud and is blamed for most of the suicide attacks and other terrorist violence in FATA, the NWFP and Punjab in 2007 and 2008 as well as the assassination of Benazir Bhutto.[14] The overwhelmingly kinetic approach that was adopted by the Pakistani military against Al-Qaeda terrorists and their tribal allies who had fled Afghanistan caused existing Pakistani terrorist outfits to spawn new groups that were dedicated to protecting foreign fighters. Once established in FATA, Al-Qaeda was able to co-opt local terrorists in South Waziristan to form the base of what would become the TTP and orchestrated two failed assassination attempts on former Pakistani President Pervez Musharraf.[15] Because the TTP acted quickly, it was able to establish itself as an alternative to the tribal elders before Islamabad was able to try to resurrect the jirga institution.[16] Since 2002, over 200 secular tribal leaders have been killed in FATA and replaced with those who subscribe to Taliban-style ideology. This has allowed the TTP to consolidate its position, to continue to shelter Al-Qaeda and to try to spread its operations and influence into Pakistan's settled areas.[17] The transition from being initial Taliban sympathizers to becoming a mainstream Taliban force in FATA began when a variety of small independent terrorist groups began to network with one another while the Pakistani security forces expended the majority of their time and resources on pursuing Al-Qaeda-linked foreign fighters. Not long after this development, many other local extremist groups began joining the Taliban movement in FATA with some serving as partners while others were followers. However, throughout this whole process the Pakistani Taliban never merged into the organizational structure of the Mullah Omar-led Afghan Taliban.[18] Due to its more decentralized nature and independence from Mullah Omar, the TTP gravitated more towards Al-Qaeda than its Afghan counterparts. This has readily been witnessed in its rhetoric as well as its tactics. However, this also arguably renders the TTP even more vulnerable than its Afghan counterparts and sectarian groups like LeJ to fractionalization and internal division. Of the former 27 nodes, not all share the same level of ideological commitment and some seem to be simply motivated by local grievances, such as the poor functioning of the colonial-era justice system in FATA and parts of the NWFP, as opposed to global jihadist ideology. Indeed, a declared partnership with Al-Qaeda by some of the TTP factions may represent opportunism rather than anything else as this relationship could grant access to Al Qaeda resources as well as the prestige of being associated with the group. As such, a more effective provision of government services and employment opportunities in FATA and neglected areas of the NWFP combined with an appeal to Pakistani nationalism could peel several factions of TTP away from Al-Qaeda and could even dismantle the outfit. Some current TTP fighters have a history of fighting on behalf of Pakistan either in Kashmir or Afghanistan and, despite the recent fighting with the Pakistani security forces, TTP still offered to fight alongside the Pakistani military in the event of an Indian invasion. Also, while implementing this strategy, a more consistent effort must be made by the Pakistani government and prominent analysts to highlight the shortcomings of Al-Qaeda's worldview, namely its complete lack of knowledge of how a modern economy functions.

TTP: hardly unified

Although members of Islamic terrorist groups such as the TTP and other jihadists share the same pro-Al-Qaeda, anti-US worldview, they are not always in sync when it comes to organizational matters. This can be explained by the existence of many extremist factions that operate under different leaders and commanders who sometimes have conflicting interests and aims. The tribal nature of the TTP became apparent when Hafiz Gul Bahadur, the *Amir* of the TTP in North Waziristan, openly warned now-deceased TTP head Baitullah Mehsud in South Waziristan not to attack Pakistani security forces. The fact that Bahadur was the deputy leader of the TTP did not make any difference when it came to the territorial and tribal limits of each TTP group and commander. Bahadur also refused to abide by a major TTP initiative to coordinate attacks against the Pakistani military to ease pressure on Mehsud's fighters. On paper, the TTP looks impressive with powerful components in all seven tribal agencies and in most of the six semi-tribal Frontier Regions and several settled districts of the NWFP. Its command structure also appears strong with Taliban groups from Swat and elsewhere sitting on the TTP's 40-member *Shura*. However, these groups also have regional and local political agendas and, as such, are always under pressure from their tribes and overall communities not to get co-opted into wider conflicts that could cause greater suffering by turning their areas into battlegrounds. Due to these considerations, when fighting against US-led coalition forces or the Pakistani military, even ideologically-driven extremist Taliban and jihadist fighters gravitate towards their own tribe and local commander.[19] Because of its fragmented nature, segments of the TTP are more extreme than others. This benefits Al-Qaeda as it allows them to often deal with TTP components in isolation thus allowing them to assert more influence. Al-Qaeda has experienced success to varying degrees in Pakistan but has found a long-term ally in the Mehsud tribe. However this can be turned against Al-Qaeda by dealing with individual tribes bilaterally but the provision of arms to non-state actors would be unwise given the many tribal rivalries that plague the region. Nonetheless, grassroots economic projects, improved access to education and healthcare and positions in the security forces could turn the tide against Al-Qaeda. In terms of the latter, the image of former TTP combatants fighting to cleanse their areas of foreign Al-Qaeda influence would indeed be a powerful one. However, most critically, it must be realized that until the most influential Islamist terrorist group, LeT (the strongest of Pakistan's 'original' jihadis who laid the initial ideological groundwork), is tackled, any actions taken against outfits like the TTP will only achieve superficial and ultimately unsustainable results as the key driver remains intact not only as a source of inspiration and ideological justification, but also for key lessons learned regarding operations, propaganda efforts and political strategies. As long as this remains, groups like the TTP will likely to continue to recycle and re-emerge in different forms thus ultimately producing a strategic stalemate in Pakistan's struggle to contain Islamist terrorism.

Many of the new leaders of the anti-US forces in Afghanistan and those increasingly focusing on Pakistan differ considerably from their Soviet-era counterparts. They tend to be despised by both the ISI and tribal elders as they are much more radical than their predecessors. Qari Ziaur Rahman is a clear example of this new generation as he does not have ISI links nor is he the son of a legendary Mujahedeen commander. Rather, he is aligned with Osama bin Laden and gained his status on the battlefield.[20] In addition, the Afghan Taliban are now mentoring and guiding their Pakistani counterparts as has been demonstrated by Mullah Omar sending envoys to FATA to negotiate with the Pakistani military alongside TTP leaders.[21] This relationship also allows the TTP to operate on both sides on the Durand Line, much to the dismay of the Pakistani security forces.[22] However, this is denied by the TTP on the grounds that they have no need to cross into Afghanistan because the Afghan Taliban is strong and does not require assistance. Nonetheless, they note that if asked for assistance, the TTP would make a decision in consultation with the people.[23] What is for certain is that since 2003, the threat from the TTP has developed into a formidable political and security challenge for both Islamabad and Kabul. Al-Qaeda, which has a presence now in South Waziristan, North Waziristan, Bajaur and possibly other agencies, has provided support to the various TTP factions in the form of ideological, strategic, tactical and logistical assistance, particularly in the development of IEDs and suicide attacks.[24]

Baitullah Mehsud

Baitullah Mehsud was considered by many to be the most influential member of the TTP and was believed to have an estimated 20,000 fighters at his disposal and a stated preference for protracted guerilla warfare. In addition to his networks in the tribal regions, Mehsud established linkages with other Pakistani terrorist groups thus allowing him to extend his influence to the cities while establishing his own parallel government with its own judicial system that is funded by both the TTP and Al-Qaeda. Mehsud's approach went far beyond attacking foreign troops in Afghanistan or security forces in Pakistan and believed that the Afghan war cannot be won without carrying out attacks inside the nations of world powers such as the United States and UK. In January 2008, Spanish police claimed that a cell of Pakistanis they arrested in Barcelona were planning suicide operations in the country and possibly throughout Europe and were dispatched by Mehsud. Although Mehsud was killed, he will quickly be replaced and his battle will continue unabated.[25] The most likely successor would be Waliur Rahman or possibly Qari Hussain, someone known for training and deploying suicide bombers and for his strong anti-Shia views.[26] These individuals, and Mehsud in particular, need to be more forcefully branded as anti-nationals by Pakistani civil society and religious scholars. At present, Pakistani politico-religious parties make far too many statements in TTP's favour that go virtually unchallenged by the majority. Increased domestic pressure on the Mehsud tribe could cause other neighbouring tribes to deny his landlocked faction access to fight in Afghanistan, an indispensable source of legitimacy.

FATA is the single most important base for Al-Qaeda's operations as it houses its leaders, trainers and planners. Also in FATA are large portions of the leadership of the Afghan Taliban, East Turkistan Islamic Movement (ETIM), IMU, Islamic Jihad Union (IJU), Libyan Islamic Fighters Group (LIFG) and a wide range of like-minded groups. Both their operational and ideological leaders are given protection by the TTP. In addition, FATA is home to considerable research and development efforts in explosives, training and global strategic development.[27] Due in part to this safe haven, the organizational strength, military strategy and the quality of leadership of the TTP has improved markedly in recent years.[28] This is problematic as the TTP shifts its focus onto Pakistan itself as it is heavily influenced by Al-Qaeda and its strategy to focus on what it views as soft Muslim states.[29] Some have even suggested that the recent financial crisis has emboldened Al-Qaeda as they have interpreted it as proof positive that the West is not invincible and that the dominant role of the United States can be shaken.[30] If Al-Qaeda and its TTP allies view the market turmoil in the United States and elsewhere as a sign of vulnerability, they must be observing Pakistan's economic difficulties with much interest. Any spectaculars on highly visible economic targets such as ports, major banks or financial institutions, or stock exchanges could send Pakistan even further into a downward spiral. Because of the severity of the consequences associated with this type of attack, Pakistan has to remain vigilant while making its civilian populace aware of the fact that some of its economic woes can be attributed to the instability caused by the TTP and Al-Qaeda, thus once again demonstrating their foreign-influenced, anti-national credentials.

TTP moves east

Indian security forces have been receiving reports claiming that a steady infiltration of TTP and Al-Qaeda fighters is occurring in Pakistan's biggest cities of Lahore and Karachi. For example, TTP posters have been seen in Karachi and Taliban spokespersons have been promising better government in Sindh. In addition, the Pakistani media has carried Taliban statements warning traders in Lahore to not sell 'immoral goods' and the TTP has carried out several high-profile attacks in the city.[31] The growth of the TTP has clearly caught the Pakistani military off guard as it was devoting much of its time to Afghanistan. The Pakistani Pashtun tribesmen were quickly radicalized by the influx of Al-Qaeda fighters and now seek to Talibanize at least northern Pakistan and create a new Sharia state that would lead to the Balkanization of the country. However, some believe that the TTP seeks to control the whole of Pakistan.[32] The TTP is now poised on the borders of Punjab province and joined by Punjabi and Kashmiri terrorist groups (including seasoned members of LeT) with this development being compounded by the desertions that are now plaguing the police and paramilitary forces.[33] The executive director of the Pakistani Center for Research and Security Studies, Dr Farrukh Saleem, claims that Pakistan has already lost 7,440 square miles (12,000 square kilometres) of territory to the TTP and has unsuccessfully tried to cease these advancements through military offensives, the secular Awami National Party (ANP) and the cultivation of pro-government militias. On the second day of *Eidul Fitr* a suicide bomber attacked ANP chief Asfandyar Wali Khan at his home about 12 miles (20 kilometres) from Peshawar. Although he escaped unharmed, Khan, who is an important US asset, fled to Islamabad and this attack was followed by a rocket attack on the residence of the Chief Minister of the NWFP.[34]

These operations are often directed by Osama bin Laden, who remains Al-Qaeda's military and spiritual inspiration while Zawahiri has developed a core group of around 100 Arab trainers that specialize in explosives, finance, communications, military training, urban warfare and propaganda.[35] Further, the TTP also has ties with Tehrik-e-Nafaz-e-Shariat (TNSM) that was led by Maulana Fazlullah, a group that was able to seize large areas of the Swat valley and forged closer ties with the TTP in terms of manpower, logistics and intelligence following a crackdown by Pakistani security forces.[36] Further, contrary to what is often stated, many of Pakistan's more lethal terrorists are well educated and do not predominantly emerge from madrassas but they are often underemployed.[37] Although a small number of madrassas are used for terrorist training, limited evidence suggests that madrassa students support jihad more than those in public or private schools in Pakistan.[38] Many of Pakistan's madrassas are operated by the JUI-F party and it appears to have some influence on the TTP in North Waziristan.[39] Another prominent Islamic party, JI, also runs a considerable madrassa network in Pakistan along the Afghan border. It has consistently demanded that Islamabad 'divorce' the United States and cease cooperation in combating terrorism in order to bring about an end to suicide attacks and a deteriorating law and order situation in Pakistan.[40] In addition, in North Waziristan there are two clerics who wield considerable influence on the TTP: Maulana Sadiq Noor and Maulana Abdul Khaliq.[41]

More Pakistani citizens died in terrorist violence in 2007 than in the previous five years combined and at least 800,000 of FATA's 3.5 million residents have fled since 2006 – terrified of both the Army and the TTP.[42] However, although the TTP has committed atrocities against fellow Muslims, Pakistan's political and religious leadership do not challenge its credentials as an Islamic movement. Some Pakistanis also believe that the TTP insurgency is the latest in a long line of anti-colonial militancy that stretches back to the mid-nineteenth century uprisings against British rule. In contrast, the Pakistani Army is seen as an American proxy and some openly doubt the existence of the TTP and claim it is an attempt to cover up what is essentially a civil war in Pakistan.[43] Even though General Kiani (Pakistan's Army Chief) may be a favourite amongst Western circles, he does not enjoy the same strong constituency in the military that Musharraf did and this could have an impact on his decision-making.[44] He had to visit several army camps in the tribal regions to address the increasing cases of defiance in the ranks, including officers, and is expected to purge these dissidents and replace them with more pro-US officers.[45] Against this backdrop, former jihadi leaders and retired military officers are attempting to build bridges between the TTP and the Pakistani government, one of which is Amir Sultan, a former ISI official and Consul General in Herat who is considered to be one of the fathers of the Afghan Taliban. However, the terrorists are not responding positively to these efforts.[46] This may partially be because of the growing indications that some former intelligence agents and serving junior-level officials of the security forces are actually assisting the terrorists. As well-known Pakistani scholar Pervez Hoodbhoy has said, 'a part of the establishment is clearly at war with another part'.[47] In another development, a jirga in Khyber agency, an area traditionally known for its anti-Taliban Sufi traditions, in October 2008 agreed to close down the activities and offices of all religious organizations except for the TTP on the grounds that they would be tolerated provided that they do not become involved in local affairs. Following this jirga, the TTP seized four containers belonging to NATO. This is also occurring while terrorist organizations in Punjab are gaining strength and Shahzad claims this can safely be termed a mass Taliban-led rebellion against Pakistan.[48] However, Shahzad, like the Pakistani government and other prominent analysts, have fundamentally misunderstood the dynamics of the current threat posed by Islamist terrorism in Pakistan. Given the TTP's fractured nature and the lack of an overall, comprehensive strategy, it is not capable of leading any kind of sustained movement. Rather, it is the actions of more established, organized and sophisticated groups like LeT that are driving the current unrest through providing best practices regarding operations and strategic communications while seasoned members serve as crucial enablers for TTP operations in the settled areas of Pakistan, namely Punjab. Without the example and resources from LeT, much of which has come from decades of operations in IHK and the rest of India (largely enabled through D-Company infrastructure), TTP would be a disjointed organization that is unable to strike outside of a very select area in FATA.

State responses

The escalation of the conflict in FATA and the NWFP is based on the strategies recently used in Iraq where the United States scaled up operations and troop numbers while offering an olive branch to local fighters to drive a wedge between Al-Qaeda and the Iraqi tribal resistance. However, this does not seem to be happening as yet and Pakistani security officials have openly warned that terrorists fighting Pakistani security forces were obtaining weapons and reinforcements from Afghanistan. This is especially true in Bajaur agency where, contrary to official claims, TTP fighters have not been routed and the insurgents as well as foreign fighters have rallied under the command of Afghan Taliban commander Qari Ziaur Rahman who oversees operations in Kunar, Nooristan, Bajaur and Mohmand agency.[49] In Bajaur, TTP militants have identified the main weakness of the Pakistani forces: the inability to control and hold territory. If Pakistani forces do try to consolidate their positions, the TTP seems confident that it can force them to retreat. Rahman has already captured over 100 Pakistani security personnel and, as this number increases, the morale of the security forces weakens. This is further compounded by the recently formed partnership between Abdul Wali, TTP commander from Mohmand agency, and Rahman, and their joint venture to send hundreds of fresh guerillas to attack the Pakistani security forces. If Pakistan loses in Bajaur, Islamabad will have trouble stopping the TTP's march towards settled parts of Pakistan (although it will not able to actually move in). This has already been seen in Peshawar with the TTP and its sophisticated weaponry forcing some police to remain in their stations. The TTP also abducted Afghanistan's Ambassador-Designate to Islamabad in the upscale Hyatabad area of Peshawar in broad daylight.[50] Rashid believes much of the problem lies in the approach taken by the Army:

> The army has still not made the necessary strategic u-turn, giving up on the Afghan Taliban leadership who live in Balochistan. The ISI still attempts to separate the favored Afghan Taliban from the disfavored Pakistani Taliban and Al Qaeda. But the truth is that all operate under a common strategy and guidelines set by Al-Qaeda.[51]

However, those who claim that the TTP is close to gaining control of Peshawar have taken an overly alarmist stance. A TTP takeover of the city is not possible for a number of reasons. First, unlike FATA, the NWFP has a regular police force that cannot be cowed completely. The area also has a heavy presence of troops. Second, and arguably more importantly, the Pashtuns in Peshawar would not submit to TTP rule as many view the FATA-based militants as uneducated, anti-development, and as second class. The TTP also offers them no agenda aside from fighting against the Pakistani government and it should be stated that the main reason that the Afghan Taliban was able to capture Kabul in 1996 is because they were invited by a civilian populace tired of civil war and continuous shelling. There is no such invitation for the TTP in Peshawar at present. Further, Rashid has completely neglected the role of LeT, a group which many Pakistanis view favourably (unlike Al-Qaeda) and will prove more difficult and unpopular to crack down on than any operation against Arab-dominated Al-Qaeda.

The TTP's rise has not been without friction. On 30 June 2008, Mullah Nazir, the commander of the TTP of the Ahmadzai Wazir tribe of South Waziristan and Hafiz Gul Bahadur Wazir, the leader of the TTP of the Uthmanzai Wazir and Daur tribes of North Waziristan, announced that they would be forming the Local Taliban Movement to more effectively fight US and NATO forces in Afghanistan. Bahadur was appointed overall commander while Nazir was made a deputy commander and Mufti Abu

Haroon became its spokesperson. The creation of the Bahadur–Wazir alliance is referred to as a 'Waziri alliance' as both Bahadur and Nazir belong to the dominant Wazir tribe that almost encircles the Mehsud tribe from all three sides in Waziristan. Nazir himself claims that the group was formed to defend the interests of the Waziris in North and South Waziristan. Mehsud's response to this development was quick and stepped up its terrorist activities against the Pakistani government and launched punitive expeditions in June 2008 to punish the pro-government Hajji Turkistan group from the neighbouring Bhittani tribe. At present Nazir and Bahadur are pro-government and against terrorist activities within Pakistan. However, this is not to suggest that they are friendly towards the United States or NATO and are actually still engaging them in Afghanistan.[52]

The major source of tension between Nazir and Mehsud was the support that Mehsud offered Uzbek militants from the IMU. This dispute came to the fore in March 2007 when Nazir purged Uzbek militants along with their local support networks from the Ahmadzai Wazir's tribal territory. These militants were granted refuge in Mehsud territory and continued their attacks against Nazir and his key commanders, one of which was eventually successful and killed Malik Khanan on 1 June 2008. By forming a partnership with Bahadur, Nazir was able to strengthen his support base and overcome the vulnerability felt after the loss of Khanan. The policy of Nazir and Bahadur is largely in step with the Afghan Taliban and has always urged the TTP to focus their energy on Afghanistan. Conversely, some TTP fighters have moved closer to Al-Qaeda and its global jihadist ideology and, due to this, prominent Afghan Taliban commanders like Mullah Omar have renounced ties with them.[53]Because of the Waziri alliance, Bahadur is the strongest Taliban commander in North and South Waziristan in terms of both manpower and influence with the Afghan Taliban. The Ahmadzai Wazir and Utmanzai Wazir tribes have a border with Afghanistan's Khost and Paktia provinces while Mehsud's tribe is landlocked. As such, they are dependent on a safe passage through Waziri territory to conduct cross-border activities in Afghanistan, an activity that is an indispensable source of legitimacy. This alliance is also attempting to steer various Taliban groups in FATA and the NWFP away from the TTP and may be able to weaken the TTP over time. This tactic has achieved some success as Haji Namdar's Amr bil Maroof wa Nahi Anir Munkir (Promotion of Virtue and Prevention of Vices) outfit in Khyber agency has possibly joined the alliance. Bahadur is actively courting other non-TTP Taliban groups in FATA such as the Shah Khalid group in Mohmand and the Jaish-i-Islami of Waliur Rahman in Bajaur. Further, the aforementioned pro-government Hajji Turkistan group of the Bhittani tribe, which borders Mehsud territory to the east, may become part of this alliance thus denying the Mehsuds critical access to the southern NWFP. If this occurs, the Mehsud tribe will be faced with a complete blockade and this could be further compounded if any dissenting Mehsud or Uzbek commanders join forces with the Waziri alliance.[54] This is a possibility as many within the Mehsud tribe blame senior leaders for bringing suffering on the tribe and making their villages war zones but are often scared to speak out. The tribe has informants in places as far away as Tank and Dera Ismail Khan where members of the tribe have migrated and become largely urbanized.[55]

The TTP and its ideology have also experienced some setbacks amongst the civilian population and the religious establishment. In November 2006, hundreds of political leaders and chiefs from the Pashtun tribes inhabiting Pakistan's border with Afghanistan met in Peshawar to demand that Islamabad cease its links with the Afghan Taliban.[56] Further, in October 2008, the Mutahidda Ulema Council (MUC), a group of Pakistani clerics known for their hard-line views, agreed that only the state can declare jihad and not groups or individuals. They also claimed that suicide bombings were *haram* (forbidden) and *najaaiz* (illegitimate).[57] However, while many hailed this ruling as a major breakthrough, the MUC has consistently endorsed the actions of LeT and other 'mujahedeen' fighting in Kashmir and they also share similar regressive Deobandi/Wahhabi views that inspire and provide ideological justification for sectarian groups such as Lashkar-i-Jhangvi. Put simply, these statements only superficially deal with a specific violent manifestation of Islamic extremism (which is a foreign export) while cynically failing to address the key domestic drivers. All of this points to a clear lack of understanding amongst the Pakistani government and the civilian populace, as well as the clerical elite, to recognize the actual dynamics of Islamic extremism and terrorism in the country and the central role that LeT and, to a lesser extent, D-Company play.

Insurgency in the NWFP: spillover from FATA or driven by local grievances?

'The NWFP is swiftly crystallizing at the core of the Islamist militant mobilization in the Pakistan-Afghanistan region'.[58] The increasing terrorist violence in the NWFP is somewhat ironic as the NWFP has historically been a region where Islamabad's grip has been strong, much more so than the traditionally ungoverned FATA. The worsening security situation in the NWFP is indicative of a greater trend of deteriorating security within the whole of Pakistan as Musharraf finds himself in an embattled state and struggling to maintain his grip on power and the relatively new civilian government is presently overwhelmed and plagued by instability. Administrative control in the districts of Tank, Swat, Bannu, Dera Ismail Khan, Lakki Marwat, Kohat, and in other parts of the NWFP, have gradually been taken over by radical Islamic groups. Further, the demoralized police force is no longer able to uphold law and order in these areas, specifically in Tank, located on the border with South Waziristan. The police have reportedly abandoned four out of the five major police posts in Tank and the Taliban have established their own court system and gained control of Darra Adam Khel in the Kohat district, a major illicit arms manufacturing hub. As such, the NWFP has begun to emerge as a safe haven for Waziristan-based militants as well as extremists from other parts of Pakistan and Afghanistan.[59] However, it should be noted that because Swat, Malakand and Dir are administratively settled areas of the NWFP, they still are not as secure for Al-Qaeda and the TTP as the tribal belt in FATA, where hospitality and providing asylum are key components of local Pashtun culture.[60] Further, as Sufi Mohammed has been released from custody and has resumed leadership of the TNSM, terrorists from other regions will find the area to be more hostile as Mohammed has spent his whole life there and has considerable grassroots support.

TNSM was previously headed by Maulana Fazlullah, Sufi Mohammed's son-in-law, but Mohammed replaced him on the grounds that Fazlullah was mishandling his position and pushing TNSM towards the TTP and Al-Qaeda and against Pakistan. Fazlullah now heads the TTP chapter in Swat, a fringe group that could spark violence with TNSM if the latter is unable to effectively implement Sharia law (a problem in itself) and bring sustainable stability to Malakand division. Although brutal and regressive in their own right, Sufi Mohammed and his TNSM do not appear inclined towards international terrorism though this is not to suggest that TTP, LeJ, Kashmir-centred or Al-Qaeda fighters will not be able to find safe havens in areas under TNSM control.

The recent insurgency in Swat was widely interpreted as being a knock-on effect of rising levels of extremism in FATA. However, the demands set out by Sufi Mohammed were viewed as reasonable by the local population: the replacement of the current backlogged and corrupt local justice system with Sharia courts as well as the removal of Western-style laws. Since Islamabad agreed to TNSM's demands for Sharia, violence levels dropped considerably although this is unlikely to remain the case. Despite the fact that Islamabad made a grave strategic error by ceding ground to a non-state actor and set a dangerous precedent, this scenario demonstrates the local, inward-looking nature of groups such as TNSM. Still, it must be noted that Sufi Mohammed was imprisoned for leading thousands of Pakistanis into Afghanistan to fight against NATO forces and, as such, can hardly be viewed as a friendly party and may tolerate the presence of other terrorist groups provided that they do not disturb the local environment.

Unsurprisingly, the NWFP's capital city, Peshawar, has become a considerable cause for concern. At the end of 1979, Afghan refugees began arriving in large numbers, thus transforming Peshawar into a hub for Afghan resistance groups and for Western aid and intelligence agencies. Today, Peshawar faces many of the same problems that it did during the Soviet invasion and an estimated one million Afghan refugees remain in the city.[61] Peshawar still serves as a major hub for displaced Al-Qaeda fighters and the city has witnessed several attacks.[62] One such attack was in March 2004 after the Pakistan Army's operation began around Wana in South Waziristan. In response, rockets were fired by tribesmen towards the runway of Peshawar

Airport, which handles both military and civilian aviation. Not long after, two missiles were also fired from a handcart that hit the Criminal Investigation Agency interrogation centre.[63] It has been said that militants in Peshawar have become so bold that the Peshawar police have openly refused to go out on patrols in certain areas and that Pakistani government officials have voiced concerns that the city is actually capable of falling to Islamic extremists.[64] However, concerns of Peshawar falling to the Pakistani Taliban are misplaced. For one, Peshawar is entirely too large for a relatively small group like the Pakistani Taliban to control. Also, although the majority of Peshawar's residents are Pashtuns, their educational levels tend to be higher than their FATA-based counterparts and most do not subscribe to Taliban-style ideology. In the event of an attempted takeover, the Pakistani Taliban would find a hostile civilian populace thus rendering them unable to carry out their aim. It is important to note that the Pakistani Taliban still can cause considerable instability, as has been demonstrated by several recent rocket attacks on government buildings in Peshawar and large-scale attacks on truck depots that handle supplies for NATO troops in Afghanistan. Nonetheless, these short-term tactical victories cannot be translated into permanent strategic gains because TTP, like Al-Qaeda, lacks a comprehensive political platform and manifesto.

The MMA

The Muttahida Majlis-e-Amal (MMA), a coalition of six Islamist opposition parties, has had a significant voice in Pakistan's national assembly and has governed over the NWFP and Balochistan. The MMA openly denounced Pakistan's military operations in the tribal areas, resisted governmental reforms of radical madrassas and criticized Islamabad's relationship with Washington and its rapprochement with India. The MMA has also been accused of allowing Afghan Taliban leaders to operate openly in Quetta and other cities in western Pakistan, thus resulting in increased violence in Afghanistan.[65]

The MMA evolved from the Pak-Afghan Defense Council that was established in October 2001 by up to 26 religious parties and some smaller groups, both Shia and Sunni, which were opposed to US military involvement in Afghanistan as well as Islamabad's new relationship with Washington. However, this council dissolved once the Taliban fell and the religious parties were unsuccessful in their efforts to galvanize wide support. As a result, the six major parties in the Council opted to form the MMA in January 2002 in order to contest the elections on a common platform.[66] The MMA resigned in 2007 during the crisis over the re-election of Musharraf but not before they allowed pro-Taliban and Al-Qaeda terrorists to establish autonomous enclaves in North and South Waziristan.[67] Although the MMA was replaced by the officially secular Awami National Party (ANP), the election loss was largely put down to the MMA's failure to improve basic quality of life issues such as roads and other infrastructure projects as opposed to the NWFP's wholesale rejection of extremism, the latter of which Islamabad tends to put forward as the explanation for the political developments in the restive region. Further, any party in the NWFP must prove its 'Islamic credentials' in order to gain legitimacy and the ANP has quietly brought in members from the previous MMA government.

Capitulation in Swat

As briefly discussed earlier, the Swat Valley has seen terrorist violence that was led by Maulana Fazlullah that included suicide bombings, beheadings and kidnappings and troops have been sent to quell the situation and several sympathetic local officials were removed. This was the first rebellion by an Islamic terror group outside of FATA and TNSM established their stronghold in Swat in 2005.[68] Following the capture of 48 paramilitary and police personnel, TNSM terrorists raised a jihadist flag over a police station and released the captives the next day. Fazlullah then deployed his fighters onto the streets of Swat, where they set fire to shops selling Western music and Indian films, assaulted barbers who shaved men's beards, drilled holes in a 1,300-year-old Buddhist carving, and even began to direct traffic. Further, the World Health Organization was forced to suspend its polio vaccination drive due to security concerns largely stemming from Fazlullah's claims that the drive was a ploy to render Muslims impotent.[69]

Before his removal and defection to the TTP, Fazlullah was believed to have had roughly 4,500 fighters under his command, a number that was bolstered by high unemployment and Islamabad's failure to address local grievances. Many Swat residents have come to prefer the Sharia law advocated by TNSM as opposed to the British-style Pakistani justice system that they see as slow, expensive and corrupt. There have also been persistent reports that fighters from Uzbekistan, Afghanistan and Waziristan have joined TNSM's ranks, seeming to suggest that this battle may be part of a wider struggle by extremist forces to destabilize northern Pakistan.[70] Others claim that in addition to these foreign terrorists, Arabs and Tajiks have become part of TNSM and some of the terrorist group's own fighters claim that Al-Qaeda is at least partially financing their operations. It is also noteworthy that Fazlullah still enjoys local support and he often draws tens of thousands to his rallies.[71] However, these dynamics are likely to change under Sufi Mohammed (at least temporarily) as it is essential that he demonstrates to Islamabad that although he is an extremist, he will not pose a security threat to Pakistan and can bring stability to his area. These promises are what released him from prison and expect him to make efforts to cleanse the ranks of his militia of foreigners and Pakistani militants with TTP sympathies. Nonetheless, Swat is hardly pacified and the relative stability that presides over the region is temporary. In the future, Swat is likely to be used as a springboard to spread into nearby areas.

Final thoughts

The civilian government and the Pakistani state as a whole face an immense challenge in its western border regions. Due to both historical and contemporary factors as well as internal and external events, there now exist a myriad of pro-Taliban, anti-Islamabad terrorist groups as well as Al-Qaeda fighters that are well-armed, have received enough training to inflict heavy losses on Pakistani security forces, and who continue to generate their own revenue through weapons and narcotics trafficking, and smuggling, and also enjoy financial and logistical support from elements within the Pakistani security apparatus and the civilian bureaucracy. Given the reach of these groups into Pakistan's major cities, namely Peshawar, Karachi, Lahore and Islamabad, and their ability to target well-guarded military installations in their own region, terrorism in the NWFP and FATA poses a very serious threat to the Pakistani state. Failure to effectively quell the unrest and bring FATA and the NWFP firmly and undisputedly under the writ of Islamabad could eventually see the Pashtun-majority regions of western Pakistan become completely ungovernable. In such an event, the Pakistan Army would find itself governing a shrinking state and largely confined to Punjab. Further, it is unlikely that Pakistan's regional rival, India, would stand idle in such a situation. India would attempt to capitalize upon Pakistan's misfortunes by either extracting a forced settlement on Kashmir in a way that greatly favours India or may even actively support these separatist movements with the intent of removing a long-time antagonist on India's western flank. It would also provide India with an opportunity to greatly weaken Chinese influence in the subcontinent, thereby increasing India's freedom of action and its sphere of influence.

Due to the clear ramifications of failing to reverse the trend of Talibanization in Pakistan, the leadership in Islamabad, the Zardari regime or otherwise, will have to prioritize this issue. Combating the Pakistani and Afghan Taliban, Al-Qaeda and other groups in FATA and the NWFP will be an enormous task that will require madrassa reform, effective hawala supervision, cutting lucrative supply lines and smuggling routes, and rooting out elements within the Pakistani government that lend support to terrorists; all highly sensitive subjects within Pakistan. Because of this, Islamabad is unlikely to crack down on groups like LeT and D-Company as they are still viewed as pro-Pakistan and forwarding vital Pakistani state interests despite the clear evidence to the contrary.

What Pakistan fundamentally fails to realize is that the distinction between Kashmir-centred outfits and groups such as TTP are artificial. Following Pakistan's official policy reversal regarding the support for irregulars and the arrest of key leaders, LeT and others have moved critical infrastructure into FATA and have ties with TTP, LeJ and possibly the Afghan Taliban. LeT spiritual head, Hafiz Saeed, has refused Islamabad's requests to go into Waziristan to persuade LeT to reverse its present course on the grounds that he would be kidnapped or killed. LeT's drift towards Pakistan itself is occurring while it still is able to utilize the international logistics networks of criminal syndicates such as D-Company thus reducing its vulnerability and helping to ensure that it can continue to function in India and Pakistan, as well as Kashmir, and will likely become the most dangerous and long-lasting terrorist group in South Asia.

What is Al-Qaeda doing in Pakistan?

One does not have to look far to find analysis on Al-Qaeda's continued presence and role in Pakistan. Most predictions tend to be dire and it seems to have nearly been accepted as a fact that Al-Qaeda poses the most serious threat to the long-term stability of Pakistan and could even cause the state to collapse. This analysis is inaccurate for a variety of reasons. First, it needs to be noted that Al-Qaeda is hardly in Pakistan by choice and is always seeking ways to engineer its return to the Middle East, the region in which it envisioned its revolution starting and where it is able to move around much more easily and have more assets. Though some Al-Qaeda members, such as Ayman al-Zawahari, have married into local tribes in the Afghan–Pakistan border region, most only have minimal loyalty towards their strategic allies, the TTP. Second, Arab-dominated Al-Qaeda is resented by many Pakistanis (unlike LeT, which is revered) and the more rational elements of society (which, admittedly, are a minority) blame the group's presence in the country for many of Pakistan's social, political, economic and security problems. The continuous stream of strongly worded newspaper editorials by some of Pakistan's most prominent intellectuals is a testimony to this. Third, when given a chance to participate in a clean and fair election that is free of large-scale vote-rigging, Pakistanis overwhelmingly shun extremist parties and this can be seen with secular parties in control in all four provinces following last year's election. All of this leads to a hostile environment for Al-Qaeda in the long term.

Al-Qaeda's politics

Many analysts have claimed that Al-Qaeda does not believe in politics as it is a Wahhabi outfit that seeks to establish a caliphate governed by strict Islamic law. However this judgement is erroneous. Naji, a key Al-Qaeda strategist, has a strongly worded statement for Al-Qaeda's fighters: 'A single political mistake (leads to) a result that is worse than one hundred military mistakes.'[72] It is noteworthy that Osama bin Laden has polled favourably and has achieved approval ratings as high as 65 per cent in Pakistan, 55 per cent in Morocco, 45 per cent in Jordan and 50 per cent in Saudi Arabia. Interestingly, while agreeing with bin Laden's political ideas, only 5 per cent would want him to be their leader.[73] This demonstrates that after over 20 years of international terrorism and a physical presence in Pakistan since at least 2001, bin Laden's politics are not nearly as sophisticated as many give him credit for. While he may find common ground with some everyday Pakistanis in his anti-American rhetoric, he has been unable to translate this into anything concrete in Pakistan. Al-Qaeda lacks overt political representation and does not even have a defined constituency. Further, anti-Americanism is hardly unique to Pakistan or the Muslim world for that matter.

On the other hand, through the use of the media, Al-Qaeda has been able to portray itself as being stronger than it actually is. For example, the Saudi government found itself on the defensive after the attacks on the Oasis compound in Khobar in 2004 because, as part of its propaganda campaign, Al-Qaeda ideologues claimed online that the attacks were an inside job even though this was highly unlikely.[74] Through the constant release of videos, Al-Qaeda is now using its own media production to cultivate an image of itself as a group that is omnipresent. Inevitably, this will require Al-Qaeda's central command in Pakistan to rely more heavily on regional affiliates. However, by doing so Al-Qaeda loses the monopoly on its message. Even in Pakistan, recent TTP videos showing children executing Pakistani security personnel and training them for suicide bombings have caused enormous damage to Al-Qaeda's image. Given its recent setbacks in Iraq that were largely blamed on its unnecessary brutality, Al-Qaeda would not likely have approved the release of such videos.

Al-Qaeda plans for the future

Naji believes that Al-Qaeda may be surprised at the sudden fall of regions into chaos in peripheries or in the centre of non-priority states. In these scenarios, there are either Islamic organizations in these regions that are able to manage this transition or there are not. In the event of the latter, Al-Qaeda believes that those regions will fall under the control of non-Islamic groups, the remnants of the ruling regimes, organized gangs and others if it does not move quickly. It feels that the key to success and consolidating power in these regions is establishing internal security as well as providing food and medical treatment. In addition, the region must be secured from enemy invasions and, after these tasks are achieved, a logistical support network for the regions must be established no matter how far away they are from each other.[75] Al-Qaeda has failed to achieve any of these objectives in Pakistan. FATA still remains a war zone as clashes between TTP and the Pakistani security forces and pro-government tribal militias (lashkars) continue and Al-Qaeda is unable to provide any kind of social services. In addition, US drone strikes continue to target Al-Qaeda cadres thus causing the organization to disperse and exert more effort on ensuring operational security rather than innovating and developing new strategies in Pakistan.

Al-Qaeda also strongly believes that in countries where there is the greatest potential for the expansion of jihadi ideology, there is authoritarianism and immense suffering amongst the people.[76] However, although Pakistan suffers from considerable economic hardship at present, there is still an elected civilian government, an active and vocal parliament and, most critically, a Pakistani political culture that will not allow the permanent repression of civil society or democracy, unlike some Arab states. Though tolerant of military dictatorships in the past, the consistent disturbances against the former Musharraf regime demonstrate a new, albeit belated, chapter in Pakistan's civil society.

Al-Qaeda is now operating in a less-permissive environment and if it can be kept on the run, the numbers it can train will decline which will eventually result in a corresponding qualitative decline in terrorist operations. Nonetheless, organizational survival, the natural desire to continue to engage in meaningful activity and the rewards of status and inflated self-image all contribute powerful incentives for Al-Qaeda to remain active. Al-Qaeda's leaders may have indeed underestimated the American response while overestimating the readiness of their sympathizers to rise up against the West. Al-Qaeda must now adapt their organization and strategy to this new reality and though religious conviction is what gives Al-Qaeda strength, its armed struggle holds it together. Its acts of terrorism provide status, power, psychological satisfaction, and attract new recruits. They also demonstrate its devotion and grants it historical significance.[77]

It is often forgotten that terrorists operate in a clandestine world and tend to measure success differently. Death and destruction are achievements in themselves and terrorists do not always feel that it is necessary to translate these actions into political progress. In these scenarios, successes seem to derive from violence and setbacks often prompt greater violence.[78] This phenomenon is being witnessed in Pakistan, but due to Al-Qaeda's failure to understand the human geography of Pakistan outside of the tribal regions, Al-Qaeda and the TTP have irreparably damaged their image in the country. Further, TTP has trapped itself in a downward spiral where increasing the tempo and scale of attacks is an indispensable component of any strategy to maintain its reputation and put down any challenges to the Mehsud's absolute rule from within the organization itself. Here it is important to note that LeT has never made these types of mistakes despite sharing much of the same type of regressive ideology with groups like TTP and Al-Qaeda and also does not suffer from internal power struggles that could lead to irrational and ultimately self-destructive actions within Pakistan itself.

Al-Qaeda in Pakistan

Many speak of foreign fighters in Pakistan and Afghanistan as possessing a type of hero status though this is actually an incorrect perception. Even for much of the Afghan war against the Soviets, the foreign volunteers were actually a burden on the Afghan fighters that did the bulk of the fighting. The Saudi- and Pakistan-funded training camps near the Afghan border further radicalized foreign fighters and brought them into direct confrontation with the Islamic practices of Afghans. This divide led to violent clashes between the Afghan fighters and Wahhabi volunteers and foreign radicals further alienated local fighters by employing extraordinarily violent tactics, much of which was considered to be extremely foolish and unnecessary.[79] Ironically, Al-Qaeda and its partners, TTP and Lashkar-i-Jhangvi, still employ the most violent and provocative attacks, namely attacks on mosques and the use of suicide bombings against soft targets, something that LeT has never done. LeT does not engage in suicide bombings as it believes that they are contrary to the code of Islamic warfare and is careful not to overtly claim or acknowledge involvement in terrorist attacks within Pakistan itself for fear of jeopardizing its image as being Pakistan's Islamic crack force against India.

Although they can pose a considerable degree of danger to Pakistan itself, poorly educated Pakistani youth were never likely to become sophisticated international operatives.[80] Nonetheless, in the 1990s bin Laden tried to destabilize the democratically elected governments of Pakistan through bribes. Some rivals of Benazir Bhutto received large amounts of money from bin Laden but balked when asked to cooperate with him politically. Even today, bin Laden is reported to still be bitter over these experiences.[81] These events again demonstrate the limits of Al-Qaeda's real political influence and its inability to advance past a basic stage despite levels of sympathy in government and the public. This is in marked contrast to the support that LeT and D-Company have been able to cultivate.

The change in Pakistani policy after 9/11 came as a great surprise for the Al Qaeda leadership and, in November 2001, bin Laden called on the people of Pakistan to overthrow the Musharraf regime and al-Zawahiri expressed hope that there could be a coup.[82] Despite the presence of considerably more Islamist-leaning generals in the Army than there are today, these calls still fell on largely deaf ears. This must have come as somewhat of a shock to Al-Qaeda as it thought it had levers in the armed forces. However, what Al-Qaeda failed to realize is that it was viewed as a foreign policy tool and subservient in nature, much like the Kashmiri irregulars. As such, Al-Qaeda was hardly in a position to make demands.

Al-Qaeda's recent tactics, such as the use of children as suicide bombers, have outraged Pakistanis and have greatly damaged Al-Qaeda's image as the 'Champions of Islam' in the country.[83] Nonetheless, Al-Qaeda and TTP have locked themselves into a self-destructive cycle where they cannot backtrack from the use of suicide bombings in the current political climate without admitting strategic weakness, something that could cause dissention in the ranks and prompt cadres to question the absolute rule of only a handful of individuals. As such, they have no alternative but to continue along the same path despite the obvious dangers to their objectives.

In December 2004, bin Laden clearly stated that democracies and constitutional governments are equally unacceptable forms of governance as they empower human rule and man-made legal systems rather than the 'law of god'. In January 2005, now-deceased AQI chief al-Zarqawi described democracy as a rival religion to Islam.[84] These two comments were major errors in Al-Qaeda's strategic communications and clearly demonstrated its failure to fully grasp the dynamics of Pakistani society. Despite continuous bouts of military rule, democratic principles remain strongly rooted in the country's political culture with few claiming that democracy is incompatible with Islam. Even the NWFP, which houses FATA and is often referred to as a hotbed for Islamic extremism, elected the secular Awami National Party (ANP) in the 2008 elections. By maintaining such inflexibility regarding its ideology, Al-Qaeda has greatly damaged itself in Iraq and has done the same in Pakistan.

Al-Qaeda is now carrying out most of its operations through its TTP proxies though the latter should hardly be viewed as subservient. As such, many suicide bombings in response to American drone strikes and military offensives by the Pakistan army are likely directed at least in part by Al-Qaeda although TTP claims responsibility. The TTP appears to have four main goals:

- overthrow the secular regime in Islamabad;
- Talibanize Pakistan and create a state that provides safe havens for Islamic terrorist groups;
- create communal unrest in India;
- partner with Al-Qaeda to carry out attacks worldwide.

The TTP is not able to Talibanize the whole of Pakistan though it can carve out chunks of Pashtun-majority territory which it can use to put continuous pressure on Punjab and Sindh. However, it would be difficult for the TTP to consistently carry out international acts of terrorism as it is a territorial group that is more vulnerable to military strikes and intelligence action than a stateless group like Al-Qaeda. In addition, in the event of a TTP escalation, there are serious concerns over whether a new commander can maintain control over all nodes of the TTP considering his remote location. The TTP is a disparate group of 27 individual tribal militias with differing interests and long-term agendas, some of which have fought against each other in the past. The outfit is hardly egalitarian and the dominance of the Mehsuds is intended to be absolute, thus opening the door for dissent and internal leadership challenges in the event of setbacks or unexpected deviations from the initial strategy. Many analysts exaggerated Baitullah Mehsud's ability to control the activities of the 26 other nodes and to convince them to set aside their more localized concerns. As such, it is likely that the TTP will suffer from competing interests and power struggles deriving from tribal tensions in the future. These are not individuals who are prepared to sacrifice their autonomy and sign up for Al-Qaeda's global operations.

Some components of TTP include purely criminal elements, as is the case in Khyber agency and, like D-Company (albeit on a smaller scale) are mostly motivated by self-interests such as the desire to control smuggling routes or exert monopolies over other illicit activities in the area. There is also credible information that suggests serious disputes over strategic direction and policy formulation not only within the larger TTP, but even within Mehsud tribe itself. In addition to being surrounded by hostile factions like the Wazirs and the Bittanis, many of the local community in areas under the control of the Mehsud tribe have grown tired of living in a constant war zone and have begun to pressure his senior lieutenants, some of which desire the leadership position for themselves anyway. If any Mehsud leader continues to be viewed with disdain within tribal society, an internal 'coup' cannot be ruled out with a leader emerging that is much less friendly towards foreigners. Further, continuous US missile strikes on Al-Qaeda leaders in Pakistan have forced the TTP's Al-Qaeda allies to maintain a low profile thereby excluding themselves from physical participation in any fighting in Pakistan or Afghanistan, something that is a key source of legitimacy.

Unlike other powerful Islamist groups, namely Shia Hizballah, Al-Qaeda does no charity work in FATA nor does it provide any kind of social services. On the contrary, the TTP has actively pushed aid workers out of their areas. As demonstrated by Hizballah, the provision of humanitarian relief tends to be a necessary precursor for any kind of overt political representation as it generates grassroots support and helps to overcome suspicions. However, even if Al-Qaeda is aware of this, it is unable to act on it as the development of any facilities will assist the targeting efforts of both the Pakistani security forces and NATO in Afghanistan. In addition, given the heavy security presence it would be extremely difficult, if not impossible, for Al-Qaeda to bring in heavy equipment to engage in reconstruction like its Hizballah competitors have in Lebanon.

The biggest threat that Al-Qaeda poses to Pakistan is its ideology that has sparked franchise groups and its ability to selectively upgrade the operational capacities of several terrorist groups in Pakistan through training and other forms of guidance. However, the departure of President Musharraf removed a critical component of Al-Qaeda's campaign as Asif Zardari was chosen by the people and enjoys a level of legitimacy that his predecessor did not and, as such, verbal attacks on his government resonate less. Further, the secular ANP is now at the helm in the NWFP. Nonetheless, Al-Qaeda remains a serious challenge to Pakistan's stability but the enduring threat is from the Kashmir-centred groups, namely Lashkar-i-Taiba, as they enjoy large amounts of domestic support despite their avocation of extremist ideology and LeT has consistent access to India through D-Company's criminal, illicit profit-generating infrastructure.

Lashkar al Zil – impressive on paper

In February 2009, reports surfaced that Al-Qaeda re-organized its paramilitary formations that were devastated during the US invasion of Afghanistan in 2001 and 2002. This group, which was formerly known as Brigade 055, is now believed to be a larger, more effective fighting unit known as the Lashkar al Zil, or Shadow Army. Lashkar al Zil is believed to be active primarily in FATA, the NWFP and in eastern and southern Afghanistan. This paramilitary force is well trained and equipped and has successfully defeated the Pakistani Army in multiple engagements and has also been active in Taliban campaigns in North and South Waziristan, Bajaur, Peshawar, Khyber and Swat. In Afghanistan, Lashkar al Zil is believed to have engaged Coalition and Afghan forces in Kunar, Nuristan, Nangarhar, Kabul, Logar, Wardark, Khost, Paktika, Paktia, Zabul, Ghazni and Kandahar provinces. Further, the TTP is reported to have integrated elements of their forces into Lashkar al Zil and it is considered a status symbol to be part of the outfit.[85]

Lashkar al Zil is organized under a military structure with units analogous to battalion, brigade and division formations found in Western armies. This military organization has a clear-cut command structure with established ranks and a senior Al-Qaeda military leader is placed in command of the greater Laskhar al Zil while experienced officers are put in command of the brigades and subordinate battalions and companies. The reformed Brigade 055 is one of a possible three to four additional brigades in the Lashkar al Zil, some consisting of former members of Saddam Hussein's Republican Guards as well as Iraqis, Saudis, Yemenis, Egyptians, North Africans and others.[86] However, if Lashkar al Zil is to prove sustainable, Al-Qaeda must be careful not to replicate its critical strategic mistakes that were made in Iraq. Pashtuns are equally allergic to foreign dominance (if not more so) and Al-Qaeda will be forced to coordinate its activities through the TTP. However, this will limit the scope of Lashkar al Zil's operations in that although the Mehsud tribe has aligned itself with Al-Qaeda, it will not allow the outfit to threaten its prestige or status as being the most powerful force in FATA.

Al-Qaeda in Iraq and the failure to evolve

Al-Qaeda in Iraq's defeat can be attributed to its ideological inflexibility, indiscriminate violence and refusal to accommodate the sensitivities and political interests of its host communities.[87] Al-Qaeda in Iraq, or AQI, is a shadow of its former self primarily because of its rejection by broad sectors of Iraq's Sunni population after three years of active and tacit cooperation. AQI's brutal extremism encouraged this backlash but AQI also made two critical strategic errors that accelerated its downfall. First, it incited a sectarian backlash from Iraqi Shia without the capability to defend Iraq's Sunnis from the onslaught that it itself provoked. Second, AQI established a formal political entity, the Islamic State of Iraq (ISI), to dominate the country after a US withdrawal without sufficient support from Iraq's Sunnis. These strategic miscalculations angered Sunni tribesmen and continuous pressure from US and Iraqi forces compounded AQI's operational weaknesses to prompt a self-reinforcing cycle of command and control failure, tactical mistakes and logistical disconnect which encouraged AQI's descent into criminal-like behaviour, further alienating local populations.[88] West Point's Fishman puts it succinctly: 'AQI's strategic sin was arrogance; the jihadist group had the power to tear society apart but was not strong enough to pull it back together again in its own image.'[89] Al-Qaeda is also attempting to decimate traditional Pashtun tribal governance and society in Pakistan, something which has led to uprisings against them by local lashkars that have so far been unable to receive adequate government support. Al-Qaeda and TTP have also played a crucial role in turning FATA into a war zone, causing considerable internal displacement and suffering. However, by failing to effectively practice counter-insurgency, many refugees direct their anger towards the Pakistani security forces as well. Nonetheless, by making the same types of mistakes in Pakistan that proved fatal in Iraq, Al-Qaeda has scuppered any chance to become a permanent factor in Pakistan.

Tribal groups in Anbar became angry with AQI's intrusion on their traditional smuggling routes and consistent attempts to uproot traditional tribal political structures. These tribal groups overlapped with many of the insurgent groups in Iraq and, in some cases, tribes used insurgent infrastructure to pursue their own narrow interests, such as obtaining lucrative reconstruction contracts.[90] On 17 September 2006, several tribes in Anbar held a press conference to publicly denounce AQI. One Sheikh explained their reasoning:

> We all say to the terrorists, leave because you do not have a place in Al-Anbar Governorate after now. We have discovered from where you get financed and who orders you to kill our Iraqi cousins. Leave now or you will be killed in an ugly way. We are determined to fight you face to face. God is great.[91]

Here it should be noted that Iraqi tribes are not somehow separated or remote. Rather, they are powerful interest groups that penetrate all aspects of Iraqi society with 85 per cent of Iraqis claiming some form of tribal affiliation. For most Iraqis, tribal affiliation exists alongside other strands of identity – religious, ethnic, regional and socio-economic – that interact in complex ways thus rendering simplistic divisions of Sunni, Shia and Kurd meaningless. As such, the tribal revolt was not a remote riot on a reservation but a major social movement with the potential to significantly influence most Iraqis regardless of where they reside.[92]

In December 2004, bin Laden identified the conflict in Iraq as a 'golden and unique opportunity' for jihadis to engage and defeat the United States and referred to the insurgency in Iraq as the central battle in a 'Third World War.' He went on further to describe Baghdad as the capital of the future caliphate.[93] However, even with thousands of active fighters in the heart of the Arab world, AQI was still unable to achieve its objectives. Logistical considerations in Pakistan are also much more complex than they are in Iraq given the geography of FATA. If even with these advantages AQI was not able to put down meaningful roots in Iraq, their chances of doing so in Pakistan are even more remote.

As briefly mentioned earlier, in pursuit of Zawahiri's aim to prepare AQI for a post-American Iraq in which his group would fill the resultant political void, he advocated the creation of a political institution (ISI) that had the unintended consequence of alienating the Iraqis that it was supposed to govern.[94] The same events will be repeated in FATA and the NWFP if Al-Qaeda attempts a similar experiment. Al-Qaeda finds itself in the unenviable predicament of needing institutions and political representation if it wants to be a permanent reality but being unable to do so without committing operational suicide. Abu Umar al-Baghdadi summarizes AQI's downfall:

> At the beginning, the organization [AQI] did not do anything wrong and the factions used to rally behind it and bless and help it. Then the organization suddenly, and in a weird manner, began to behave strangely. It began to liquidate scholars – scholars of Shariah and others. It began to say that they are affiliated with the [Iraqi] Islamic Party and began to kill them based on suspicions . . . This was followed by attacks on the very livelihoods of Muslim Sunnis – they planted charges in front of houses, schools, and hospitals, and under electric generators without any consideration for the importance of [these facilities] for the society . . . They also went too far in the issue of *Al-Tatarrus* [killing of fellow Muslims in the pursuit of infidel casualties], exceeding all limits.[95]

Somewhat incredibly, Al-Qaeda is making these same mistakes in Pakistan. Baitullah Mehsud began scaling up attacks on mosques, schools and hospitals in FATA, NWFP and even settled areas to shore up his own authority and to quash dissent. However, Al-Qaeda was perceived to be so close to him that Mehsud's actions were a reflection on Al-Qaeda. Many Pakistanis also view the group as the chief strategist and the brain behind much of TTP's activities.

Another AQI commander himself also produced a detailed list of lessons learned. The most critical were:

- use of unreliable smugglers in Syria;
- unrealistic expectations of foreign fighters due to Al-Qaeda propaganda;
- poor cooperation between Emirs (leaders);
- tension between foreign fighters and Iraqi members of AQI;
- suicide bombers reneging;
- command structure that diluted authority;
- unnecessary bureaucracy;
- poor use of financial resources.[96]

Globally distributed propaganda created unrealistic expectations among arriving foreign fighters, many of whom were unprepared for the hardships and frustrations of insurgency. Instead, they expected to immediately participate in glorious attacks like those seen in Al-Qaeda's videos. These expectations led to disputes with local fighters accustomed to the careful planning, logistics problems and general drudgery of insurgency. Further, the author of the lessons learned document faults bureaucratic AQI Emirs who were more concerned with protecting their own human and material resources than distributing people and funds where they were needed most.[97] The same tendencies are evident in the TTP as it is an unnatural alliance of strongmen who derive their authority from local sources.

Many foreign fighters in Iraq had a sense of moral superiority relative to their Iraqi counterparts who tended to be less ideologically motivated. Many local fighters had never studied Al-Qaeda's ideology and did not understand the foreigners' motivations – a failure of Al-Qaeda's usual indoctrination practices that the author suggests was caused by the pace of military operations in Iraq. This failure to indoctrinate local fighters ensured that their motivations remained tribal, nationalistic and financial, which hastened their clash with more ideological foreign fighters.[98] In addition, foreign fighters accounted for the vast majority of suicide bombings in Iraq and, although Saudis were greater in number, the rates for Libyan and Moroccan nationals were higher.[99] Similar to Iraq, Al-Qaeda fighters tend to look down on their Pashtun counterparts as they are viewed as less educated, poorly trained and less dedicated to Al-Qaeda's cause. Though religion undoubtedly plays a critical role, Taliban groups in both Pakistan and Afghanistan are primarily Pashtun social/political movements and a response to political disenfranchisement. Many Pashtuns in Afghanistan view themselves as the rightful rulers of the country and are still bitter over their removal from power while Pakistani Pashtuns, especially in FATA, have suffered from marginalization ever since independence. These factors, not simply religious extremism, are what provide the critical oxygen for these outfits and will weigh in more heavily in any future strategy. This will inevitably lead to disputes with Al-Qaeda and will frustrate any efforts for it to become a permanent force in Pakistan.

As AQI cells proliferated across Iraq, the group's experienced leadership cadre was diluted and communication became more difficult to a point where the strategic intent of AQI's high command was not clear to local cells. This problem intensified after less qualified people rose to positions of authority after local Emirs were killed or captured. In addition, ISI fell into the trap of favouring some cells over others without proper analysis of their actual needs.[100] Al-Qaeda is still doing this in Pakistan as it tends to favour the Mehsud faction, thus lessening the probability of other factions taking greater risks to ensure Al-Qaeda's security or to further its agenda in Pakistan.

AQI's setbacks have caused a strategic problem for Al-Qaeda's global movement as their decline demonstrated that most Muslims reject jihadi ideas when applied on the battlefield or offered as governing principles. While efforts to create or co-opt franchise organizations such as AQI generate the impression of global reach, they also dangerously expose the entire movement to the mistakes of local command. Nonetheless, Al-Qaeda at present has a relatively secure (though hardly permanent) safe haven in parts of Pakistan, which makes it more difficult to target directly and also allows Al-Qaeda to build systems that are more resistant to disruption even if strikes on leadership are effective. Further, the relatively low operational space in Pakistan allows better training and indoctrination of Al-Qaeda cadres and offers critical opportunities to build redundant communications systems. These capabilities mean that Al- Qaeda in Pakistan is more able to replace its leadership than AQI was. In the case of the latter, leadership strikes played a critical role in AQI's demise but, due to ground realities, these strikes are unlikely to have a comparable strategic impact in Pakistan.[101]

Foreign fighters continue to support AQI's operations in Iraq although the majority of AQI's logistics network outside the country are most likely being used to move people, goods and money to other potential conflict theatres.[102] Clearly, the most attractive location is Pakistan/Afghanistan given the increasing NATO troop presence and the scaled up cross-border attacks on Al-Qaeda's central command. However, it is going to be more difficult for a continuous supply of foreign fighters to reach FATA in Pakistan because of its remoteness, proximity to a range of security forces and intelligence agencies, and the overall heightened state of security. As such, many aspiring international terrorists may come to view other conflict theatres in the Middle East as more realistic options.

Conclusion

Al-Qaeda is unable to gain any kind of political space in Pakistan and this is unlikely to change as, unlike more successful Islamist terror groups such as Hizballah, Al-Qaeda provides no social services that are often a precursor for overt political representation by generating goodwill and overcoming suspicions. In addition, though many Pakistanis may agree with Al-Qaeda's fundamental tenet of resistance to US 'dominance', bin Laden's politics are not sophisticated enough the translate this basic commonality into concrete political representation in Pakistan, something that is also unlikely to change as Al-Qaeda has made grave errors in strategic communications by denouncing democracy and constitutional governance in a country where these principles are deeply rooted in the political culture and have survived despite decades of military rule.

Al-Qaeda has chosen a poor partner in the TTP, which is a disparate organization of 27 local militias that is highly vulnerable to factionalism and lacks ideological commitment and shared objectives. Al-Qaeda and TTP have also made numerous mistakes in target selection and have trapped themselves in a downward spiral where increasing the tempo and scale of attacks is an indispensable component of the TTP's strategy to maintain its authority and relevance. This is occurring while both groups have fundamentally failed to understand Pakistani society and this will lead to further targeting mistakes, thus hastening their decline.

Al-Qaeda has shown itself to have a weak capacity for storing, analysing and disseminating knowledge as it has made several of the same mistakes in Pakistan that proved fatal in Iraq. The most critical errors include disrupting local governance and turning areas into war zones without adequate consultation with local populations, failure to establish political representation with local support, choosing unreliable and vulnerable partners with tribal tendencies, continued use of indiscriminate violence despite popular opposition, and maintaining complete inflexibility regarding ideology. Despite its mistakes, Al-Qaeda still has a relative safe haven in Pakistan that allows it to ensure that it is more resistant to leadership strikes and other forms of military actions than its counterparts in Iraq. However, it will prove more difficult to ensure a steady supply of recruits to Pakistan than other theatres in the Middle East given geographical and other considerations.

Al-Qaeda is not likely to be a permanent reality in Pakistan. It is not there by choice and would prefer to be in the Middle East where its revolution was intended to start. Further, sympathetic political parties in Pakistan are marginalized and their goal of taking over Pakistan through their TTP proxies or at least gaining substantial political space is unattainable. Pakistan is likely to experience some difficulties on account of Al-Qaeda and the TTP in the years to come, but if history is anything to go by the state will not succumb to them. Despite claims by many, nationalism is strong in all corners of Pakistan and there is no possibility of Islamabad or its people ever surrendering the right to rule to a group of foreigners who have no idea how to govern or even how a modern economy functions. Pakistanis had the opportunity to witness Afghanistan firsthand in the 1990s and would never allow such an experiment with Islamic extremism in their own country. On the other hand, LeT is local and is still widely believed to serve vital Pakistani state interests in the eyes of some. It is not viewed with inherent suspicion by many, most likely because it has a source of legitimacy by fighting in Kashmir but does not have an overt political agenda, and this is precisely what makes LeT so dangerous. Hafiz Saeed, like many other terrorist/insurgent leaders, has prioritized his persona and image over the Kashmir issue and will not be sidelined without a fight. This individual and the group that he represents, along with D-Company, are able to cause the most serious long-term instability in Pakistan.

This chapter sought to highlight the fatal organizational and doctrinal contradictions that plague both TTP as well as Al-Qaeda in order to demonstrate that neither is able to export its revolution outside of Pakistan's tribal areas to the rest of the country. As previously discussed, TTP is an unnatural conglomerate of 27 nodes with tribal tendencies and a poor understanding of politics, strategy or basic issues of governance. Inevitably, this has led the TTP to make extremely poor decisions regarding targeting and propaganda efforts and this directly impacts Al-Qaeda's image in Pakistan due to the perception that Al-Qaeda directs much of the TTP's activities. Conversely, LeT has not made any such mistakes despite sharing the same extremist ideology and also does not suffer from serious friction with D-Company and thus must be viewed as the key driver of Islamist terrorism in the country. In addition, unlike Al-Qaeda, LeT has consistently demonstrated the ability to acquire, store and disseminate knowledge throughout its rank-and-file and this plays a major role in maintaining its positive and at times heroic image within Pakistan. Further, given its relationship with JuD, LeT is intimately involved in the provision of social services, something that Al-Qaeda is unable to do while TTP still does not seem to recognize its importance. Based on these realities it is clear that, contrary to most mainstream analyses, LeT and D-Company pose the greatest threat to Pakistan's security and that of the region.

The next chapter will closely analyse the role that D-Company plays in the Pakistani economy in order to shed light on why some within the establishment view Ibrahim and his syndicate as indispensable strategic assets whose presence should be tolerated. It is this reliance on 'easy' money instead of making crucial economic reforms that further solidifies D-Company's presence in the country. This has negative implications not only for the future development of Pakistan's economy, but also for Islamabad's efforts to deal with Islamist terror groups and for its relations with India.

7 The Pakistani economy

Imbalances and contradictions, incomplete Islamization and D-Company as a strategic asset

Overview

> Pakistan's travails are rooted in the imbalances of its political economy. The ever-escalating, non-development sector, growing economic disparities, a narrow tax base, and massive defaults on loans and assets combine to make Pakistan more and more dependent on foreign loans. The fiscal system remained in the doldrums.[1]

Domestic political crises and a stagnant economy have left Pakistan feeling vulnerable to India. In the last five years of the twentieth century, Pakistan's per capita growth was 0.5 per cent while Sri Lanka's was 3.7 per cent, Bangladesh's 3.4 per cent and India's 4 per cent. Despite large amounts of US and Western aid aimed at reviving the economy, Pakistan still suffers from high rates of unemployment and poverty.[2] Poverty is especially problematic in Pakistan as the rural populations, much as is the case with India, are falling further behind urban centres.[3]

The gap between rich and poor has widened greatly while the number of poor has multiplied substantially. Although poverty levels have declined from an estimated level of 55–60 per cent half a century ago, the dramatic rise in the absolute number of poor is a root cause of social problems and likely has contributed to the breakdown of law and order as well as the growth of sectarian violence in the country. Pakistan's disappointing performance in poverty alleviation is the result of multiple policy failures. For example, the neglect of social and human development is a major driver of poverty and Pakistan lags behind many other developing countries in this regard, including many of its South Asian neighbours. There are also gaps in the delivery of public goods and the delivery of services to the poor is considerably lower than the higher income groups. Further, low levels of social spending and low priority for human resource development by the governing elite, inattention to pro-poor policies, high population growth, excessive focus on urban areas and neglect of rural areas, ineffective use of resources and excessive centralization have all contributed to the rise in poverty. Some methods to help reverse this trend include devolving authority to elected district governments for the delivery of public sector services and taking steps to lower inflation. Critically, Pakistan's rate of population growth is much higher than in either India or Bangladesh and is a burden on the economy and social services and family planning measures are likely in order.[4]

Corruption

Like in many other developing nations, corruption in Pakistan is problematic but taking measures to curb it will help to reduce economic distortions and alleviate the distress among the poor who are often the biggest victims of the use of public power for private gain. Increasing accountability and moving decision-making closer to the people are critical initial steps as is formulating and implementing decentralization strategies. Further, discretionary power of public offices must be reduced and the empowerment of NGOs can help. Nonetheless, the issue of low salaries for high influence-wielding yet low-level public officials must be addressed, especially amongst the police, revenue and irrigation departments.[5] Despite their extremist rhetoric, TNSM in Swat has a reputation for relatively clean governance and for being intolerant of corruption and other forms of vice. Further, their recent 'victory' of establishing more efficient Sharia courts in Malakand has won them a considerable amount of goodwill amongst the local populace at Islamabad's expense. Not only does official corruption distort the Pakistani economy and harm growth, it also helps to create political space for subversive elements.

Domestic and external debt plague Pakistan and, at the end of June 1998, total debt was 100 per cent of GDP and interest payments on the public debt accounted for 47 per cent of total government spending. In addition, by the end of June 2001, Pakistan's external debt accounted for 55 per cent of GDP, having grown at an average annual rate of 5.4 per cent throughout the 1990s.[6] Not surprisingly, investor confidence in Pakistan's economy is at its lowest level since the 1950s. The Asian Financial Crisis and economic sanctions placed on Pakistan after its 1998 nuclear tests resulted in the decrease of foreign investment in Pakistan, thus greatly denting the economy.[7] Further, internal unrest and tensions with India discourage investment and further perpetuate the image of South Asia as an unstable region and the 1999 Kargil conflict is believed to have cost Pakistan millions in potential foreign investment.[8] In addition, a lack of infrastructure, corruption, outdated regulations, unnecessary bureaucracy, difficulties in enforcing contracts, the inability to protect intellectual property rights and a weak rule of law have all harmed the investment climate.[9] In recent times, investment in Pakistan has only accounted for 14–15 per cent of GDP and fixed investment aimed at creating new production facilities and jobs has also remained slightly less than 14 per cent of GDP.[10]

The events of 9/11 caused great damage to Pakistan's economy as freight charges to and from Pakistan increased due to the perception that Pakistan was in a war zone. Also, several airlines ceased services to Pakistan resulting in a reduction of available air cargo capacity. Third, domestic textile and garment manufacturers had export orders cancelled and experienced a drop in new orders due to a decreased external demand. Increased regional stability caused further economic woes for Pakistan as it has to cope with an increased influx of refugees, maintaining law and order, and with conventional defence concerns. In addition, risk premiums increased on sovereign debt and Pakistan suffered from a shortfall in revenue collection due to a slowdown in imports.[11] However, 9/11 also brought about large amounts of foreign aid, especially from the United States and the United Kingdom, some of which has been used for infrastructure and other projects designed to raise social indicators. Nonetheless, it appears as if the costs of 9/11 for Pakistan's economy outweigh the aid provided by overseas donors.

Islamization of the economy: Pakistan's experience

In rural areas, the enforcement of the rule of law and land reform are in order and although *zakat* and other social safety nets have been strengthened in recent years, they are still inadequate. More generally, fiscal policy must be used as an instrument of redistribution of income in favour of the poor. Effective taxation on the wealthy in Pakistan is very light mainly due to weaknesses in the tax administration machinery and, as such, income tax collection accounts for only around 1.5 per cent of GDP.[12] However, given the state's dependence on the landed elite, land reform has not been implemented in Pakistan in any meaningful fashion. At present, 30 per cent of Pakistan's farmland is held by 0.5 per cent of the landowners. In order to compensate for this shortcoming, the state has sought to promote equity through other channels such as taking over religious lands and endowments as well as the collection of religious taxes and distribution of the proceeds. By the end of the 1980s, the distribution of religious taxes approximated the level of all government subsidies, thus demonstrating how central 'Islamization' measures have become to the state's redistribution process.[13]

The Islamization of redistribution, or the creation of an Islamic welfare system, has by itself Islamized national politics to the advantage of Islamist groups. These Islamic parties have openly challenged the state's intrusion into their domain but have also capitalized on the situation to augment their power by demanding concessions. In the political arena, the Islamist parties received support from the middle and lower middle classes in addition to the country's industrial leaders and entrepreneurs, all of whom are unhappy with the current redistribution measures even though they have benefited from the pro-industry policies of the state. Further, the control of distributive services attached to the religious institutions increased state capacity and reach in place of segments of the landed elite and attempted to compensate for the shortcomings in land reform measures. The consequences of these actions were a galvanized resistance by religious parties and their supporters. Though *zakat* and *ushr* laws may have assisted the state's revenues and increased its capacity to provide social welfare services to a modest extent, these and other provisions exacted a heavy political cost in terms of entrenching Islamization in state policy and national politics, intensifying sectarian conflict and expanding state capacity. Regarding the latter, this will eventually create tensions between the state and its Islamist allies as well.[14]

Karachi: a microcosm of Pakistan's economic difficulties

Roughly five million Karachi residents live in slums and transport, water supply and housing remain woefully inadequate. As the demand for these services is greater than the government supply, a massive sub-economy has developed where everything is available for a price.[15] All in all, Pakistan's underground economy has been estimated to be worth up to US$1.4 billion per year.[16] Foreign investors often avoid Karachi due to violence and the cease in the flow of foreign money has badly hit local industry and many businesses have had to shorten their operating hours.[17] The global economic downturn and high oil prices have greatly harmed import-dependent Pakistan and inflation is rampant and the country's foreign reserves are dangerously low. Pakistan also suffers from high levels of company and consumer debt, something that is likely to slow growth even further as this will have a knock-on effect on consumer spending and domestic investment by the private sector.

Dawood Ibrahim is essential to Pakistan's economy and is highly influential in Pakistan's stock market. He has invested heavily in real estate, especially in Karachi, and even gave financial assistance to the Central Bank during a crisis. Also, in an effort to account for Pakistan's monetary shortages, Ibrahim and ISI are largely believed to be involved in the drug trade.[18] ISI's involvement in narcotics trafficking, even while its own civilian populace suffers from the influx of Afghan opiates in the form of addiction, disease and increased levels of violence at major transit points and distribution centres, is clearly to generate revenue for the Pakistani state. Pakistan does not have a viable economy at this stage and is dependent upon overseas remittances and foreign aid to stay afloat. In order to avoid additional financial difficulties, Pakistan has had to turn to illicit activities to fill state coffers and to avoid becoming even more dependent on outside donors and as FDI inflows remain low in Pakistan, ISI will continue with these activities.

Illicit revenue

D-Company's networks in Afghanistan, the United Arab Emirates, India and Pakistan itself would greatly enhance trafficking capabilities. As such, the syndicate is likely viewed as an indispensable component of Pakistan's effort to pull its economy back from a crisis state. Further, not only does D-Company play a role in keeping Pakistan's economy afloat, it also works with ISI and funds LeT to encourage instability and to carry out attacks in IHK and throughout India. In addition, recent political squabbling and an escalating terrorist campaign have resulted in volatile markets as well as a weakening rupee, thus further solidifying Pakistan's dependence upon Ibrahim.

Most experts are in agreement that the 'opium tsunami' that has swept across the region shows no signs of abating in the near future. At present, a significant portion of the unrefined, morphine-based opiates produced in Afghanistan pass through Pakistan, which serves as a central conduit to Turkey and Iran; two main routes to the European market.[19] D-Company and elements in ISI are very likely involved in this trade as it is a relatively low-cost but highly profitable way to finance some of its operations, such as IHK and those along the Afghan–Pak border regions. They would have to utilize the resources and expertise of D-Company, especially in Karachi. ISI would look to D-Company not only for operational assistance such as access to smuggling and hawala routes, but also for specialized knowledge such as money laundering and smuggling techniques. By using Ibrahim's global network that spans several continents, it greatly increases the profit potential and assists ISI in furthering Pakistani state interests vis-à-vis India.

Recent developments and future directions

The Pakistani economy has been growing steadily at around 7 per cent since 2001 when Pakistan began to receive large amounts of aid.[20] However, some analysts note that although Pakistan's economy has picked up in recent times, gains are still very modest. Pakistan's behaviour regarding terrorism, proliferation and democracy will largely influence how much investment and foreign aid flows into Pakistan. Some even go so far as to suggest that Pakistan's present gains are largely because of debt rescheduling, foreign grants and overseas remittances. Further, in order for any positive economic growth to occur, the domestic scene in Pakistan must remain stable.[21] Regardless, overall economic activity has dramatically decreased, inflation is rising and many Pakistanis have begun to stock up on staple food items like sugar and wheat. Further, Pakistani businessmen, with their deep links in the Gulf and Europe, fear that instability will result in a flight of capital similar to what happened in the 1970s and the 1980s; capital that may not return in the way it has in the past.[22]

Although Pakistan was experiencing relatively substantial growth under the military government of Pervez Musharraf, there was a severe lack of investment in infrastructure that was needed to keep pace with this development and much of this growth was in consumer financing. As a result, Pakistan suffers from load-shedding and lost production, especially in the critical textile manufacturing and garment industries. This has cost Pakistan much in terms of foreign currency earnings and has harmed the nation's narrow tax base. Unemployment rates, already at unacceptable levels, are on the rise throughout Pakistan and are estimated to be as high as 70 per cent in the

Tribal Regions. Job-creating fixed investment is also extremely low. As these unflattering figures continue to grow, so too does the operating space of D-Company, LeT and the raft of other extremist groups that have their base in the country and look to LeT for inspiration and guidance. Unemployed, marginalized youths and young adults can make ready recruits for terrorist and criminal organizations, especially if they can be convinced that their less than desirable circumstances are the direct result of the actions of a particular government, organization or even an individual.

Inflation under General Musharraf was mostly contained through heavy and ultimately unsustainable state subsidies on oil and other petroleum products. However, these subsidies were still unable to shield Pakistanis from happenings on the international market. According to some statistics, in March 2008 the price of fuel rose by 17.7 per cent, food by 20.6 per cent and the price of bread (*roti* – a staple food item in Pakistan) nearly doubled.[23] Though some of these rises can be attributed to external events outside of Islamabad's control, some of these rises still could be stemmed by improving agricultural efficiency and the supply chain. This would likely involve the privatization of several major state-owned companies, something that the socialist-leaning Pakistan People's Party (PPP) may be reluctant to do as downsizing some of these bloated organizations would lead to unemployment and could damage the party's self-styled image of being a party of the masses. However, the business-friendly Pakistan Muslim League – Nawaz (PML-N) may serve as somewhat of a counterbalance, especially given the sway that it holds in Punjab, Pakistan's breadbasket. This is one of the few positives of this otherwise awkward relationship.

While the cameras of the international media are firmly fixed on the events transpiring in the Tribal Regions and the possible build-up of forces along the Indian border following the Mumbai attacks, the low-level insurgency in Balochistan continues relatively unabated and the province still remains largely excluded from the political mainstream – a legacy of military rule. Balochistan is critical to the Pakistani economy and provides much of the nation's gas (the province also is believed to have large unproven reserves) and coal and is home to Pakistan's Gwadar port. Violence against symbols of Islamabad has been on the rise since 2004 and is likely to intensify if the Baloch lose faith in the elected government. The Balochistan Liberation Army (BLA) has claimed most of the attacks on government targets as well as communication links and energy grids throughout Balochistan and, as such, is considered the most lethal. Marri and Bugti tribesmen account for the majority of the BLA's membership, some of whom were involved in the insurgency in the 1970s, and many armed Marri tribesman who have originally been living in exile in Afghanistan have begun to return to Balochistan. The primary difference between the earlier Baloch struggles and the present is that Islamabad now faces a better organized nationalist movement under the command of younger leadership that is drawn from tribal leaders as well as from the literate Baloch middle class that did not exist in the 1970s.

The BLA is also a better armed, more disciplined and better funded group than that of the past.[24] As such, ensuring an uninterrupted gas supply from this province will require Pakistan to divert resources that could be used to establish Islamabad's writ over the Tribal Regions.

In 2009 rural Pakistan is still largely feudal and home to Pakistan's most dangerous sectarian groups that have the potential to threaten the very fabric of the Pakistani state. Stories of bonded labour and other forms of exploitation are not uncommon and as agricultural efficiency declines while food prices increase, there are concerns that these sectarian groups, especially Sunni outfits such as Lashkar-e-Jhangvi, will gain strength and cause further destabilization. It is difficult to overstate the importance of rectifying the imbalances in Pakistan's countryside as it will deal a major blow to terrorist recruitment and may cut down on the amount of extremists entering the Pakistani Army. Years of underinvestment in irrigation systems and modern equipment and techniques must be reversed and will require more active participation from the private sector. Further, related infrastructure must be developed in order to promote agri-business and to ensure that Pakistani farmers have greater access to markets.

Aid is needed in Pakistan, namely in the Tribal Regions, but handouts funnelled through external agencies will not prove to be a long-term solution. The private sector in Pakistan must step up to fill the void and create jobs but will need encouragement from Western governments in the form of increased market access, more favourable tariff regimes, technology transfers, assistance for Pakistani firms in their efforts to come into line with industry best practices, and debt forgiveness. It is essential that Islamabad plays the role of neutral regulator and does not apply its hand too heavily. Islamabad must also encourage private firms to invest in agriculture and provide incentives such as tax breaks and cheap credit. Although the Pakistani government can not completely shield its populace from inflation, it can soften the blow on food prices by improving its agricultural sector and distribution networks, and steadily moving towards self-sufficiency. Further, the new government cannot allow infighting to distract it from its responsibilities to address the accumulated grievances of the people of Balochistan. Failure to do so will inevitably harm Pakistan's economic stability in the future and efforts must be made to locate and release all Balochi political prisoners and to engage in sustained efforts to bring the province into the political mainstream. In addition, Western governments and international financial institutions, specifically the Asian Development Bank (ADB) and the sometimes-controversial International Monetary Fund (IMF), have a role to play in strengthening the legislation governing foreign investment, clamping down on corruption, improving the business climate, increasing discipline in government expenditures, correcting imbalances and bringing about currency stability. The benefits that would be reaped from these actions would be immense and could deny terrorist groups much needed operating space and the pools of disaffected potential recruits that their organizations are dependent upon. A stake in the future and something to lose is as powerful a counter-terrorism tool as any.

Ibrahim in Karachi: a permanent reality?

Some claim that Pakistan has given 'economic citizenship' to Ibrahim with the understanding that he will maintain a minimum deposit in foreign currency in local banks in Pakistan in order to be granted refuge.[25] Some Indian analysts claim that, in the early 1990s, Ibrahim helped Pakistan to finance its clandestine procurement of nuclear and missile technology components and also believes that he controls the entire Pakistani drug mafia on behalf of ISI and contributes a 'huge amount of money to ISI coffers every year'.[26] While it is likely impossible to independently verify these claims, what is clear is that D-Company plays a major role in the Pakistani economy though it would be a stretch to suggest any kind of dependency. Unsurprisingly, Islamabad denies Ibrahim's existence in Pakistan despite overwhelming evidence to the contrary. One such example of Ibrahim's residence in Pakistan was the blasts at Kawish Crown Plaza in Karachi in 2003. After the explosions, both the Inspector General of the Sindh Police and de facto Sindh Home Minister admitted Ibrahim's presence in Pakistan and claimed that he was the actual owner of building.[27] This particular event demonstrated that not only does Ibrahim enjoy safe haven in Pakistan, he has also made sizeable investments there, thus solidifying his presence in Pakistan's economy and making him much more difficult to dispose of. Because of this and other events, D-Company, Pakistan and LeT are likely to remain in a trilateral nexus as D-Company is a viewed as a strategic asset, although its activities and links with LeT in India actually undermine Pakistan's security.

ISI is accused of using D-Company's illegal hawala channels to finance subversive activities in India, such as the circulation of counterfeit Indian rupees, funding contract killers, paying agents, informers and police/jail officials, and to compensate the families of their associates killed by the police.[28] ISI is also believed to use Ibrahim to spot RAW agents. Further, ISI utilizes some of Ibrahim's contacts in India and, according to Indian security agencies, ISI uses Anees Ibrahim's (Dawood's younger brother) network to smuggle arms into India. Anees is believed to not only have links to LeT and JeM, but also to militants in Nagaland in northeast India.[29] However, once again, these are accusations that have yet to be independently verified.

In the event that LeT chooses to expand on a larger scale (which seems to be the case, especially following the November 2008 Mumbai attack), Ibrahim's global links and assets could be used to generate revenue and to strengthen LeT's operational capacities and his resources in the Middle East and Europe could act as the explosives and munitions supply for LeT.[30] Although it is indeed important not to sensationalize issues such as these, the outward expansion of LeT with D-Company assistance is accelerating, especially as Pakistan refuses to cease support for Ibrahim or extradite him to India. Pakistan is likely reluctant to hand over any terrorist to India, even if their movement is no longer active (as is the case with Sikh terrorism), for fear that this would signal to other groups that Islamabad is no longer a reliable partner. There is also another potentially troublesome reason for Pakistan's refusal to cooperate with Indian authorities: 'Pakistan's reluctance to hand over people, even those with internationally acknowledged criminal records, is, to India, clear evidence that Islamabad has no intention of renouncing terrorism as an instrument of state policy vis-à-vis India.'[31]

Pakistan's struggle to develop and maintain a legitimate economy as a result of corruption, a lack of the rule of law, and the image of South Asia (and Pakistan in particular) as an unstable region has forced Pakistan to look to illegitimate sources of financing. By engaging in state-sponsored organized criminal activity and working with transnational syndicates such as D-Company, Pakistan has managed to stave off outright financial collapse and has been able to continue its funding of various insurgencies in the region, namely in IHK. At present, Pakistan's domestic situation will remain unstable for the foreseeable future as Pakistan will have to counter the unrest in Balochistan, FATA and the NWFP all while combating sectarian violence in its major cities (although it continues to fail to move against the source, which is LeT). Further, Pakistan's gradual return to democracy, if present trends continue, will be characterized by occasional upheavals by both rival political factions and an army that is determined to hold its grip on power and remain the authoritative voice on all major policy matters. As such, foreign investment will not return to Pakistan in substantial sums any time soon. Nonetheless, Pakistan's major unresolved conflict, Kashmir, will require continued funding in order to remain a LIC. Without D-Company and its global network, this will not be possible.

Ibrahim, although considered an international terrorist, is believed to forward a vital Pakistani state interest by assisting terrorists to pin down Indian troops, thus preventing India from fully capitalizing upon its conventional superiority to make larger strategic moves within the subcontinent and to be able to dedicate more resources to the myriad of insurgencies that plague the northeast and the Naxal Belt in eastern and central India. Islamabad also believes that Ibrahim plays a critical role in ensuring that the Pakistani economy stays afloat and provides enough hard currency to prevent a collapse and to ensure the modest standard of living for a segment of Pakistan's population. D-Company's earnings also help to supplement Pakistan's high defence spending and fund LeT.

Pakistan's continued tolerance of D-Company and its active encouragement of the syndicate's relationship with LeT can be best characterized as deficient, short-term strategic thinking. While Pakistan likely believes that D-Company plays a key role in the country's economic development, its presence actually further solidifies the imbalances and contradictions that landed Pakistan in this economic difficulty in the first place. Further, through its enablement of LeT terrorist activities in India and the accompanied prestige and contagion effect that comes along with it, D-Company also fans sectarian tensions and encourages Deobandi/Wahhabi ideology with negative implications for Pakistan's ability to develop and implement sound, modern economic policies. Further, as D-Company is primarily a profit-oriented organization that assists terrorist groups only when it is in the syndicate's interest to do so, D-Company has no incentive to see this situation alter and will continue to expand and put down deeper roots in Pakistan.

Concluding thoughts

Indian misrule such as rigged elections, forced disappearances and other abuses combined with Pakistan's strategy of indirect proxy warfare has created an environment that has enabled the trilateral nexus between D-Company, LeT and Pakistan to flourish in Kashmir while Islamabad becomes less and less relevant. As long as the status quo remains, Kashmir will remain plagued by multiple insurgent groups, criminal gangs, underdevelopment and overall despair. This will ensure that Kashmir continues to provide a steady pool of recruits to carry out attacks against Indian targets in Kashmir and elsewhere. However, as Islamabad refuses to cease its support for irregulars and continues to feel vulnerable to its much larger neighbour, India is unlikely to meet Pakistani requests such as the validation of troop positions, demilitarization of the Siachen Glacier, etc. As such, a disproportionate amount of the Indian security forces are likely to remain pinned down and subject to guerrilla attacks. Further, Kashmir will not be granted the autonomy that it is guaranteed under the Indian constitution and this will fuel greater disillusionment with the legitimate political process amongst Kashmiris. As a result, the current social, political and economic environment in Kashmir shows little signs of change and the disputed territory will continue to pose a major challenge to stability in South Asia.

ISI's support for terrorist and insurgent groups in India is well known. ISI supplied mostly Chinese weaponry in the form of machine guns, grenades and mines (including Claymore mines) to the Khalistan movement in Punjab via underground networks and have consistently trained, armed and funded Kashmir-centred terrorist groups since at least 1989. In the early 1990s, ISI formed a partnership with D-Company and jointly planned and executed the 1993 Mumbai Blasts. Following these attacks, ISI facilitated the development of ties between LeT and D-Company, thus forming a trilateral nexus that often functions independently of the political system and greatly complicates diplomacy between New Delhi and Islamabad on a wide range of issues. At present, D-Company provides logistical support to LeT in Kashmir by smuggling predominantly Chinese weapons that are likely in the possession of the Pakistani government as Ibrahim already possesses the expertise and contacts required to transport arms into and through India.

Further, the sheer size and scale of the weapons that were smuggled into Mumbai by D-Company via the high seas in 1993 demonstrates that the syndicate is capable of trafficking enough firepower to fight a LIC for an extended period of time. Unless a sincere effort is made by Islamabad to either disrupt these smuggling routes or shut them down entirely, D-Company and LeT will continue to partner to carry out extreme acts of violence within India, thus greatly inhibiting the peace process and contributing to the mutual suspicion and hostility that often characterizes relations between New Delhi and Islamabad.

Although LeT was initially a Kashmir-centred group that was dependent upon ISI, through its partnership with D-Company it has now developed its own pan-Islamic agenda and sources of funding. It has also maintained ties with ISI despite being proscribed in Pakistan and has strengthened its partnership with D-Company, TTP and Al-Qaeda, thereby greatly increasing its operational capabilities and emerging as the greatest long-term threat to Pakistan. In addition, LeT will continue to receive funding and weaponry from D-Company as their operations have now become intertwined and Ibrahim is dependent upon Pakistan for refuge and his support for LeT's operations has essentially become D-Company's 'rent' for its safe haven and favourable business environment with Pakistan. However, D-Company will continue to prioritize profit generation and its networks will only secondarily be used for acts of terrorism within India. Further, it is unclear whether D-Company is willing to extend consistent access to its network within India to any terrorist group aside from LeT as it does not appear to be in the syndicate's interest to do so. This dynamic shares characteristics of Shelley's traditional definition of symbiosis but remains a distinct fold nonetheless.

ISI will not cease its support for LeT despite official declarations to the contrary by Islamabad and the fact that the support is further lessening ISI's influence. Pakistan's use of irregulars has proven to be highly cost-effective in the past as it has enabled Islamabad to pin down one-third of the Indian Army. Because of this, India's conventional superiority has been degraded and has a limited capacity to engage in conflicts elsewhere, such as India's northeast or other areas of instability as well as the disputed Sino-Indian border region. Further, elements within ISI will work with LeT modules across India through D-Company infrastructure as it attempts to gradually weaken India over time while further indigenizing LeT and encouraging the development of IM. If Islamic hard-line elements remain in ISI and the Pakistani Army, these occurrences will be a permanent reality. However, if Islamabad is to successfully continue these efforts, they will need D-Company's expertise and networks within India. Put bluntly, if the impasse over Kashmir is not resolved and the Indo-Pak border is not normalized, these ties are likely to strengthen, especially between D-Company and LeT. Islamabad has not abandoned its support for terrorism and ISI aims to keep at least a reservist force within Pakistan in the event of a conflict with India. Unfortunately, Islamabad seems to be unaware of the fact that the longer LeT receives support from ISI and D-Company, the less influence that Pakistan will be able to exert over LeT in the future. If the current trend continues, future efforts to reign in LeT will be unsuccessful as the group will have become multinational with a wide variety of state and non-state sponsors and sources of funding and will have fighters and other resources dispersed throughout several countries.

Dawood Ibrahim will remain in Pakistan for the foreseeable future even though he is the most wanted man in India. First, Ibrahim is not widely regarded as a criminal in Pakistan as he is largely seen as a protector of the Muslim community in India. Second, Ibrahim is believed by Islamabad to be an important asset for Pakistan's economy in addition to its intentions to encourage instability in Kashmir and throughout India. Also, even if there was a genuine desire to dismantle D-Company and sever its links with LeT, it would not be possible as most of Pakistan's energy and resources are dedicated to combating sectarian violence, containing a resurgent Taliban in FATA and several areas of the NWFP without realizing that it is LeT that provides the ideological underpinning for the activities of these newer groups. Pakistan must also deal with the low-level nationalist insurgency in Balochistan. As such, analysts and policymakers will have to factor the nexus between ISI, D-Company and LeT into the equation for the foreseeable future.

If the threat of LeT and its operational partners are to be neutralized, its core cause and key source of legitimacy must be removed. The Kashmir issue, although not the only rallying point, is unquestionably the major motivator of LeT's activities in the subcontinent and its effective resolution would deal a major blow to the ideology of the group as well as its recruitment and financing efforts. Nonetheless, it is important to note that the group would still remain in one form or the other as it has already established some international links and would still pose a security threat to India albeit in a less serious form, at least initially. However, as neither India nor Pakistan seems willing to take the first step for fear of the other exploiting the situation to make strategic gains, it is reasonable to believe that the Kashmir conflict will not be resolved in the near or medium term and that LeT will continue to operate with clandestine support from Pakistan.

Much like LeT, D-Company will not be abandoned by Pakistan unless there is a dramatic strategic and ideological shift within the political leadership and security apparatus and Pakistan begins to experience strong yet sustainable economic growth that is not the result of foreign aid, debt restructuring or one-off foreign investments. These events are highly unlikely and, as such, D-Company will continue to serve several vital missions within Pakistan by supporting LeT and maintaining Islamabad's 'insurance policy' vis-à-vis India, making sizeable investments in Pakistan, and by generating revenue for the state through illicit activities. Because of this, D-Company will remain a key non-state actor in the region and will serve as a major irritant in bilateral relations between India and Pakistan that also stifles meaningful economic reform in Pakistan.

Pakistan has to realize that it is in its own interests to cease its material and ideological support for LeT and D-Company and take immediate action to shut down their activities. LeT will eventually completely cease to be accountable to Islamabad and will begin to develop its own objectives much like many former Islamic combatants did following the Soviet withdrawal. It is nothing short of astonishing that the leadership in Pakistan has not come to realize that supporting non-state actors, especially those with independent ambitions, to forward state interests is a highly dangerous strategy that has few examples of long-term success. Inevitably, LeT will become more independent in its decision-making and will maintain relations with D-Company, Al-Qaeda and other like-minded groups as part of its quest to become the most powerful terrorist group in South Asia.

By granting D-Company a safe haven in Pakistan and allowing Ibrahim's syndicate to operate with near impunity, Islamabad is doing more to ensure that the Pakistani economy remains underdeveloped, imbalanced, dependent on foreign aid and remittances, and unattractive to most foreign investors. By engaging in illicit activities such as smuggling, arms and narcotics trafficking, and illegal hawala transactions, Ibrahim has played a critical role in establishing a parallel black market economy in Pakistan that competes with and inhibits the growth of the legitimate. In addition, the longer D-Company is given a free hand while the fundamentals of Pakistan's economy show few signs of improvement, the greater Ibrahim's presence will be solidified. Also, his residency on Pakistani soil serves as a major blemish on Pakistan's international image and puts forth the impression, right or wrong, that Pakistan is tolerant of corruption and is willing to shelter entire criminal syndicates if it suits their interest. This is at least partially responsible for investor confidence in Pakistan being at its lowest levels in decades, thus depriving Pakistan of much-needed foreign capital and greatly inhibiting their own counter-terrorism efforts. Without foreign investment, Pakistan is unlikely to bring about the dramatic drop of poverty rates necessary to deal a blow to the recruitment efforts of both domestic and international terrorist groups in the country. However, it is of note that it is not uncommon for nations that are facing increasingly desperate circumstances to resort to more extreme methods and to deal with questionable non-state actors in order to stay afloat.

It is tempting to view some of these developments as new, unprecedented phenomena not witnessed before in Pakistan as well as the region. However, this is not the case as Pakistan has hosted regional subversive organizations since at least the time of the Soviet invasion and has consistently used them to further state interests. Nonetheless, through bridging the gap between D-Company and LeT, Pakistan has greatly accelerated LeT's progress towards operational independence and D-Company's metamorphosis from a profit-driven, non-ideological group to a hybrid organization that, while prioritizing profits, is willing to enable terrorism within India. As Pakistan's socio-economic conditions continue to worsen alongside its faltering political system, these elements may eventually come to fill some of the void. Such a development could have a knock-on effect elsewhere, thus greatly harming regional stability. The danger is not Pakistan becoming a 'failed state', a term which is often used rather carelessly, but rather developments in Pakistan setting a precedent for terrorist and insurgent groups in South Asia, something that would further complicate diplomacy between regional states, namely India and Pakistan, make a viable solution to the Kashmir dispute an even more distant objective, and would ensure that the political and economic potential of the region remains unrealized.

Key policy points

By granting continued refuge to D-Company and allowing the syndicate to maintain its ties with Lashkar-i-Taiba (LeT), Pakistan is accelerating LeT's evolution into South Asia's most dangerous terrorist group while inadvertently decreasing its own relevance. As such, LeT will begin to exhibit even more independence in its decision-making, will continue to nurture the emergent Indian Mujahedeen (IM) through D-Company criminal infrastructure, and will plot further terrorist spectaculars on Indian soil. Involvement with D-Company and its logistical network also renders LeT less vulnerable to any kind of decapitating strike and the group can continue to function in one form or the other even if abandoned by Islamabad entirely.

D-Company's continued prioritization of illicit profit-generating actives while also enabling and occasionally participating in Pakistan-backed terrorist activities with LeT in India represents a new dynamic of Shelley's model, namely her definition of symbiosis. Contrary to this traditional definition and the analysis of many, D-Company has not descended into a hybrid-type organization that assigns equal priority to both crime and terrorism or has shifted its primary focus to terrorism itself. Rather, D-Company supports terrorist groups, namely LeT, when it is in its business interests to do so. In the case of the trilateral nexus with LeT and Pakistan, D-Company's support for LeT ensures its continued safe haven and favourable business environment in Pakistan. It is for the same reasons that it is unclear whether D-Company would be willing extend consistent access to its networks in India to Islamist terror groups based in Bangladesh or India itself. When it comes to LeT attacks in IHK and throughout India, it is ironically the profit motive which enables terrorism.

LeT is not likely to sacrifice its independence and come under Al-Qaeda's umbrella. Rather, LeT will continue to develop into a distinctive, South Asia-centric terrorist group in its own right while receiving aid from elements in Pakistan's security and intelligence apparatus as well as retired personnel. LeT has forged selective partnerships with fellow Pakistani and other regional terrorist and insurgent groups in addition to criminal syndicates whose activities undermine Pakistan's own security and escalate terrorist campaigns throughout South Asia. LeT's development challenges the long-held notion that irregulars can be sustainably used to achieve limited objectives in an asymmetric conflict against a conventionally superior adversary. This should serve as a clear warning to other state sponsors of terrorism.

Given its mostly Pashtun membership and lack of a nationwide support base, the Tehrik-i-Taliban Pakistan (TTP) is unlikely to be able to capture any major urban centres, including Peshawar. Peshawar has a regular police force that cannot be cowed completely and the area also has a heavy presence of troops. Second and arguably more importantly, the Pashtuns in Peshawar would not submit to TTP rule as many view these tribal militants as uneducated, anti-development, and as second-class. Further, TTP's close links with Al-Qaeda have greatly damaged its image and TTP has little operational experience outside of the Federally Administered Tribal Areas (FATA). TTP is an unwieldy conglomerate of 27 local Taliban groups with minimal support in the settled areas of Pakistan. It is also vulnerable to internal disputes and rivalries as all 27 nodes have tribal tendencies and local constituencies to account for.

LeT, not Al-Qaeda or the TTP, poses the greatest long term threat to Pakistan. LeT still enjoys high levels of domestic sympathy due to its involvement in the Kashmir dispute despite its recently developed links with anti-state elements like TTP and Al-Qaeda. Further, given its predominantly Punjabi membership, decades of state patronage and military training, extensive experience engaging Indian security forces, ties to criminal syndicates such as D-Company, and its rapidly increasing regional ambitions, LeT poses the greatest long-term threat to Pakistan. It is capable of carrying out highly sophisticated attacks in Pakistan and, as was demonstrated by its involvement in the November 2008 Mumbai attacks, could also drag Pakistan into a conventional war with India.

Behind LeT, the anti-Shia Lashkar-i-Jhangvi (LeJ) poses the next most serious threat to Pakistan. LeJ has extensive experience in terrorist activities in both rural and urban environments from its time in Punjab and FATA. LeJ has members who speak Urdu, Punjabi, Seraiki, Bangla, Balochi and Pashtu and has survived the loss of several leaders due to arrest or killings but was still able to re-organize. As LeJ is not a territorial group, it lacks external baggage which allows it to focus its undivided attention on its core mission of carrying out attacks against Pakistan's Shia and India, thus posing a major long-term threat to Pakistan and the region. The type of sectarian violence that LeJ engages in and its use of suicide bombings has the potential to greatly weaken Pakistan's national unity if unchecked.

Al-Qaeda is not likely a permanent reality in Pakistan despite its current safe haven. The biggest threat that Al-Qaeda poses to Pakistan is its ideology that has sparked franchise groups and its ability to selectively upgrade the operational capacities of several terrorist groups in Pakistan through training and other forms of guidance. Aside from this, Al-Qaeda has been unable to obtain any kind of overt political space in the country. This is unlikely to change as, unlike groups like Hizballah, Al-Qaeda provides no social services and its politics are not sophisticated enough to translate feelings of anti-Americanism into anything concrete in Pakistan. Al-Qaeda has also made grave errors in strategic communications by denouncing democracy and constitutional governance in a country where these principles are deeply rooted in the political culture and have survived despite decades of military rule. In addition, Al-Qaeda chose an unreliable partner in the TTP and the group has shown itself to have a weak capacity for storing, analysing and effectively disseminating knowledge as it has made many of the same mistakes in Pakistan that proved fatal in Iraq. As such, although Al-Qaeda currently enjoys a safe haven, it is unlikely to remain in Pakistan permanently.

Although LeT and others have high hopes for the Indian Mujahedeen, the outfit remains relatively primitive in terms of operational capacity and information operations. LeT's rise to prominence has largely followed a more sophisticated understanding of politics and strategic thought thus causing the group to come to view violence as a tool rather than an end in itself. IM's urban terrorism campaign currently appears to be reactive and driven by anger rather than by more complex strategic objectives, something that LeT undoubtedly seeks to change. At present, IM's attacks do not require a safe haven outside of India but if the group intends to evolve then the role of both Pakistan and Bangladesh will become more prominent. As many of LeT's cadres are Pakistani and IM is still somewhat of a disjointed organization, D-Company's logistical network will be critical, especially in major urban centres such as Mumbai. This network can be utilized for recruiting, smuggling weapons and militants in and out of India, and providing pre-operation and post-operation services like surveillance, reconnaissance and assisting terrorists in moving through India undetected. Without this network, LeT is not likely able to achieve its objectives in India and the growth of IM will be inhibited thus limiting it to inconsistent low-tech terrorism which has few lasting effects and does not influence policy.

Notes

Introduction

1 Mickolus, Edward, 'What Constitutes State Support to Terrorists?', *Terrorism and Political Violence*, Vol. 1, Issue 3, 1989, p. 288.
2 Mickolus, 1989.
3 Byman, Daniel, Chalk, Peter, Hoffman, Bruce, Rosenau, William and Brannan, David, 'Trends in Outside Support for Insurgent Movements', RAND Corporation, 2001. For a more in-depth discussion, also see Byman, Daniel, *Deadly Connections: States that Sponsor Terrorism*, Cambridge University Press, 2005.
4 Byman *et al.*, 2001.
5 Byman, Daniel, 'The Changing Nature of State Sponsorship of Terrorism', Analysis Paper, No. 16, May 2008. Saban Center for Middle East Policy, Brookings Institute, pp. 25–6.
6 Byman, 2008.
7 Byman, Daniel, 'Passive Support of Terrorism', MIT Security Studies Seminar, 6 October 2004, p. 1.
8 Byman, 2004.
9 El-Hokayem, Emile, 'Hizballah and Syria: Outgrowing the Proxy Relationship', *The Washington Quarterly*, Spring 2007, p. 36.
10 Byman, Daniel, 'Proxy Power: Understanding Iran's Use of Terrorism', *Slate*, 26 July 2006. Online, available at: www.slate.com/id/2146532.
11 Byman, 2006.
12 Byman, 2006.
13 Byman, 2006.
14 Curtis, Glenn and Karacan, Tara, 'The Nexus Among Terrorists, Narcotics Traffickers, Weapons Proliferators and Organized Crime Networks in Western Europe', Congressional Research Service, December 2002.
15 Shelley, Louise, Picarelli, John T., Irby, Allison, Hart, Douglas M., Craig-Hart, Patricia A., Williams, Phil, Simon, Steven, Abdullaev, Nabi, Stanislawski, Bartosz and Covill, Laura, 'Methods and Motives: Exploring Links Between Transnational Organized Crime & International Terrorism', National Institute of Justice, September 2005, pp. 5–6.
16 Shelley *et al.*, 2005.
17 Shelley *et al.*, 2005.
18 Shelley *et al.*, 2005.
19 Shelley *et al.*, 2005.
20 Shelley *et al.*, 2005.
21 Makarenko, Tamara, 'The Crime-Terror Continuum: Tracing the Interplay between Transnational Organised Crime and Terrorism', *Global Crime*, Vol. 6, No. 1, 2004, pp. 129–45.

22 Makarenko, 2004.
23 Makarenko, 2004.
24 Makarenko, 2004, p. 133.
25 Makarenko, 2004.
26 Makarenko, 2004, p. 135.
27 Makarenko, 2004.
28 Makarenko, 2004, p. 136.
29 Makarenko, 2004, p. 138.
30 Makarenko, 2004.
31 Makarenko, 2004.
32 Stern, Jessica, 'Pakistan's Jihad Culture', *Foreign Affairs*, November/December 2000, p. 53.
33 Stern, 2000.
34 Treverton, Greg, Matthies, Carl, Cunningham, Karla J., Goulka, Jeremiah, Ridgeway, Greg and Wong, Anny, 'Film Piracy, Organized Crime, and Terrorism', RAND Coporation, 2009, pp. xi–xiv.
35 Stern, 2000.

1 Analysis of current research

1 Badmus, I.A., 'The Vale of Tears: Kashmir, the Source of Indo-Pakistani Tensions Since 1947', *Anthropologist*, Vol. 2, No. 8, 2006, pp. 103–9.
2 Misra, Ashutosh, 'The Problem of Kashmir and the Problem in Kashmir: Divergence Demands Convergence', *Strategic Analysis*, Vol. 29, No. 1, 2005.
3 Palit, P.S., 'The 9/11 Report: Reaffirming Pakistan-Terror Nexus', *Strategic Analysis*, Vol. 28, No. 3, 2004.
4 Warikoo, K., 'Islamist Extremism: Challenge to Security in South Asia', *Strategic Analysis*, Vol. 30, No. 1, 2006.
5 Misra, 2005, p. 16.
6 Misra, 2005.
7 Jamwal, N.S., 'Terrorists' Modus Operandi in Jammu and Kashmir', *Strategic Analysis*, Vol. 27, No. 3, 2003(a).
8 Jamwal, 2003(a).
9 Samii, Cyrus, 'Seizing the Moment in Kashmir', *SAIS Review*, Vol. XXVI, No. 1, Winter–Spring 2006, p. 66.
10 Bhatt, Shakti, 'State Terrorism vs. Jihad in Kashmir', *Journal of Contemporary Asia*, Vol. 33, 2003.
11 Malik, Mohan, 'The China Factor in the India-Pakistan Conflict', *Parameters*, Vol. 33, 2003.
12 Jamwal, 2003(a).
13 Marwah, Ved, 'India's Internal Security Challenges', *Strategic Analysis*, Vol. 27, No. 4, 2003.
14 Kartha, Tara, 'Countering Transnational Terrorism', *Strategic Analysis*, Vol. 23, No. 11, 2006.
15 Ganguly, Sumit, 'Will Kashmir Stop India's Rise?', *Foreign Affairs Magazine*, Vol. 85, No. 4, July–August 2006, p. 5.
16 Racine, Jean Luc, 'The Uncertain Triangle: India, China, and Pakistan – The Regional and International Dimensions', Centre for the Study of India and South Asia, Paris, 2001, p. 8.
17 Warikoo, 2006.
18 Warikoo, 2006.
19 Mazari, Shireen, 'Current Situation & Trends of Terrorism in South Asia', *Strategic Studies*, Vol. XXIV, No. 2, Summer 2004.

20 Mazari, Shireen, 'Future of Terrorism: A Critical Appraisal', *Strategic Studies*, Issue XXVI, No. 1, Spring 2006.
21 Samii, 2006.
22 Gill, John, 'Regional Concerns, Global Ambitions', *Strategic Asia 2003–2004*, National Bureau of Asian Research, Seattle, 2004.
23 Gill, 2004.
24 Tellis, Ashley, 'The Changing Political-Military Environment: South Asia', RAND Corporation, Santa Monica, California, 2001.
25 Subrahmanyam, K., 'Arms and Politics', *Strategic Analysis*, Vol. 29, No. 1, 2005.
26 Pillsbury, Michael, 'China's Strategic Outlook – A Case Study of Japan and India', in *Asian Security and China 2000–2010*, ed. Santhanam, K. and Kondapalli, S., Institute for Defence Studies and Analyses, Shipra Publications, New Delhi, 2004, pp. 79–115.
27 Pillsbury, 2004, p. 102.
28 Wenmu, Zhang, 'The Issue of South Asia in Major Power Politics', *Hong Kong Ta Kung Pao*, 23 September 1998.
29 Mannan, Md. Abdul, 'China's Policy toward South Asia – a Bangladesh Perspective', in *Asian Security and China 2000–2010*, ed. Santhanam, K. and Kondapalli, S., Institute for Defence Studies and Analyses, Shipra Publications, New Delhi, 2004, pp. 301–9.
30 Mannan, 2004.
31 Budania, Rajpal, 'The Emerging International Security System: Threats, Challenges, and Opportunities for India', *Strategic Analysis*, Vol. 27, No. 1, 2003.
32 Racine, 2001.
33 Tellis, 2001.
34 Tellis, 2001, p. 227.
35 Tellis, 2001.
36 'China's Missile Exports and Assistance to Pakistan', Center for Nonproliferation Studies, Monterey Institute of International Studies, Monterey, California, 2000.
37 Spector, Leonard, Yuan, Jing-Dong and Saunders, Phillip, 'Hearing on China's Proliferation Policies and Practices', Prepared Statement before the U.S.-China Economic and Security Review Commission, Center for Nonproliferation Studies, Monterey Institute of International Studies, Monterey, California, 24 July 2003.
38 Spector *et al.*, 2003.
39 Chalk, Peter, 'Light Arms Trading in SE Asia', *Jane's Intelligence Review*, 2001, p. 4.
40 Williams, Phil, 'Criminals, Militias, and Insurgents: Organized Crime in Iraq', Strategic Studies Institute, U.S. Army War College, June 2009, p. vii.
41 Williams, 2009, p. vii.
42 Williams, 2009, pp. 221–3.
43 Williams, 2009, pp. 221–3.
44 Williams, 2009, pp. 221–3.
45 Williams, 2009, pp. 221–3.
46 Defense Intelligence Testimony, initially cited in Williams, 2009, pp. 221–3.
47 Williams, 2009, pp. 243–4.
48 Long, Austin, 'The Anbar Awakening', *Survival*, Vol. 50, No. 2, April 2008, pp. 67–94, especially p. 77.
49 Long, 2008.
50 Bergen, Peter, Felter, Joseph, Brown, Vahid and Shapiro, Joseph, *Bombers, Bank Accounts, & Bleedout: Al Qaida's Road In and Out of Iraq*, Combating Terrorism Center, West Point, 2008, pp. 7–8.

51 Bergen *et al.*, 2008, pp. 7–8.
52 Bergen *et al.*, 2008, pp. 9–10.
53 Bergen *et al.*, 2008, pp. 9–10.

2 Misgovernance and proxy warfare in Kashmir: laying the groundwork for the crime–terror nexus

1 Ganguly, Sumit, 'Will Kashmir Stop India's Rise?', *Foreign Affairs*, Vol. 85, No. 4, July/August 2006.
2 Haqqani, Husain, 'Pakistan's Endgame in Kashmir', *India Review*, Vol. 2, No. 3, July 2003.
3 International Crisis Group, 'Kashmir: The View From Islamabad', Asia Report No. 68, 4 December 2003(a).
4 International Crisis Group, 'Kashmir, The View From New Delhi', Asia Report No. 69, 4 December 2003(b).
5 Misra, Ashutosh, 'The Problem of Kashmir and the Problem in Kashmir: Divergence Demands Convergence', *Strategic Analysis*, Vol. 29, No. 1, January–March 2005.
6 Ganguly, 2006.
7 Ganguly, Sumit, 'Explaining the Kashmir Insurgency: Political Mobilization and Institutional Decay', *International Security*, Vol. 21, No. 2, Fall 1996. Malik, Mohan, 'The China Factor in the India-Pakistan Conflict', *Parameters*, Vol. 33, 2003.
8 Ganguly, 2006, p. 2.
9 Ganguly, 2006.
10 Raju, A. Subramanyam, 'Third-Generation Indian Perceptions of the Kashmir Issue', RCSS Policy Studies 18, Regional Centre for Strategic Studies, Colombo, April 2001, p. 14.
11 Verghese, B.G., 'A Jammu and Kashmir Primer – From Myth to Reality', CPR Occasional Paper 14, Centre for Policy Research, New Delhi, 2006. Violent attacks include firings, grenades, bombs, IEDs, rocket attacks, arson, abductions, hangings and arms snatching.
12 Parthasarathy, G., 'Pugwash Initiative on Kashmir – Opinions Differ on Troop Pullout', *The Tribune*, 9 August 2007.
13 Vohra, A.M., 'J&K: Demilitarization and Joint Management', Article 2057, 4 July 2006, Institute of Peace and Conflict Studies, New Delhi, p. 1.
14 Roughneen, Simon, 'The Simmering Conflict Over Kashmir: The Blame Game of the Subcontinent', Paper 493, 12 December 2002, South Asia Analysis Group, New Delhi.
15 Mandelbaum, Michael, 'Kashmir – the Perpetual Tinderbox', *Newsday*, 22 February 2002.
16 Ganguly, 1996, p. 1.
17 Ganguly 1996, p. 4.
18 Ganguly, 1996.
19 Ganguly, 1996, p. 9.
20 Ganguly, 1996.
21 Samii, Cyrus, 'Seizing the Moment in Kashmir', *SAIS Review*, Vol. 26, No. 1, 2006, p. 68. Indian-Held Kashmir is often referred to as IJK.
22 Samii, 2006.
23 Verghese, 2006.
24 Chandran, Suba, 'Elections in Kashmir- XI: Real Threat Comes From the People', Article 841, 26 August 2002, Institute of Peace and Conflict Studies, New Delhi.

25 'Kashmiri Parties in Coalition Bid', BBC, 29 December 2008. Online, available at: www.bbc.co.uk.
26 'Clashes Mark Final Kashmir Poll', BBC, 24 December 2008. Online, available at: www.bbc.co.uk.
27 Samii, 2006.
28 Roughneen, 2002.
29 Samii, 2006.
30 'Centre Afraid of Stable Regimes in JK: Omar', *Daily Excelsior*, 29 August 2007.
31 Ganguly, 1996.
32 A combing operation generally refers to a systematic search of a large area through the use of numerous security force personnel, sometimes numbering in the hundreds.
33 Amnesty International, 'India – Torture, Rape, and Deaths in Custody', 1992.
34 'Amnesty Urges Kashmir Grave Probe, BBC News, 7 April 2008. Online, available at: http://news.bbc.co.uk/1/hi/world/south_asia/7334965.stm.
35 'Fake encounter' is term that is often used in Kashmir and throughout India. It refers to situations in which Indian security forces either apprehend a suspect and execute them on the spot or when an innocent person is killed and claimed to be a militant in order to collect monetary and other benefits. In both cases, evidence is often destroyed and investigations are misled, if they even occur at all.
36 Andley, Priyashree, '"Zero Tolerance" for Fake Encounters: A Reality Check in J&K', Article 2210, 17 February 2007, Institute of Peace and Conflict Studies, New Delhi.
37 Jha, Sanjay, 'Delhi Blasts, Terror Networks and India's Internal Security', *Strategic Analysis*, Vol. 29, No. 4, October–December 2005.
38 Chandran, Suba, 'People, State, Fear, and Counter-Militancy', Article 1989, 12 April 2006, Institute of Peace and Conflict Studies, New Delhi.
39 International Crisis Group, 2003(b).
40 Raju, 2001.
41 Warikoo, K., 'Islamist Extremism: Challenge to Security in South Asia', *Strategic Analysis*, Vol. 30, No. 1, January–March 2006.
42 Warikoo, 2006.
43 Bahadur, Kalim, 'Regional Implications of the Rise of Islamic Fundamentalism in Pakistan', *Strategic Analysis*, Vol. 30, No. 1, January–March 2006.
44 Cohen, Stephen, 'India, Pakistan, and Kashmir', paper presented at the University of Texas, December 2001, p. 29.
45 John, Wilson, 'The Jihadi Factor in India-Pakistan Peace Process', ORF Issue Brief 6, May 2006, Observer Research Foundation, New Delhi.
46 John, 2006.
47 Samii, 2006.
48 John, 2006, p. 2.
49 Haqqani, 2003.
50 John, 2006.
51 Lavroy, Peter, 'Pakistan's Kashmir Policy after the Bush visit to South Asia', *Strategic Insights*, Vol. 4, Issue 4, April 2006.
52 Samii, 2006.
53 Verghese, 2006.
54 Samii, 2006.
55 Samii, 2006.
56 Haqqani, 2003.
57 Jamwal, N.S., 'Terrorists' Modus Operandi in Jammu and Kashmir', *Strategic Analysis*, Vol. 27, No. 3, July–September 2003.

58 The 9/11 Commission Report. Final Report of the National Commission on Terrorist Attacks Upon the United States.
59 'Our Homegrown Suicide Bombers', *Hindustan Times*, 11 December 2005.
60 Jamwal, 2003.
61 Jamwal, 2003.
62 'Afghan Link to Seoul Drug Arrests', BBC News, 4 July 2008. Online, available at: http://news.bbc.co.uk/1/hi/world/asia-pacific/7489171.stm.
63 Marwah, Ved, 'India's Internal Security Challenges', *Strategic Analysis*, Vol. 27, No. 4, October–December 2003.
64 Jamwal, 2003.

3 The crime–terror nexus and Chinese arms in Indian-Held Kashmir

1 Sections of this chapter have appeared in Clarke, Ryan, "D-Company: A Study of the Crime-Terror Nexus in South Asia", *International Journal of Business and Globalization*, Vol. 4, No. 3, 2010, and Clarke, Ryan, "Bad Company: South Asia's Regional Criminal Organization", *Jane's Intelligence Review*, Vol. 21, No. 9, September 2009.
2 Kumar, Neeraj, 'Organized Crime', *PoliceSpeak*, 1999. Online, available at: www.india-seminar.com/1999/483.htm.
3 Charles, Molly, 'The Growth and Activities of Organised Crime in Bombay', *International Social Science Journal*, Vol. 53, No. 3, 2001(a), pp. 359–67. For a more in-depth, yet somewhat controversial historical overview, see Ghosh, Amitav, *Sea of Poppies*, John Murray General Publishing Division, London, 2008.
4 Charles, Molly, 'The Drug Scene in India', presentation at 'Drug Abuse: A Symposium on Social Processes, Narcotics, and the State', Bombay, August, 2001(b). Online, available at: www.india-seminar.com/2001/504/504%20molly%20charles.htm.
5 For an interesting firsthand narrative, see Mehta, Suketu, *Maximum City: Bombay Lost and Found*, Penguin Books, New Delhi, 2004.
6 Smith, Chris, 'Light Weapons and Ethnic Conflict in South Asia', in *Lethal Commerce: The Global Trade in Small Arms and Light Weapons*, ed. Boutwell, J., Klare, M. and Reed, L., Committee on International Security Studies, American Academy of Arts and Sciences, Cambridge, Massachusetts, 1995, pp. 61–81.
Raghavan, T.C.A., 'The Problem of Black Money', Institute of Peace and Conflict Studies, Article no. 398, New Delhi, 2000.
7 Singh, Shankar, 'Transnational Organized Crime: The Indian Perspective', UNAFEI Annual Report for 2000 and Resource Material Series No. 59, pp. 570–87, 2002.
8 Singh, 2002. Bolan, Kim, 'Sikh Separatist Threat on Rise in Canada: Indian PM Warns of Resurgent Threat in Canada', *Vancouver Sun*, 11 March 2008. Online, available at: www.canada.com/vancouversun/news/story.html?id=2be0865c-29ba-4dab-9bcc-d945e75007c1&k=79664.
9 Lal, Rollie, 'South Asian Organized Crime', *Orbis: A Journal of World Affairs*, Vol. 49, No. 2, Spring 2005, pp. 293–304.
10 Lal, 2005.
11 Mehta, 2004.
12 Charles, 2001(a).
13 Chengappa, Raj and Raval, Sheela, 'War on Terror: Getting Dawood', *India Today International*, 3 November 2003, pp. 10–16.
14 Lal, 2005.
15 Lal, 2005. The methodology used to generate these figures has not been made

clear by Lal and, as such, they should only be viewed as a semi-educated estimate as opposed to established fact.

16 Mehta, 2004.
17 Chengappa and Raval, 2003, p. 11.
18 Chengappa and Raval, 2003.
19 Mehta, 2004. Lal, 2005.
20 Charles, 2001(a).
21 Chengappa and Raval, 2003.
22 Charles, 2001(a).
23 'Gulshan Kumar Killer Escapes after Temporary Release from Jail', *Express India*, 23 May 2009. Online, available at: www.expressindia.com.
24 John, Wilson, 'Pakistan's Nuclear Underworld – An Investigation', Observer Research Foundation, New Delhi, 2005.
25 Lele, Ajey, 'A Shift from Crime to Terrorism: Assessing D-Company', SSPC Paper, Society for the Study of Peace and Conflict, December 2005, p. 10.
26 Bolan, 2008.
27 Smith, Chris, 'The Diffusion of Small Arms and Light Weapons in Pakistan and Northern India', Brassey's Centre for Defence Studies, London, 1993.
28 'India: Arms and Abuses in Indian Punjab and Kashmir', Human Rights Watch, 1994.
29 Smith, 1995.
30 Kartha, Tara, 'Tools of Terror: Light Weapons and India's Security', Knowledge World in association with the Institute for Defence Studies and Analyses, New Delhi, 1999.
31 'Pak Likely to Smuggle in More Arms', *Indian Express*, 19 April 1993.
32 'India: Arms and Abuses', 1994.
33 Smith, 1993.
34 Rahman, M. and Baweja, Harinder, 'Making Headway', *India Today*, Vol. XVIII, No. 12, 30 April 1993.
35 Mehta, 2004.
36 Hussain, Fawaz, 'Terror in Bombay', *India Today*, Vol. XVIII, No. 12, 31 March 1993.
37 Rahman, M. and Pathak, Rahul, 'The Conspiracy Unravels', *India Today*, Vol. XVIII, No. 12, 30 June 1993.
38 Rahman and Pathak, 1993.
39 Rahman and Baweja, 1993.
40 Mehta, 2004.
41 Ramachandran, V.K., 'Blasts of Terror', *Frontline*, Vol. 10, 9 April 1993. Padmanabhan, R., 'Sitting on Bombs: Thane Reveals More', *Frontline*, Vol. 10, 23 April 1993(a). 'The Man Who Knew Too Much', The Telegraph, 1 October 2006. Online, available at: www.telegraphindia.com.
42 Rahman and Pathak, 1993.
43 'Mumbai Bombing Sentencing Delay', BBC, 13 September 2006. Online, available at: www.bbc.co.uk.
44 Ramachandran, 1993.
45 Lal, 2005.
46 Mehta, 2004.
47 Padmanabhan, R., 'Nexus Galore: The Complicated Trail of the Blasts', *Frontline*, Vol. 10, 21 May 1993(b).
48 Padmanabhan, R., 'Movie Mafia: The Underworld and "Bollywood"', *Frontline*, Vol. 10, 21 May 1993(c). 'Indian Court Sentences 5 in Mumbai Blasts, Including Bollywood Producer', Voice of America (VOA) News, 1 June 2007.
49 Lal, 2005. Mehta, 2004.
50 Padmanabhan, 1993(a).

51 Mehta, 2004, p. 128
52 Rahman and Baweja, 1993.
53 Gupta, Shekar, 'The Memons: India's Most Wanted Family', *India Today*, Vol. XVIII, No. 12, 15 April 1993.
54 Hussain, 1993.
55 Nair, P.M., *Combating Organised Crime*, Konark Publishers, New Delhi, 2002, p. 75.
56 Smith, 1993.
57 Smith, 1993. 'India: Arms and Abuses', 1994.
58 Smith, 1995, p. 69.
59 Kartha, 1999.
60 India, 1994.
61 India, 1994.
62 Smith, 1995. India, 1994.
63 Smith, 1995.
64 Smith, 1995.
65 Kartha, 1999.

4 Lashkar-i-Taiba: the fallacy of subservient proxies and the future of Islamist terrorism in India

1 Sections of this chapter have appeared in Clarke, Ryan, "Lashkar-i-Taiba: The Fallacy of Subservient Proxies and the Future of Islamist Terrorism in India", Strategic Studies Institute, U.S. Army War College, March 2010, and Clarke, Ryan, "Lashkar-i-Taiba: Roots, Logistics, Partnerships, and the Fallacy of Subservient Proxies", *Terrorism and Political Violence*, Vol. 22, Iss. 3, July 2010.
2 Raman, B., 'Lashkar-e-Toiba: Spreading the Jehad', *The Hindu Business Line*, 5 January 2001(a). Online, available at: www.hinduonnet.com/businessline/2001/01/05/stories/040555ra.htm.
3 Shafqat, Saeed, 'From Official Islam to Islamism: The Rise of Dawat-ul-Irshad and Lashkar-e-Taiba', in *Pakistan – Nationalism without a Nation?*, ed. Jaffrelot, C., Manohar Publishers & Distributors, New Delhi, 2002, pp. 131–49.
4 Raman, 2001(a).
5 'Profile: Lashkar-e-Toiba', BBC News, 17 March 2006. Online, available at: http://news.bbc.co.uk/1/hi/world/south_asia/3181925.stm.
6 John, Wilson, 'Lashkar-e-Toiba: New Threats Posed by an Old Organization', *Terrorism Monitor*, Vol. 3, Issue 4, 24 February 2005.
7 The primary objective of a fidayeen mission is to inflict as many human casualties as possible. Most often, a militant attacks a target until they themselves are killed. However, unlike suicide bombings, there is a small chance of survival although it is minimal.
8 'Profile', 2006.
9 'Lashkar-e-Toiba', BBC News, 25 November 2002. Online, available at: http://news.bbc.co.uk/1/hi/world/south_asia/2510613.stm. John, 2005.
10 'Lashkar-e-Toiba – "Army of the Pure"', South Asia Terror Portal, 2001. Online, available at: www.satp.org/satporgtp/countries/india/states/jandk/terrorist_outfits/lashkar_e_toiba.htm.
11 'ISI Hand in 7/11 Mumbai Blasts, Say Police', *The Hindu*, 1 October 2006. Online, available at: www.hindu.com/2006/10/01/stories/2006100113440100.htm. Lakshman, Kanchan, 'The ISI Exposed', *South Asia Intelligence Review*, Vol. 5, No. 12, 2 October 2006.
12 Aftergood, Steven, 'Lashkar-e-Taiba (Army of the Righteous)', Federation

of American Scientists, 21 May 2004. Online, available at: www.fas.org/irp/world/para/lakshar.htm.

13 Interview with Bukhari Syed Adnan Ali Shah (Hereinafter Pakistani Security Analyst 1). International Centre for Political Violence and Terrorism Research, Singapore, 14 March 2008.

14 'Lashkar-e-Toiba', 2002.

15 'Profile', 2006. Yasmeen, Samina, 'Pakistan's Kashmir Policy: Voices of Moderation?', *Contemporary South Asia*, Vol. 12, No. 2, June 2003. Jama'at ud Dawa has also now been proscribed following the November 2008 Mumbai attacks.

16 Jha, Sanjay, 'Delhi Blasts, Terror Networks, and India's Internal Security', *Strategic Analysis*, Vol. 29, No. 4, 2005.

17 McGirk, Tim, 'Lay Down Your Guns', *Time Magazine*, 12 May 2003. Online, available at: www.time.com/time/magazine/article/0,9171,451022,00.html.

18 Khan, M., 'Pakistani Militant's Fluctuating Fate', BBC News, 24 October 2006. Online, available at: http://news.bbc.co.uk/1/hi/world/south_asia/6067694.stm.

19 Pakistani Security Analyst 1, 2008.

20 John, 2005.

21 Kak, M.L., 'ISI Plan to Restructure UJC', *The Tribune*, 1 February 2003. Online, available at: www.tribuneindia.com/2003/20030201/j&k.htm#1.

22 Jha, 2005.

23 'Lashkar-e-Toiba', 2002.

24 Raman, 2001(a).

25 Sreedhar, K. and Manish, Sudhir, *Jihadis in Jammu and Kashmir – a Portrait Gallery*, Sage Publications, New Delhi, 2003.

26 Both quotes from Raman, B., 'The Lashkar-e-Toiba (LeT)', South Asia Analysis Group, Paper No. 374, 2001(b), pp. 3–4.

27 'Lashkar-e-Toiba', 2001. Ismail, Noor, 'The Role of Kinship in Indonesia's Jemmah Islamiya', *Terrorism Monitor*, Vol. 4, Issue 11, 2 June 2006.

28 'Lashkar-e-Toiba', 2001.

29 Raman, B., 'LeT Issues Fatwa to Kill the Pope', *International Terrorism Monitor*, Paper no. 133, South Asia Analysis Group, 2006.

30 Aftergood, 2004.

31 Sreedhar and Manish, 2003.

32 Hardaker, David, 'The World Today – Background to Lashkar-e-Toiba', ABC Online, 5 November 2003. Online, available at: www.abc.net.au/worldtoday/content/2003/s982752.html.

33 Raman, 2001(b).

34 Kaul, Ashima, 'The Proliferation of Small Arms in J&K', *Control Arms India Update*, Vol. 1, No. 2, 2005.

35 Hardaker, 2003.

36 'ISI Agent Held in Hyderabad', *The Hindu*, 2 April 2007. Online, available at: www.thehindu.com/2007/04/02/stories/2007040217231100.htm.

37 Singh, Thangjam, 'Could Pune be a Future Terrorist Target?', *IDSA Strategic Comments*, 17 August 2006, Institute for Defence Studies and Analyses, New Delhi.

38 Marwah, Ved, 'India's Internal Security Challenges', *Strategic Analysis*, Vol. 27, No. 4, 2003.

39 Swami, Praveen and Shehzad, Mohammed, 'Lashkar Raising Islamist Brigades for Iraq', *The Hindu*, 13 June 2004. Online, available at: www.hindu.com/2004/06/13/stories/2004061306050100.htm.

40 'Profile', 2006. 'Lashkar-e-Toiba', 2002.

41 Sreedhar and Manish, 2003.

42 Brew, Nigel, 'Lashkar-e-Taiba (LeT) and the Threat to Australia', Research

Note, No. 36, 16 February 2004. Information Analysis and Advice for the Parliament, Department of Parliamentary Services, Canberra.
43 'Lashkar-e-Toiba', 2001.
44 Hasnain, Ghulam, 'Inside Jihad', *Time Asia*, Vol. 157, No. 5, 5 February 2001. Khan, 2006.
45 John, 2005.
46 Stern, Jessica, 'Pakistan's Jihad Culture', *Foreign Affairs*, November/December 2000.
47 Sreedhar and Manish, 2003.
48 Pakistani Security Analyst 1, 2008. Interview with Mahsud Saif Ullah Khan (Hereinafter Pakistani Security Analyst 2), International Centre for Political Violence and Terrorism Research, Singapore, 14 March 2008.
49 'LeT Recruiting Afghan Refugees to Support Taliban in Afghanistan', *Terrorism Focus*, Vol. 3, Issue 39, 10 October 2006.
50 Schriek, Daan Van Der, 'Nuristan: Insurgent Hideout in Afghanistan', *Terrorism Monitor*, Vol. 3, Issue 10, 19 May 2005.
51 Raman, 2006. John, 2005.
52 John, 2005.
53 Sreedhar and Manish, 2003.
54 'Lashkar-e-Toiba', 2002.
55 'Lashkar Militant Admits Killing Sikhs in Chittisinghpura', Rediff, 31 December 2000, p. 1. Online, available at: www.rediff.com/news/2000/dec/31sikh.htm.
56 'Who are the Kashmir Militants?', BBC News, 19 February 2003. Online, available at: http://news.bbc.co.uk/1/low/world/south_asia/1719612.stm.
57 'Profile', 2006.
58 'Profile', 2006.
59 'Pakistan Freezes Militant Funds', BBC News, 24 December 2001. Online, available at: http://news.bbc.co.uk/1/hi/world/south_asia/1726813.stm.
60 Aftergood, 2004.
61 'Lashkar-e-Toiba', 2002.
62 Aftergood, 2004.
63 Brew, 2004.
64 'Profile', 2006.
65 'Lashkar-e-Toiba', 2001.
66 'Pakistan's "Role in Mumbai Attacks"', BBC News, 30 September 2006. Online, available at: http://news.bbc.co.uk/1/hi/world/south_asia/5394686.stm.
67 Ahmed, Zubair, 'Mumbai Marks a Grim Anniversary', BBC News, 10 July 2007. Online, available at: http://news.bbc.co.uk/1/hi/world/south_asia/6288916.stm.
68 'LeT Threat to Dalai Lama', *Daily Excelsior*, 2 April 2007. Online, available at: www.dailyexcelsior.com/web1/07apr02/news.htm#9.
69 'Anatomy of Evil', *The Indian Express*, 11 July 2007. Online, available at: www.indianexpress.com/story/204473.html.
70 'Anatomy', 2007.
71 'Anatomy', 2007.
72 'Anatomy', 2007.
73 'Man Arrested in Nepal with Fake Indian Currency', *Dawn*, 1 August 2007. Online, available at: www.dawn.com/2007/08/01/top21.htm.
74 'LeT Suspect Nabbed', *The Times of India*, 13 July 2007. Online, available at: http://timesofindia.indiatimes.com/cities/LeT_suspect_nabbed/articleshow/2199336.cms.
75 Singh, M., 'Growing Fundamentalism in the Northeast', *IDSA Strategic Comments*, 19 February 2007(a), Institute for Defence Studies and Analyses, New Delhi.

76 Bhat, Anil, 'From Inverted Crescent to Full Moon & Jihadi Pincer', *The Statesman*, 26 June 2007. Online, available at: http://thestatesman.co.in/page.arcview.php?clid=14&id=188731&usrsess=1.
76 Singh, 2007(a).
78 Singh, Thangjam, 'The LeT Menace in Delhi', *IDSA Strategic Comments*, May 11, 2007(b), Institute for Defence Studies and Analyses, New Delhi.
79 Aftergood, 2004.
80 Sreedhar and Manish, 2003.
81 Aftergood, 2004.
82 'Profile', 2006.
83 Khan, 2006.
84 Swami, Praveen, 'Quake Came as a Boon for Lashkar Leadership', *The Hindu*, 17 November 2005. Online, available at: www.thehindu.com/2005/11/17/stories/2005111705951200.htm.
85 Partlow, Joshua and Khan, Kamran, 'Charity Funds Said to Provide Clues to Alleged Terrorist Plot', *Washington Post*, 15 August 2006.
86 'Meet the Lashkar-e-Tayiba's Fundraiser', Rediff, 28 July 2006. Online, available at: www.rediff.com///news/2006/jul/28lashkar.htm.
87 Stern, 2000.
88 Brew, 2004.
89 Shehzad, Mohammad, 'Banned LeT Collects Millions in Charity, Hides', *South Asia Tribune*, Issue 35, 23–29 March 2003.
90 Tandy, Karen, 'Afghanistan: Law Enforcement Interdiction Efforts in Transshipment Countries to Stem the Flow of Heroin', Testimony before the Subcommittee on Criminal Justice, Drug Policy and Human Resources, U.S. House of Representatives, Washington, DC, 26 February 2004. Online, available at: www.usdoj.gov/dea/pubs/cngrtest/ct022604.htm. '70% Afghan Narcotics Move through Pakistan', *Daily Times*, 22 March 2005. Online, available at: www.dailytimes.com.pk/default.asp?page=story_22-3-2005_pg7_35.
91 Lal, Rollie, 'South Asian Organized Crime and Terrorist Networks', *Orbis*, Vol. 49, Issue 2, Spring 2005.
92 Lal, 2005.
93 Mustafa, Malik, 'Proliferation of Small Arms and Light Weapons: Case Study – South Asia', *Strategic Studies*, Vol. XXV, No. 2, Summer 2005.
94 'A Godfather's Lethal Mix of Business and Politics', U.S. News and World Report, 27 November 2005. Online, available at: www.usnews.com/usnews/news/articles/051205/5terror.b.htm.
95 Swami, Praveen, 'Flawed Justice', *Frontline*, Vol. 23, Issue 19, 23 September – 6 October 2006(a).
96 Swami, Praveen, 'Harnessing Hate', *Frontline*, Vol. 23, Issue 15, 29 July – 11 August 2006(b).
97 Swami, Praveen, 'Nairobi Arrest Points to Deepening Lashkar-Dawood Links', *The Hindu*, 22 July 2006(c). Online, available at: www.hindu.com/2006/07/22/stories/2006072225171800.htm.
98 Watson, Paul and Barua, Siddhartha, 'Camps Thrive in Pakistan, India Charges', *Los Angeles Times*, 11 January 2002.
99 Mishra, Bisheshwar, 'ISI, Dawood Help LeT Set a Global Network', *The Times of India*, 2 July 2003, p. 1. Online, available at: http://timesofindia.indiatimes.com/articleshow/56386.cms.
100 Mishra, 2003.
101 Mir, Amir, 'Catch Me If You Can', *Mid Day*, 9 November 2003.
102 Pike, Jonathan, 'Directorate for Inter-Services Intelligence [ISI]', Federation of American Scientists, 2002. Online, available at: www.fas.org/irp/world/pakistan/isi.

103 Bedi, Rahul, 'Vital Intelligence on the Taliban May Rest with its Prime Sponsor – Pakistan's ISI', Jane's Information Group, 1 October 2001. Online, available at: www.janes.com/security/international_security/news/misc/janes011001_1_n.shtml.
104 Harrison, Selig, 'Stop Building Up Pakistani Military Capacities Against India', *The International Herald Tribune*, 20 December 2001. Online, available at: www.iht.com/articles/2001/12/20/edsig_ed3_.php.
105 'Kashmir: An Insurgency Wedged Between Two Nuclear Powers', *Jane's Intelligence Backgrounder*, 2001.
106 Interview with Pakistani diplomat (Hereinafter Pakistani Diplomat 1), Pakistan High Commission, Singapore, 13 February 2009.
107 Both quotes from Hardy, Roger, 'Pakistan's "Culture of Jihad"', BBC News, 5 August 2002, p. 4. Online, available at: http://news.bbc.co.uk/1/hi/in_depth/world/2002/islamic_world/2173818.stm.
108 'Kashmir', 2001.
109 Stern, 2000. Hardaker, 2003.
110 Khan, 2006.
111 Chossudovsky, Michel, 'The Foiled UK Terror Plot and the "Pakistani Connection"', *Global Research*, 14 August 2006.
112 Singh, 2007(b).
113 Raman, 2001(b).
114 Smucker, Phillip, 'Al-Qaeda Thriving in Pakistani Kashmir', *Christian Science Monitor*, 2 July 2002. Online, available at: www.csmonitor.com/2002/0702/p01s02-wosc.html. Swami and Shehzad, 2004.
115 Mir, Amir, 'The Jihad Lives On', *Asia Times*, 11 March 2005. Online, available at: www.atimes.com/atimes/South_Asia/GC11Df07.html.
116 Riedel, Bruce, 'Terrorism in India and the Global Jihad', Brookings Institute, 30 November 2008.
117 Jenkins, Brian, 'Terrorists Can Think Strategically – Lessons Learned from the Mumbai Attacks', Testimony presented before the Senate Homeland Security and Governmental Affairs Committee, 28 January 2009.
118 Rabasa, Angel, Blackwill, Robert D., Chalk, Peter, Cragin, Kim, Fair, Christine, Jackson, Brian A., Jenkins, Brian Michael, Jones, Seth, Shestak, Nathaniel and Tellis, Ashley J., 'The Lessons of Mumbai', Occasional Paper, RAND Corporation, Washington, DC, 2009.
119 Jenkins, 2009.
120 Rabasa *et al.*, 2009.
121 Rabasa *et al.*, 2009.
122 Rabasa *et al.*, 2009.
123 Interview with Indian security analyst Dr Arabinda Acharya (Hereinafter Indian Security Analyst 1), International Centre for Political Violence and Terrorism Research, Singapore, 16 April 2009.
124 Rabasa *et al.*, 2009.
125 Jenkins, 2009.
126 Rabasa *et al.*, 2009.
127 'Lawyer Named for Mumbai Suspect', BBC News, 30 March 2009. Online, available at: www.bbc.co.uk.
128 Rabasa *et al.*, 2009.
129 Rabasa *et al.*, 2009.
130 Rabasa *et al.*, 2009.
131 Scheuer, Michael, 'Islamabad Rides a Terror Tiger', *Asia Times*, 20 September 2008. Online, available at: www.atimes.com.
132 Swami, Praveen, 'India's Elections and the Islamist Terror Threat', *Asian Conflict Reports*, Issue 4, April 2009.

133 Swami, 2009.
134 Scheuer, 2008.
135 Scheuer, 2008.
136 Roul, Animesh, 'Lashkar-e-Taiba Resumes Operations Against Indian Forces in Jammu and Kashmir', *Terrorism Monitor*, Vol. VII, Issue 8, 3 April 2009.
137 Roul, 2009.
138 Shazad, Syed Saleem, 'The Rise and Rise of the Neo-Taliban', *Asia Times*, 2 April 2009(a). Online, available at: www.atimes.com.
139 Shazad, 2009(a).
140 Shahzad, Syed Saleem, 'Pakistan Braces for More Attacks', *Asia Times*, 1 April 2009(b).
141 Shahzad, 2009(b)
142 Ali, Farhana and Shehzad, Mohammed, 'Lashkar-i-Tayyiba Remains Committed to Jihad', *CTC Sentinel*, Vol. 2, Issue 3, March 2009.
143 Ali and Shehzad, 2009.
144 Srivastava, Siddharth, 'India Faces Terror From Another Front', *Asia Times*, 13 November 2008. Online, available at: www.atimes.com.
145 Srivastava, 2008.
146 Chowdhury, Khaled Iqbal, 'BDR Mutiny and Its Security Implications', Bangladesh Institute of Peace and Security Studies (BIPSS) Special Report, Dhaka, March 2009.
147 Interview with Bangladeshi security analyst Shafqat Munir (Hereinafter Bangladeshi Security Analyst 1), International Centre for Political Violence and Terrorism Research, Singapore, 15 April 2009.
148 Bangladeshi Security Analyst 1, 2009.
149 Bangladeshi Security Analyst 1, 2009.
150 'Bombs Explode Across Bangladesh', BBC News, 17 August 2005.
151 For a more in-depth discussion, see Burr, J. Millar and O'Collins, Robert, *Alms for Jihad: Charity and Terrorism in the Islamic World*, Cambridge University Press, 2006.
152 Bangladeshi Security Analyst 1, 2009.
153 Interview with Pakistani security analyst Khurram Iqbal (Hereinafter Pakistani Security Analyst 3), International Centre for Political Violence and Terrorism Research, Singapore, 10 April 2009. Bangladeshi Security Analyst 1, 2009.
154 Bangladeshi Security Analyst 1, 2009.
155 Kumar, Anand, 'Bangladesh: Islamists Attempt to Regroup', Paper 2351, South Asia Analysis Group, 30 August 2007, New Delhi. Online, available at: www.southasiaanalysis.org/default.asp.
156 Rashid, Ahmed, *Taliban: Militant Islam, Oil and Fundamentalism in Central Asia*, Yale University Press, 2001, pp. 17–31.
157 Deyer, Simon, 'Concern Mounts Over Bangladesh Madrassas After Bombs', *Daily Times*, 29 September 2005. Online, available at: www.dailytimes.com.pk.
158 Bangladeshi Security Analyst 1, 2009.
159 Rabasa *et al.*, 2009.

5 LeT and D-Company in Pakistan: selective justice, sectarianism and artificial distinctions

1 'Definition of Crime', *Compact Oxford English Dictionary*. Online, available at: wwww.askoxford.com (accessed 5 November 2007).
2 'Crime', *Merriam-Webster Dictionary*. Online, available at: www.merriam-webster.com (accessed 17 November 2007).

3 However, it is important to note that this situation is by no means unique to Pakistan. Many nations, including major world powers, have used and continue to use subversive elements to forward state objectives.
4 Fair, Christine and Chalk, Peter, 'United States Internal Security Assistance to Pakistan', *Small Wars and Insurgencies*, Vol. 17, Issue 3, 2006, p. 334.
5 Jones, Seth, Oliker, Olga, Chalk, Peter, Fair, Christine, Lal, Rollie and Dobbins, James, 'Securing Tyrants or Fostering Reform?', Prepared for the Open Society Institute by the RAND National Security Research Division, 2006.
6 Roul, Animesh, 'Lashkar-e-Jhangvi: Sectarian Violence in Pakistan and Ties to International Terrorism', *Terrorism Monitor*, Vol. 3, Issue 11, 2 June 2005(a), p. 6.
7 Berry, LaVerle, *et al.*, 'Nations Hospitable to Organized Crime and Terrorism', Federal Research Division, Library of Congress, October 2003. Khairi, Umber, 'Karachi: Volatile Metropolis', BBC, 11 April 2006. Online, available at: http://news.bbc.co.uk.
8 Khairi, 2006.
9 Jones *et al.*, 2006, p. 135.
10 'Pakistan's Unseen Conflict', *Jane's Intelligence Digest*, 7 February 2003.
11 Kronstadt, Alan, 'Pakistan-U.S. Anti-Terrorism Cooperation', Congressional Research Service, Library of Congress, 28 March 2003.
12 Chellaney, Brahma, 'Fighting Terrorism in Southern Asia: The Lessons of History', *International Security*, Vol. 26, No. 3, Winter 2001–2.
13 Jones *et al.*, 2006.
14 Jones, Seth, 'Counterinsurgency in Afghanistan', RAND Corporation, 2008.
15 Fair and Chalk, 2006.
16 Esser, Daniel, 'The City as Arena, Hub, and Prey – Patterns of Violence in Kabul and Karachi', *Environment and Urbanization*, Vol. 16, No. 2, 2004. Khairi, 2006. Maqbool, Imran, 'Pearl Murder Suspect Dies in Bomb Blast', *Independent*, 20 December 2002. Online, available at: www.independent.co.uk.
17 Esser, 2004. Maqbool, 2002.
18 Shahzad, Syed Saleem, 'Karachi: Where Terrorists Hide and Thrive', *Terrorism Monitor*, Vol. 2, Issue 17, 9 September 2004.
19 Shahzad, 2004.
20 Khairi, 2006.
21 Ispahani, Mahnaz, 'Religious Sword Over Pakistan', *Los Angeles Times*, 21 May 2004. Online, available at: www.latimes.com.
22 'The State of Sectarianism in Pakistan', International Crisis Group, Asia Report No. 95, April 2005.
23 International Crisis Group, 2005.
24 Zahab, Mariam Abou, 'The Regional Dimension of Sectarian Conflicts in Pakistan', in *Pakistan: Nationalism Without a Nation*, ed. Jaffrelot, Christopher, Zed Books, London, 2002, pp. 115–31.
25 Irfani, Suroosh, 'Pakistan's Sectarian Violence: Between the "Arabist Shift" and Indo-Persian Culture', in *Religious Radicalism and Security in South Asia*, ed. Limaye, Satu, Malik, Mohan and Wirsing, Robert, Asia-Pacific Center for Security Studies, Honolulu, 2004, pp. 147–71.
26 International Crisis Group, 2005, p. 5.
27 International Crisis Group, 2005.
28 Irfani, 2004.
29 Haqqani, Husain, 'Pakistan's Terrorism Dilemma', in *Religious Radicalism and Security in South Asia*, ed. Limaye, Satu, Malik, Mohan and Wirsing, Robert, Asia-Pacific Center for Security Studies, Honolulu, 2004, pp. 351–65.
30 Nasr, Vali, 'Regional Implications of Shi'a Revival in Iraq', *The Washington Quarterly*, Vol. 27, No. 3, Summer 2004, pp. 7–24.

31 Nasr, Vali, *The Shia Revival – How Conflicts within Islam Will Shape the Future*, W.W. Norton & Company, New York, 2006, pp. 81–119.
32 Nasr, 2004.
33 Nasr, 2006, p. 88.
34 Nasr, 2006.
35 Nasr, 2004.
36 International Crisis Group, 2005.
37 International Crisis Group, 2005.
38 Khan, Afzal, 'The War on Terror and the Politics of Violence in Pakistan', *Terrorism Monitor*, Vol. 2, Issue 13, 1 July 2004(a).
39 Gilani, Tariq, 'US-Pakistan Relations: The Way Forward', *Parameters*, Winter 2006–7.
40 Amnesty International, 'Pakistan: Concern about Escalating Sectarian Violence', Public Statement, 13 April 2006.
41 Mir, Amir, 'Sectarian Monster', *South Asia Intelligence Review*, Vol. 3, No. 47, 6 June 2005.
42 'Pakistan: 2006 Overview', MIPT Terrorism Knowledge Base, 2007(a). Online, available at: www.tkb.org.
43 Mir, 2005.
44 Idris, Iffat, 'Pakistan's Sectarian Menace', *Outlook India*, 21 August 2003.
45 Idris, 2003.
46 Shah, Mehtab, 'Sectarianism – a Threat to Human Security: A Case Study of Pakistan', *The Round Table*, Vol. 94, No. 382, October 2005, p. 623.
47 Ali, Mukhtar, 'Sectarian Conflict in Pakistan – A Case Study of Jhang', RCSS Policy Studies 9, Regional Centre for Strategic Studies, Colombo, 2000.
48 Chellaney, 2001–2, p. 104.
49 Chellaney, 2001–2.
50 Mir, 2005.
51 Stern, Jessica, 'Pakistan's Jihad Culture', *Foreign Affairs*, November/December 2000, p. 4.
52 Lakshman, Kanchan, 'NWFP: Extremist Encroachment', *South Asia Intelligence Review*, Vol. 5, No. 45, 21 May 2007.
53 Talbot, Ian, 'Pakistan in 2002: Democracy, Terrorism, and Brinkmanship', *Asian Survey*, Vol. 43, No. 1, A Survey of Asia in 2002, January–February 2003.
54 Kronstadt, Alan and Vaughn, Bruce, 'Terrorism in South Asia', Congressional Research Service, Library of Congress, 9 August 2004.
55 'Human Rights Watch World Report 2006 – Pakistan', Human Rights Watch, New York, 2007.
56 International Crisis Group, 2005.
57 Ahmed, Mumtaz, 'Revivalism, Islamisation, Sectarianism and Violence in Pakistan', in *Pakistan 1997*, ed. Baxter, Craig and Kennedy, Charles, Westview Press, Boulder, 1998, p. 118.
58 International Crisis Group, 2005.
59 Interview with Pakistani security analyst Khurram Iqbal (Pakistani Security Analyst 3), International Centre for Political Violence and Terrorism Research, Singapore, 10 April 2009.
60 International Crisis Group, 2005.
61 International Crisis Group, 2005.
62 International Crisis Group, 2005.
63 International Crisis Group, 2005.
64 Pakistani Security Analyst 3, 2009.
65 Pakistani Security Analyst 3, 2009.
66 International Crisis Group, 2005.

67 International Crisis Group, 2005.
68 'Pakistan Security Report 2008', Pakistan Institute for Peace Studies, Islamabad, 2009.
69 Pakistani Security Analyst 3, 2009.
70 International Crisis Group, 2005.
71 Pakistani Security Analyst 3, 2009.
72 'Balochistan: Conflicts and Players', Pakistan Institute for Peace Studies, Islamabad, 2008.
73 Pakistan Institute for Peace Studies, 2008.
74 'Sipah-e-Sahaba', South Asia Terror Portal, 2001(a). Online, available at: www.satp.org.
75 'Sipah-e-Sahaba Pakistan (SSP)', MIPT Terrorism Knowledge Base, 30 September 2007(b). Online, available at: www.tkb.org. Roul, Animesh, 'Sipah-e-Sahaba: Formenting Sectarian Violence in Pakistan', *Terrorism Monitor*, Vol. 3, Issue 2, 27 June 2005(a).
76 Roul, 2005(a).
77 South Asia Terror Portal, 2001(a).
78 Roul, 2005(a).
79 South Asia Terror Portal, 2001(a).
80 'Blast at SSP Rally Kills 40 in Multan', *Daily Times*, 8 October 2004. Online, available at: www.dailytimes.com.pk.
81 Roul, Animesh, 'Lashkar-e-Jhangvi: Sectarian Violence in Pakistan and Ties to International Terrorism', *Terrorism Monitor*, Vol. 3, Issue 11, 2 June 2005(b). 'Treasury Department Statement Regarding the Designation of Lashkar i Jhangvi', Office of Public Affairs, U.S. Treasury Department, 30 January 2003. Online, available at: www.ustreas.gov.
82 Roul, 2005(b). Because of the unhindered continuation of its activities, the group is still commonly referred to by its acronym, SSP.
83 Stern, 2000.
84 Roul, 2005(a), p. 6.
85 'Lashkar-e-Jhangvi', South Asia Terror Portal, 2007. Online, available at: www.satp.org.
86 Irfani, 2004.
87 Haniffa, Aziz, 'US Designates Lashkar-e-Jhangvi a Terrorist Outfit', Rediff, 31 January 2003. Online, available at: www.rediff.com. 'Lashkar-e-Jhangvi (LJ)', MIPT Terrorism Knowledge Base, 2007(c). Online, available at: www.tkb.org.
88 Roul, 2005(a).
89 'Lashkar-e-Toiba', GlobalSecurity, 2005. Online, available at: www.globalsecurity.org.
90 MIPT Terrorism Knowledge Base, 2007(c).
91 Roul, 2005(a).
92 Shahzad, 2004.
93 Pakistani Security Analyst 3, 2009.
94 International Crisis Group, 2005.
95 'Tehreek-e-Jafria Pakistan', South Asia Terror Portal, 2001(b), p. 1. Online, available at: www.satp.org.
96 South Asia Terror Portal, 2001(b).
97 Pakistan Institute for Peace Studies, 2008.
98 'Sunni Group Vows to Behead Iranians', *The Washington Times*, 16 January 2006.
99 'People's Resistance Movement of Iran Rejects Allegations of Alquida Ties', IntelliBriefs, 20 February 2009. Online, available at: http://intellibriefs.blogspot.com.

100 'The Secret War Against Iran', ABC News, 3 April 2007. Online, available at: www.abcnews.com.

101 Several prominent analysts have openly chastised Islamabad for allowing Iran and Saudi Arabia to fight a proxy war on its soil in the past.

6 Breakdown of order in FATA: driven by the Pakistani Taliban and Al-Qaeda but ideologically underwritten by LeT

1 Kronstadt, Alan and Vaughn, Bruce, 'Terrorism in South Asia', Congressional Research Service, Library of Congress, 9 August 2004.

2 Chouvy, Pierre-Arnaud, 'Opiate Smuggling Routes from Afghanistan to Europe and Asia', *Jane's Intelligence Review*, 1 March 2003.

3 Bukhari, Syed, 'Democracy Under Threat in Pakistan?', RSIS Commentaries, S. Rajaratnam School of International Studies, Singapore, 29 October 2007, p. 3.

4 'Al Qaeda Command Base in Pakistan Being Funded From Iraq', *Daily Times*, 21 May 2007. Online, available at: www.dailytimes.com.pk.

5 'Pakistan's Tribal Areas: Appeasing the Militants', International Crisis Group, Asia Report No. 125, December 2006.

6 International Crisis Group, 2006.

7 International Crisis Group, 2006.

8 'Pakistan: 2006 Overview', MIPT Terrorism Knowledge Base, 2007(a).

9 Raman, B., 'Musharaff's Fate in bin Laden's Hands', International Terrorism Monitor, Paper No. 300, South Asia Analysis Group, 4 November 2007, p. 2.

10 Marquand, Robert and Baldauf, Scott, 'Will Spies Who Know Tell the U.S.?', *Christian Science Monitor*, 3 October 2001. Online, available at: www.csmonitor.com.

11 Fair, Christine and Chalk, Peter, 'United States Internal Security Assistance to Pakistan', *Small Wars and Insurgencies*, Vol. 17, Issue 3, 2006.

12 Kronstadt and Vaughn, 2004. Atal, Subodh, 'Hunting Terrorists in Our Ally's Backyard: Pakistan', CATO Institute Release, Washington, DC, 16 March 2003.

13 International Crisis Group, 2006.

14 Sulaiman, Sadia, 'Empowering "Soft" Taliban Over "Hard" Taliban: Pakistan's Counter-Terrorism Strategy', *Terrorism Monitor*, Vol. 6, No. 15, 25 July 2008.

15 Gunaratna, Rohan and Bukhari, Syed Adnan Ali Shah, 'Making Peace with Pakistani Taliban to Isolate Al-Qaeda: Success and Failures', *Peace and Security Review*, Vol. 1, No. 2, Second Quarter 2008.

16 Abbas, Hassan, 'A Profile of Tehrik-i-Taliban Pakistan', *CTC Sentinel*, Vol. 1, No. 2, January 2008. Combatting Terrorism Center, West Point.

17 Gunaratna and Bukhari, 2008.

18 Abbas, 2008.

19 Yusufzai, Rahimullah, 'The Impact of Pashtun Tribal Differences on the Pakistani Taliban', *Terrorism Monitor*, Vol. 6, No. 3, 7 February 2008(a).

20 Shahzad, Syed Saleem, 'A Fighter and a Financer', *Asia Times*, 23 May 2008(a). Online, available at: www.asiatimes.com.

21 Rashid, Ahmed, 'How to Succeed and Fail in FATA', *Daily Times*, 5 February 2008(a). Online, available at: www.dailytimes.com.pk.

22 Yusufzai, Rahimullah, 'A Who's Who of the Insurgency in Pakistan's Northwest Frontier Province: Part One – North and South Waziristan', *Terrorism Monitor*, Vol. 6, No. 18, 22 September 2008(b).

23 'Taliban Ready to Give Up Arms: TTP', *Daily Times*, 16 October 2008. Online, available at: www.dailytimes.com.pk.
24 Sulaiman, 2008. Gunaratna and Bukhari, 2008.
25 Shahzad, Syed Saleem, 'In Life or Death, Baitullah's Fight Ensures', *Asia Times*, 3 October 2008(b). Online, available at: www.atimes.com.
26 Yusufzai, 2008(b).
27 Gunaratna and Bukhari, 2008.
28 Abbas, 2008.
29 Masood, Talat, 'Redirecting the War on Terror', *Daily Times*, 23 October 2008. Online, available at: www.dailytimes.com.pk.
30 'Militants See Global Financial Crisis as Sign of West's Weakness', *Daily Times*, 23 October 2008. Online, available at: www.dailytimes.com.
31 'Taliban, Qaida Trying to Take Over Pakistan', *Times of India*, 15 October 2008. Online, available at: http://timesofindia.indiatimes.com.
32 Rashid, Ahmed, 'Pakistan On The Brink', *Yale Global*, 19 September 2008(b). Qadri, Mustafa, 'In Pakistan, Sympathy for the Taliban', *Foreign Policy in Focus*, 17 September 2008.
33 Rashid, 2008(b). These desertions may not be the result of ideology or ethnic commonalities with TTP fighters but rather due to higher salaries offered by the TTP.
34 Shahzad, Syed Saleem, 'Pakistan, US Await Militant Showdown', *Asia Times*, 7 October 2008(c). Online, available at: www.atimes.com.
35 Rashid, Ahmed, 'How a Battered al-Qaeda was Rebuilt', *Daily Telegraph*, 3 September 2007. Online, available at: www.telegraph.co.uk.
36 Abbas, 2008.
37 Fair, Christine, 'The Educated Militants of Pakistan: Implications for Pakistan's Domestic Security', *Contemporary South Asia*, Vol. 16, No. 1, 1 March 2007, pp. 93–106.
38 Fair, Christine, 'Militant Recruitment in Pakistan: A New Look at the Militacy-Madrasah Connection', *Asia Policy*, No. 4, July 2007, pp. 107–34.
39 Yusufzai, 2008(b).
40 'JI General Secretary Asks Government to Disown U.S. War', *Daily Times*, 11 October 2008. Online, available at: www.dailytimes.com.pk.
41 Yusufzai, 2008(b).
42 Bergen, Peter, 'A Man, A Plan, Afghanistan', *The New Republic*, 24 September 2008. Rashid, 2008(b).
43 Qadri, 2008.
44 Shahzad, Syed Saleem, 'Dissention in Pakistan's Ranks', *Asia Times*, 13 September 2008(d). Online, available at: www.atimes.com.
45 Shahzad, 2008(c)
46 Shahzad, Syed Saleem, 'The Fight Goes On, Militants Tell Pakistan', *Asia Times*, 1 October 2008(e). Online, available at: www.atimes.com.
47 In Abbas, 2008, p. 4.
48 Shahzad, Syed Saleem, 'Militants Shake Off Pakistan's Grip', *Asia Times*, 25 September 2008(f). Online, available at: www.asiatimes.com.
49 Shahzad, 2008(f).
50 Shazad, 2008(e).
51 Rashid, 2008(b), p. 2
52 Sulaiman, 2008.
53 Sulaiman, 2008.
54 Sulaiman, 2008.
55 Yusufzai, 2008(a).
56 Rashid, Ahmed, 'Pashtuns in Pakistan Speak Out Against The Taliban Insur-

gency In Afghanistan', EurasiaNet, 27 November 2006. Online, available at: www.eurasianet.org.

57 Scheuer, Michael, 'Pakistani Islamist Fatwa Refutes Taliban's Jihad', *Terrorism Focus*, Vol. 5, No. 36, 22 October 2008.

58 Lakshman, 2007, p. 4.

59 Lakshman, 2007.

60 Nasir, Sohail, 'Al-Qaeda's Operational Corridor on the NFWP', *Terrorism Monitor*, Vol. 4, Issue 6, 23 March 2006.

61 Khan, Khwaja, 'Peshawar: The Obdurate Bastion of Soviet-era Mujahideen', *Terrorism Monitor*, Vol. 2, Issue 17, 9 September 2004.

62 Kronstadt and Vaughn, 2004.

63 Khan, 2004.

64 Khan, Ismail, 'Emboldened Militants Set Sights on Peshawar', *Dawn*, 25 June 2008. Online, available at: www.dawn.com/2008/06/25/top1.htm.

65 Kronstadt and Vaughn, 2004.

66 'Pakistan: The Mullahs and the Military', International Crisis Group, Asia Report No. 49, March 2003.

67 Raman, B., 'Jihadi Resistance, Sabotage in NWFP', International Terrorism Monitor Paper No. 295, South Asia Analysis Group, 29 October 2007.

68 Walsh, Declan, 'Fear and Brutality Inside the Fiefdom of Islamist Shock Jock', Guardian Unlimited, 5 November 2007. Online, available at: www.guardian.co.uk. 'Pakistan Army Pounds Fighters', Al-Jazeera, 28 October 2007. Online, available at: http://english.aljazeera.net.

69 Walsh, 2007.

70 Walsh, 2007.

71 Gannon, Kathy, 'Militants Gaining Ground in Pakistan', *The Detroit News*, 1 November 2007. Online, available at: www.detnews.com.

72 Naji, Abu Bakr, 'The Management of Savagery – the Most Critical Stage Through Which the Umma Will Pass', Translated by McCants, William, John M. Olin Institute for Strategic Studies, Harvard University, 23 May 2006, p. 37.

73 Fallows, James, 'Al-Qaeda Then and Now', in *Al-Qaeda Now – Understanding Today's Terrorists*, ed. Greenberg, Karen, Cambridge University Press, 2005, pp. 3–27.

74 Bergen, Peter, 'Al-Qaeda's Media Strategy', in *Al-Qaeda Now – Understanding Today's Terrorists*, ed. Greenberg, Karen, Cambridge University Press, 2005, pp. 112–35.

75 Naji, 2006.

76 Naji, 2006.

77 Jenkins, Michael, 'Countering al Qaeda', Rand Corporation, Santa Monica, 2002.

78 Jenkins, 2002.

79 Brown, Vahid, 'Foreign Fighters in Historical Perspective: The Case of Afghanistan', in *Bombers, Bank Accounts, & Bleedout – Al-Qa'ida's Road In and Out of Iraq*, ed. Bergen, Peter, Felter, Joseph, Brown, Vahid and Shapiro, Joseph, Combating Terrorism Center, West Point, 22 July 2008.

80 Jenkins, 2002.

81 Lalani, Arif, 'The Real Twin Towers – Al-Qaeda's Influence on Saudi Arabia and Pakistan', in *Al-Qaeda Now – Understanding Today's Terrorists*, ed. Greenberg, Karen, Cambridge University Press, 2005, pp. 135–59.

82 Lalani, 2005.

83 Lalani, 2005, p. 141

84 Blanchard, Christopher, 'Al Qaeda: Statements and Evolving Ideology', Congressional Research Service, Washington, DC, 9 July 2007.

85 Roggio, Bill, ' Al Qaeda's Paramilitary "Shadow Army"', *The Long War Journal*, 9 February 2009. Online, available at: www.longwarjournal.org.
86 Roggio, 2009.
87 Phillips, Andrew, 'How al Qaeda Lost Iraq', *Australian Journal of International Affairs*, Vol. 63, Issue 1, March 2009.
88 Fishman, Brian, 'Dysfunction and Decline – Lessons Learned from Inside Al Qa'ida in Iraq', The Combating Terrorism Center, West Point, 16 March 2009.
89 Fishman, 2009, p. 2.
90 Fishman, 2009.
91 Al-Iraqiyah Television, 18 September 2006.
92 Kilcullen, David, 'Field Notes on Iraq's Tribal Revolt Against Al-Qa'ida', *CTC Sentinel*, Vol. 1, Issue 11, October 2008.
93 Blanchard, 2007.
94 Fishman, 2009.
95 Umar al-Baghdadi, Abu, 'A Word of Truth – a Message to the Lion Leader Usamah bin Ladin, May God Protect Him', 12 October 2006.
96 In Fishman, 2009, pp. 16–21.
97 In Fishman, 2009.
98 In Fishman, 2009.
99 Bergen, Peter, 'Bombers, Bank Accounts, & Bleedout – Al-Qa'ida's Road In and Out of Iraq', in *Bombers, Bank Accounts, & Bleedout – Al-Qa'ida's Road In and Out of Iraq*, ed. Bergen, Peter, Felter, Joseph, Brown, Vahid and Shapiro, Joseph, Combating Terrorism Center, West Point, 22 July 2008, pp. 5–11. Combating Terrorism Center, West Point, 22 July 2008.
100 In Fishman, 2009.
101 Fishman, 2009.
102 Fishman, 2009.

7 The Pakistani economy: imbalances and contradictions, incomplete Islamization and D-Company as a strategic asset

1 Malik, Iftikhar, 'Pakistan in 2001: The Afghanistan Crisis and the Rediscovery of the Frontline State', *Asian Survey*, Vol. 42, No. 1, A Survey of Asia in 2001, January–February 2002, p. 208.
2 Andersen, Walter, 'A Selective War on Terrorism?', *Strategic Asia 2004–2005*, National Bureau of Asian Research, Seattle, Washington, 2004.
3 'Pakistan Country Overview 2006', World Bank, Washington, DC, 2007.
4 Hasan, Parvez, 'Poverty and Social Justice: Some Challenges for Islamization', in *Islamization and the Pakistani Economy*, ed. Hathaway, Robert and Lee, Wilson, Woodrow Wilson International Center for Scholars, Washington, DC, 2004, pp. 57–65.
5 Hasan, 2004.
6 Shah, M. Ali, 'Overview of Recent Economic Issues in Pakistan', *Strategic Studies*, Vol. XXI, No. 1, Spring 2002.
7 Shah, 2002.
8 Gill, John, 'Pakistan – A State Under Stress', *Strategic Asia 2003–2004*, National Bureau of Asian Research, Seattle, Washington, 2003. Lawson, Alastair, 'Kashmir: The Economic Fallout', BBC, 13 July 1999. Online, available at: www.bbc.co.uk.
9 Gill, 2003. 'Pakistan', Investment Climate Statements 2007, U.S. Department of State, 2007. Online, available at: www.state.gov/e/eeb/ifd/2007/82596.htm.
10 Andersen, 2004.

11 Shah, 2002.
12 Hasan, 2004.
13 Nasr, Vali, 'Islamization, the State, and Development', in *Islamization and the Pakistani Economy*, ed. Hathaway, Robert and Lee, Wilson, Woodrow Wilson International Center for Scholars, Washington D.C., 2004, pp. 91–101.
14 Nasr, 2004.
15 Khairi, Umber, 'Karachi: Volatile Metropolis', BBC, 11 April 2006. Online, available at: http://news.bbc.co.uk.
16 Blood, Peter, 'Pakistan-US Relations', Congressional Research Service, Library of Congress, Washington, DC, 12 February 2002.
17 Shah, 2002.
18 Berry, LaVerle, Curtis, Glenn E., Gibbs, John N., Hudson, Rex A., Karacan, Tara, Kollars, Nina and Miró, Ramón, 'Nations Hospitable to Organized Crime and Terrorism', Federal Research Division, Library of Congress, October 2003.
19 Fair, Christine and Chalk, Peter, United States Internal Security Assistance to Pakistan', *Small Wars and Insurgencies*, Vol. 17, Issue 03, 2006.
20 Rashid, Ahmed, 'Musharraf takes Pakistan to the Brink', BBC, 14 November 2007. Online, available at: www.bbc.co.uk.
21 Gill, 2003.
22 Rashid, 2007.
23 Clarke, Ryan, 'The Pakistani Economy: A Much-Neglected Front in the Struggle Against Terrorism', News Brief, 19 December 2008, Royal United Services Institute, London.
24 'Baloch Liberation Army (BLA)', MIPT Terrorism Knowledge Base, 2007. Online, available at: www.tkb.org. 'Pakistan: The Worsening Conflict in Balochistan', Asia Report No. 119, International Crisis Group, 14 September 2006.
25 Sahni, Ajai, 'Fellow Travelers of Terrorism', *South Asia Intelligence Review*, Vol. 1, No. 22, 16 December 2002.
26 Lele, Ajej, 'A Shift from Crime to Terrorism: Assessing D-Company', SSPC Paper No. 4, Society for the Study of Peace and Conflict, New Delhi, December 2005, p. 8.
27 'Dawood in Karachi, Admits Pakistan', Rediff, 21 September 2003. Online, available at: www.rediff.com.
28 'ISI Pressured Dawood to Carry Out Mumbai Blasts', Rediff, 22 December 2002. Online, available at: www.rediff.com.
29 Bhatnagar, Ashwini, 'Dusk descends on Don', *The Sunday Tribune*, 3 February 2002. Online, available at: www.tribuneindia.com.
30 Sharma, Rajeev, 'LeT Turning Global – Dawood's Links Come to the Fore', *The Tribune*, 19 January 2003. Online, available at: www.tribuneindia.com.
31 Ramachandran, Sudha, 'Pakistan in a Twist in War of Lists', *Asia Times*, 5 February 2002, p. 4. Online, available at: www.atimes.com.

Bibliography

Primary sources

'Balochistan: Conflicts and Players', Pakistan Institute for Peace Studies, Islamabad, 2008.

Chalk, Peter, 'Light Arms Trading in SE Asia', *Jane's Intelligence Review*, 2001.

'Crime', *Merriam-Webster Dictionary*. Online, available at: www.merriam-webster.com (accessed 17 November 2007).

'Definition of Crime', *Compact Oxford English Dictionary*. Online, available at: www.askoxford.com (accessed 5 November 2007).

Interview with Bukhari Syed Adnan Ali Shah (Pakistani Security Analyst 1). International Centre for Political Violence and Terrorism Research, Singapore, 14 March 2008.

Interview with Mahsud Saif Ullah Khan (Pakistani Security Analyst 2), International Centre for Political Violence and Terrorism Research, Singapore, 14 March 2008.

Interview with Pakistani diplomat (Pakistani Diplomat 1), Pakistan High Commission, Singapore, 13 February 2009.

Interview with Pakistani security analyst Khurram Iqbal (Pakistani Security Analyst 3), International Centre for Political Violence and Terrorism Research, Singapore, 10 April 2009.

Interview with Bangladeshi security analyst Shafqat Munir (Bangladeshi Security Analyst 1), International Centre for Political Violence and Terrorism Research, Singapore, 15 April 2009.

Interview with Indian security analyst Dr Arabinda Acharya (Indian Security Analyst 1), International Centre for Political Violence and Terrorism Research, Singapore, 16 April 2009.

Mehta, Suketu, *Maximum City: Bombay Lost and Found*, Penguin Books, New Delhi, 2004.

Naji, Abu Bakr, 'The Management of Savagery – the Most Critical Stage Through Which the Umma Will Pass', translated by McCants, William, John M. Olin Institute for Strategic Studies, Harvard University, 23 May 2006.

'Pakistan Security Report 2008', Pakistan Institute for Peace Studies, Islamabad, 2009.

Raju, A. Subramanyam, 'Third-Generation Indian Perceptions of the Kashmir Issue', RCSS Policy Studies 18, Regional Centre for Strategic Studies, Colombo, April 2001.

Rashid, Ahmed, *Taliban: Militant Islam, Oil and Fundamentalism in Central Asia*, Yale University Press, 2001, pp. 17–31.

Sahni, Sati, *Kashmir Underground*, Har-Anand Publications, New Delhi, 1999.

Schriek, Daan Van Der, 'Nuristan: Insurgent Hideout in Afghanistan', *Terrorism Monitor*, Vol. 3, Issue 10, 19 May 2005.

Sreedhar, K. and Manish, Sudhir, *Jihadis in Jammu and Kashmir – a Portrait Gallery*, Sage Publications, New Delhi, 2003.

'Treasury Department Statement Regarding the Designation of Lashkar i Jhangvi', Office of Public Affairs, U.S. Treasury Department, 30 January 2003. Online, available at: www.ustreas.gov.

Umar al-Baghdadi, Abu, 'A Word of Truth – a Message to the Lion Leader Usamah bin Ladin, May God Protect Him', 12 October 2006.

Secondary sources

Historical

Ahmed, Zubair, 'Mumbai Marks a Grim Anniversary', BBC News, 10 July 2007. Online, available at: http://news.bbc.co.uk/1/hi/world/south_asia/6288916.stm.

Badmus, I.A., 'The Vale of Tears: Kashmir, the Source of Indo-Pakistani Tensions Since 1947', *Anthropologist*, No. 8, Vol. 2, 2006, pp. 103–9.

Bergen, Peter, Felter, Joseph, Brown, Vahid and Shapiro, Jacob, *Bombers, Bank Accounts, & Bleedout: Al Qaida's Road In and Out of Iraq*, Combating Terrorism Center, West Point, 2008.

Brown, Vahid, 'Foreign Fighters in Historical Perspective: The Case of Afghanistan', in *Bombers, Bank Accounts, & Bleedout – Al-Qa'ida's Road In and Out of Iraq*, ed. Bergen, Peter, Felter, Joseph, Brown, Vahid and Shapiro, Jacob, Combating Terrorism Center, West Point, 22 July 2008.

Chellaney, Brahma, 'Fighting Terrorism in Southern Asia: The Lessons of History', *International Security*, Vol. 26, No. 3, Winter 2001–2.

Cohen, Stephen, 'India, Pakistan, and Kashmir', paper presented at the University of Texas. December 2001.

Ganguly, Sumit, 'Explaining the Kashmir Insurgency: Political Mobilization and Institutional Decay', *International Security*, Vol. 21, No. 2, Fall 1996.

Ghosh, Amitav, *Sea of Poppies*, John Murray General Publishing Division, London, 2008.

Gunaratna, Rohan and Bukhari, Syed Adnan Ali Shah, 'Making Peace with Pakistani Taliban to Isolate Al-Qaeda: Success and Failures', *Peace and Security Review*, Vol. 1, No. 2, Second Quarter 2008.

Long, Austin, 'The Anbar Awakening', *Survival*, Vol. 50, No. 2, April 2008, pp. 67–94.

Misra, Ashutosh, 'The Problem of Kashmir and the Problem in Kashmir: Divergence Demands Convergence', *Strategic Analysis*, Vol. 29, No. 1, 2005.

Rahman, M. and Baweja, Harinder, 'Making Headway', *India Today*, Vol. XVIII, No. 12, 30 April 1993.

Rahman, M. and Pathak, Rahul, 'The Conspiracy Unravels', *India Today*, Vol. XVIII, No. 12, 30 June 1993.

Ramachandran, V.K., 'Blasts of Terror', *Frontline*, Vol. 10, 9 April 1993.

Shafqat, Saeed, 'From Official Islam to Islamism: The Rise of Dawat-ul-Irshad and Lashkar-e-Taiba', in *Pakistan – Nationalism without a Nation?*, ed. Jaffrelot, C., Manohar Publishers & Distributors, New Delhi, 2002, pp. 131–49.

Williams, Phil, 'Criminals, Militias, and Insurgents: Organized Crime in Iraq', Strategic Studies Institute, U.S. Army War College, June 2009.

Zaidi, S. Hussain, *Black Friday: The True Story of the Bombay Bomb Blasts*, Penguin Books, New Delhi, 2002.

Descriptive

'70% Afghan Narcotics Move Through Pakistan', *Daily Times*, 22 March 2005. Online, available at: www.dailytimes.com.pk/default.asp?page=story_22-3-2005_pg7_35.

Abbas, Hassan, 'A Profile of Tehrik-i-Taliban Pakistan', *CTC Sentinel*, Vol. 1, No. 2, January 2008. Combatting Terrorism Center, West Point.

'A Godfather's Lethal Mix of Business and Politics', U.S. News and World Report, 27 November 2005. Online, available at: www.usnews.com/usnews/news/articles/051205/5terror.b.htm.

'Afghan Link to Seoul Drug Arrests', BBC News, 4 July 2008. Online, available at: http://news.bbc.co.uk/1/hi/world/asia-pacific/7489171.stm.

Aftergood, Steven, 'Lashkar-e-Taiba (Army of the Righteous)', Federation of American Scientists, 21 May 2004. Online, available at: www.fas.org/irp/world/para/lakshar.htm.

Ali, Farhana and Shehzad, Mohammed, 'Lashkar-i-Tayyiba Remains Committed to Jihad', *CTC Sentinel*, Vol. 2, Issue 3, March 2009.

Al-Iraqiyah Television, 18 September 2006.

'Al Qaeda Command Base in Pakistan Being Funded From Iraq', *Daily Times*, 21 May 2007. Online, available at: www.dailytimes.com.pk.

Amnesty International, 'India – Torture, Rape, and Deaths in Custody', 1992.

Amnesty International, 'Pakistan: Concern about Escalating Sectarian Violence', Public Statement, 13 April 2006.

'Amnesty Urges Kashmir Grave Probe, BBC News, 7 April 2008. Online, available at: http://news.bbc.co.uk/1/hi/world/south_asia/7334965.stm.

'Anatomy of Evil', *The Indian Express*, 11 July 2007. Online, available at: www.indianexpress.com/story/204473.html.

Atal, Subodh, 'Hunting Terrorists in Our Ally's Backyard: Pakistan', CATO Institute Release, Washington, DC, 16 March 2003.

'Baloch Liberation Army (BLA)', MIPT Terrorism Knowledge Base, 2007. Online, available at: www.tkb.org.

Bedi, Rahul, 'Vital Intelligence on the Taliban May Rest with its Prime Sponsor – Pakistan's ISI', Jane's Information Group, 1 October 2001. Online, available at: www.janes.com/security/international_security/news/misc/janes011001_1_n.shtml.

Berry, LaVerle, Curtis, Glenn E., Gibbs, John N., Hudson, Rex A., Karacan, Tara, Kollars, Nina and Miró, Ramón, 'Nations Hospitable to Organized Crime and Terrorism', Federal Research Division, Library of Congress, October 2003.

Bhat, Anil, 'From Inverted Crescent to Full Moon & Jihadi Pincer', *The Statesman*, 26 June 2007. Online, available at: http://thestatesman.co.in/page.arcview.php?clid=14&id=188731&usrsess=1.

Bhatnagar, Ashwini, 'Dusk Descends on Don', *The Sunday Tribune*, 3 February 2002. Online, available at: www.tribuneindia.com.

Bhatt, Shakti, 'State Terrorism vs. Jihad in Kashmir', *Journal of Contemporary Asia*, Vol. 33, 2003.

'Blast at SSP Rally Kills 40 in Multan', *Daily Times*, 8 October 2004. Online, available at: www.dailytimes.com.pk.

Bolan, Kim, 'Sikh Separatist Threat on Rise in Canada: Indian PM Warns of Resurgent Threat in Canada', *Vancouver Sun*, 11 March 2008. Online, available at: www.canada.com/vancouversun/news/story.html?id=2be0865c-29ba-4dab-9bcc-d945e75007c1&k= 79664.

'Bombs Explode Across Bangladesh', BBC News, 17 August 2005. Online, available at: www.bbc.co.uk.

Blood, Peter, 'Pakistan-US Relations', Congressional Research Service, Library of Congress, Washington, DC, 12 February 2002.

'Centre Afraid of Stable Regimes in JK: Omar', *Daily Excelsior*, 29 August 2007.

Charles, Molly, 'The Drug Scene in India', presentation at 'Drug Abuse: A Symposium on Social Processes, Narcotics, and the State', Bombay, August 2001. Online, available at: www.india-seminar.com/2001/504/504%20molly%20charles.htm.

Charles, Molly, 'The Growth and Activities of Organised Crime in Bombay', *International Social Science Journal*, Vol. 53, No. 3, 2001, pp. 359–67.

Chengappa, Raj and Raval, Sheela, 'War on Terror: Getting Dawood', *India Today International*, 3 November 2003, pp. 10–16.

'China's Missile Exports and Assistance to Pakistan', Center for Nonproliferation Studies, Monterey Institute of International Studies, Monterey, California, 2000.

Chossudovsky, Michel, 'The Foiled UK Terror Plot and the "Pakistani Connection"', *Global Research*, 14 August 2006.

Chouvy, Pierre-Arnaud, 'Opiate Smuggling Routes from Afghanistan to Europe and Asia', *Jane's Intelligence Review*, 1 March 2003.

'Clashes Mark Final Kashmir Poll', BBC, 24 December 2008. Online, available at: www.bbc.co.uk.

'Dawood in Karachi, Admits Pakistan', Rediff, 21 September 2003. Online, available at: www.rediff.com.

Deyer, Simon, 'Concern Mounts Over Bangladesh Madrassas After Bombs', *Daily Times*, 29 September 2005. Online, available at: www.dailytimes.com.pk.

'Feds Seize "Incredible Arsenal" – U.S. Agent Says China was Aware of Weapons Smuggling Operation', CNN News Service, 23 May 1996. Online, available at: www.edition.cnn.com/US/9605/23/china.arms.

Gannon, Kathy, 'Militants Gaining Ground in Pakistan', *The Detroit News*, 1 November 2007. Online, available at: www.detnews.com.

Haniffa, Aziz, 'US Designates Lashkar-e-Jhangvi a Terrorist Outfit', Rediff, 31 January 2003. Online, available at: www.rediff.com.

Hardaker, David, 'The World Today – Background to Lashkar-e-Toiba', ABC Online, 5 November 2003. Online, available at: www.abc.net.au/worldtoday/content/2003/s982752.html.

Hardy, Roger, 'Pakistan's "Culture of Jihad"', BBC News, 5 August 2002. Online, available at: http://news.bbc.co.uk/1/hi/in_depth/world/2002/islamic_world/2173818.stm.

'Human Rights Watch World Report 2006 – Pakistan', Human Rights Watch, New York, 2007.

Idris, Iffat, 'Pakistan's Sectarian Menace', *Outlook India*, 21 August 2003.

'India: Arms and Abuses in Indian Punjab and Kashmir', Human Rights Watch, 1994.

'Indian Court Sentences 5 in Mumbai Blasts, Including Bollywood Producer', Voice of America (VOA) News, 1 June 2007.

'ISI Pressured Dawood to Carry Out Mumbai Blasts', Rediff, 22 December 2002. Online, available at: www.rediff.com.

Ispahani, Mahnaz, 'Religious Sword Over Pakistan', *Los Angeles Times*, 21 May 2004. Online, available at: www.latimes.com.

'JI General Secretary Asks Government to Disown U.S. War', *Daily Times*, 11 October 2008. Online, available at: www.dailytimes.com.pk.

Kak, M.L., 'ISI Plan to Restructure UJC', *The Tribune*, 1 February 2003. Online, available at: www.tribuneindia.com/2003/20030201/j&k.htm#1.

'Kashmir: An Insurgency Wedged Between Two Nuclear Powers', *Jane's Intelligence Backgrounder*, 2001.

'Kashmiri Parties in Coalition Bid', BBC, 29 December 2008. Online, available at: www.bbc.co.uk.

Kaul, Ashima, 'The Proliferation of Small Arms in J&K', *Control Arms India Update*, Vol. 1, No. 2, 2005.

Khairi, Umber, 'Karachi: Volatile Metropolis', BBC, 11 April 2006. Online, available at: http://news.bbc.co.uk.

Khan, Afzal, 'The War on Terror and the Politics of Violence in Pakistan', *Terrorism Monitor*, Vol. 2, Issue 13, 1 July 2004.

Khan, Ismail, 'Emboldened Militants Set Sights on Peshawar', *Dawn*, 25 June 2008. Online, available at: www.dawn.com/2008/06/25/top1.htm.

Khan, Khwaja, 'Peshawar: The Obdurate Bastion of Soviet-era Mujahideen', *Terrorism Monitor*, Vol. 2, Issue 17, 9 September 2004.

Khan, M., 'Pakistani Militant's Fluctuating Fate', BBC News, 24 October 2006. Online, available at: http://news.bbc.co.uk/1/hi/world/south_asia/6067694.stm.

Kilcullen, David, 'Field Notes on Iraq's Tribal Revolt Against Al-Qa'ida', *CTC Sentinel*, Vol. 1, Issue 11, October 2008.

Kronstadt, Alan, 'Pakistan-U.S. Anti-Terrorism Cooperation', Congressional Research Service, Library of Congress, 28 March 2003.

Kronstadt, Alan and Vaughn, Bruce, 'Terrorism in South Asia', Congressional Research Service, Library of Congress, 9 August 2004.

Kumar, Anand, 'Bangladesh: Islamists Attempt to Regroup', Paper 2351, South Asia Analysis Group, 30 August 2007, New Delhi. Online, available at: www.southasiaanalysis.org/default.asp.

Lakshman, Kanchan, 'The ISI Exposed', *South Asia Intelligence Review*, Vol. 5, No. 12, 2 October 2006.

Lakshman, Kanchan, 'NWFP: Extremist Encroachment', *South Asia Intelligence Review*, Vol. 5, No. 45, 21 May 2007.

Lal, Rollie, 'South Asian Organized Crime and Terrorist Networks', *Orbis*, Vol. 49, Issue 2, Spring 2005.

'Lashkar-e-Jhangvi', South Asia Terror Portal, 2007. Online, available at: www.satp.org.

'Lashkar-e-Jhangvi (LJ)', MIPT Terrorism Knowledge Base, 2007. Online, available at: www.tkb.org.

'Lashkar-e-Toiba – "Army of the Pure"', South Asia Terror Portal, 2001. Online, available at: www.satp.org/satporgtp/countries/india/states/jandk/terrorist_outfits/lashkar_e_toiba.htm.

'Lashkar-e-Toiba', BBC News, 25 November 2002. Online, available at: http://news.bbc.co.uk/1/hi/world/south_asia/2510613.stm.

'Lashkar-e-Toiba', GlobalSecurity, 2005. Online, available at: www.globalsecurity.org.

'Lashkar Militant Admits Killing Sikhs in Chittisinghpura', Rediff, 31 December 2000. Online, available at: www.rediff.com/news/2000/dec/31sikh.htm.

Lawson, Alastair, 'Kashmir: The Economic Fallout', BBC, 13 July 1999. Online, available at: www.bbc.co.uk.

'Lawyer Named for Mumbai Suspect', BBC News, 30 March 2009. Online, available at: www.bbc.co.uk.

'LeT Recruiting Afghan Refugees to Support Taliban in Afghanistan', *Terrorism Focus*, Vol. 3, Issue 39, 10 October 2006.

'LeT Suspect Nabbed', *The Times of India*, 13 July 2007. Online, available at: http://timesofindia.indiatimes.com/cities/LeT_suspect_nabbed/articleshow/2199336.cms.

'LeT Threat to Dalai Lama', *Daily Excelsior*, 2 April 2007. Online, available at: www.dailyexcelsior.com/web1/07apr02/news.htm#9.

McGirk, Tim, 'Lay Down Your Guns', *Time Magazine*, 12 May 2003. Online, available at: www.time.com/time/magazine/article/0,9171,451022,00.html.

'Man Arrested in Nepal with Fake Indian Currency', *Dawn*, 1 August 2007. Online, available at: www.dawn.com/2007/08/01/top21.htm.

'The Man Who Knew Too Much', *Telegraph*, 1 October 2006. Online, available at: www.telegraphindia.com.

Maqbool, Imran, 'Pearl Murder Suspect Dies in Bomb Blast', *Independent*, 20 December 2002. Online, available at: www.independent.co.uk.

Marquand, Robert and Baldauf, Scott, 'Will Spies Who Know Tell the U.S.?', *Christian Science Monitor*, 3 October 2001. Online, available at: www.csmonitor.com.

Masood, Talat, 'Redirecting the War on Terror', *Daily Times*, 23 October 2008. Online, available at: www.dailytimes.com.pk.

'Meet the Lashkar-e-Tayiba's Fundraiser', Rediff, 28 July 2006. Online, available at: www.rediff.com///news/2006/jul/28lashkar.htm.

'Militants See Global Financial Crisis as Sign of West's Weakness', *Daily Times*, 23 October 2008. Online, available at: www.dailytimes.com.

Mir, Amir, 'Catch Me If You Can', *Mid Day*, 9 November 2003.

Mir, Amir, 'The Jihad Lives On', *Asia Times*, 11 March 2005. Online, available at: www.atimes.com/atimes/South_Asia/GC11Df07.html.

Mir, Amir, 'Sectarian Monster', *South Asia Intelligence Review*, Vol. 3, No. 47, 6 June 2005.

Mishra, Bisheshwar, 'ISI, Dawood Help LeT Set a Global Network', *The Times of India*, 2 July 2003. Online, available at: http://timesofindia.indiatimes.com/articleshow/56386.cms.

'Mumbai Bombing Sentencing Delay', BBC, 13 September 2006. Online, available at: www.bbc.co.uk.

Mustafa, Malik, 'Proliferation of Small Arms and Light Weapons: Case Study – South Asia', *Strategic Studies*, Vol. XXV, No. 2, Summer 2005.

'Our Homegrown Suicide Bombers', *Hindustan Times*, 11 December 2005.

Padmanabhan, R., 'Movie Mafia: The Underworld and "Bollywood"', *Frontline*, Vol. 10, 21 May 1993.

Padmanabhan, R., 'Nexus Galore: The Complicated Trail of the Blasts', *Frontline*, Vol. 10, 21 May 1993.
Padmanabhan, R., 'Sitting on Bombs: Thane Reveals More', *Frontline*, Vol. 10, 23 April 1993.
'Pak Likely to Smuggle in More Arms', *Indian Express*, 19 April 1993.
'Pakistan', Investment Climate Statements 2007, U.S. Department of State, 2007. Online, available at: www.state.gov/e/eeb/ifd/2007/82596.htm.
'Pakistan Army Pounds Fighters', Al-Jazeera, 28 October 2007. Online, available at: http://english.aljazeera.net.
'Pakistan Country Overview 2006', World Bank, Washington, DC, 2007.
'Pakistan Freezes Militant Funds', BBC News, 24 December 2001. Online, available at: http://news.bbc.co.uk/1/hi/world/south_asia/1726813.stm.
'Pakistan's "Role in Mumbai Attacks"', BBC News, 30 September 2006. Online, available at: http://news.bbc.co.uk/1/hi/world/south_asia/5394686.stm.
'Pakistan: 2006 Overview', MIPT Terrorism Knowledge Base, 2007. Online, available at: www.tkb.org.
'Pakistan's Unseen Conflict', *Jane's Intelligence Digest*, 7 February 2003.
Parthasarathy, G., 'Pugwash Initiative on Kashmir – Opinions Differ on Troop Pull-out', *The Tribune*, 9 August 2007.
Partlow, Joshua and Khan, Kamran, 'Charity Funds Said to Provide Clues to Alleged Terrorist Plot', *Washington Post*, 15 August 2006.
'People's Resistance Movement of Iran Rejects Allegations of Alquida Ties', IntelliBriefs, 20 February 2009. Online, available at: http://intellibriefs.blogspot.com.
Pike, Jonathan, 'Directorate for Inter-Services Intelligence [ISI]', Federation of American Scientists, 2002. Online, available at: www.fas.org/irp/world/pakistan/isi.
'Profile: Lashkar-e-Toiba', BBC News, 17 March 2006. Online, available at: http://news.bbc.co.uk/1/hi/world/south_asia/3181925.stm.
Qadri, Mustafa, 'In Pakistan, Sympathy for the Taliban', *Foreign Policy in Focus*, 17 September 2008.
Raghavan, T.C.A., 'The Problem of Black Money', Institute of Peace and Conflict Studies, Article no. 398, New Delhi, 2000.
Ramachandran, Sudha, 'Pakistan in a Twist in War of Lists', *Asia Times*, 5 February 2002. Online, available at: www.atimes.com.
Raman, B., 'Jihadi Resistance, Sabotage in NWFP', International Terrorism Monitor Paper No. 295, South Asia Analysis Group, 29 October 2007.
Raman, B., 'Lashkar-e-Toiba: Spreading the Jehad', *The Hindu Business Line*, 5 January 2001. Online, available at: www.hinduonnet.com/businessline/2001/01/05/stories/040555ra.htm.
Raman, B., 'LeT Issues Fatwa to Kill the Pope', *International Terrorism Monitor*, Paper no. 133, 2006, South Asia Analysis Group.
Raman, B., 'The Lashkar-e-Toiba (LeT)', South Asia Analysis Group, Paper No. 374, 2001.
Rashid, Ahmed, 'How a Battered al-Qaeda was Rebuilt', *Daily Telegraph*, 3 September 2007. Online, available at: www.telegraph.co.uk.
Rashid, Ahmed, 'Musharraf takes Pakistan to the Brink', BBC, 14 November 2007. Online, available at: www.bbc.co.uk.
Rashid, Ahmed, 'Pakistan On The Brink', *Yale Global*, 19 September 2008.
Rashid, Ahmed, 'Pashtuns in Pakistan Speak Out Against The Taliban Insurgency

In Afghanistan', EurasiaNet, 27 November 2006. Online, available at: www.eurasianet.org.

Roggio, Bill, 'Al Qaeda's Paramilitary "Shadow Army"', *The Long War Journal*, 9 February 2009. Online, available at: www.longwarjournal.org.

Roul, Animesh, 'Lashkar-e-Taiba Resumes Operations Against Indian Forces in Jammu and Kashmir', *Terrorism Monitor*, Vol. VII, Issue 8, 3 April 2009.

Sahni, Ajai, 'Fellow Travelers of Terrorism', *South Asia Intelligence Review*, Vol. 1, No. 22, 16 December 2002.

Scheuer, Michael, 'Pakistani Islamist Fatwa Refutes Taliban's Jihad', *Terrorism Focus*, Vol. 5, No. 36, 22 October 2008.

Shah, M. Ali, 'Overview of Recent Economic Issues in Pakistan', *Strategic Studies*, Vol. XXI, No. 1, Spring 2002.

Shahzad, Syed Saleem, 'A Fighter and a Financer', *Asia Times*, 23 May 2008. Online, available at: www.asiatimes.com.

Shahzad, Syed Saleem, 'Dissention in Pakistan's Ranks', *Asia Times*, 13 September 2008. Online, available at: www.atimes.com.

Shahzad, Syed Saleem, 'In Life or Death, Baitullah's Fight Ensures', *Asia Times*, 3 October 2008. Online, available at: www.atimes.com.

Shahzad, Syed Saleem, 'Karachi: Where Terrorists Hide and Thrive', *Terrorism Monitor*, Vol. 2, Issue 17, 9 September 2004.

Shahzad, Syed Saleem, 'Militants Shake Off Pakistan's Grip', *Asia Times*, 25 September 2008. Online, available at: www.asiatimes.com.

Shahzad, Syed Saleem, 'Pakistan Braces for More Attacks', *Asia Times*, 1 April 2009.

Shahzad, Syed Saleem, 'Pakistan, US Await Militant Showdown', *Asia Times*, 7 October 2008. Online, available at: www.atimes.com.

Shahzad, Syed Saleem, 'The Fight Goes On, Militants Tell Pakistan', *Asia Times*, 1 October 2008. Online, available at: www.atimes.com.

Sharma, Rajeev, 'LeT Turning Global – Dawood's Links Come to the Fore', *The Tribune*, 19 January 2003. Online, available at: www.tribuneindia.com.

Shehzad, Mohammad, 'Banned LeT Collects Millions in Charity, Hides', *South Asia Tribune*, Issue 35, 23–29 March 2003.

Singh, M., 'Growing Fundamentalism in the Northeast', *IDSA Strategic Comments*, 19 February 2007, Institute for Defence Studies and Analyses, New Delhi.

Singh, Shankar, 'Transnational Organized Crime: The Indian Perspective', UNAFEI Annual Report for 2000 and Resource Material Series No. 59, 2002, pp. 570–87.

Singh, Thangjam, 'Could Pune by a Future Terrorist Target?', *IDSA Strategic Comments*, 17 August 2006, Institute for Defence Studies and Analyses, New Delhi.

Singh, Thangjam, 'The LeT Menace in Delhi', *IDSA Strategic Comments*, 11 May 2007, Institute for Defence Studies and Analyses, New Delhi.

'Sipah-e-Sahaba', South Asia Terror Portal, 2001. Online, available at: www.satp.org.

'Sipah-e-Sahaba Pakistan (SSP)', MIPT Terrorism Knowledge Base, 30 September 2007. Online, available at: www.tkb.org.

Smith, Chris, 'Light Weapons and Ethnic Conflict in South Asia', in *Lethal Commerce: The Global Trade in Small Arms and Light Weapons*, ed. Boutwell, J., Klare, M. and Reed, L., Committee on International Security Studies, American Academy of Arts and Sciences, Cambridge, Massachusetts, 1995, pp. 61–81.

Smith, Chris, 'The Diffusion of Small Arms and Light Weapons in Pakistan and Northern India', Brassey's Centre for Defence Studies, London, 1993.

Smucker, Phillip, 'Al-Qaeda Thriving in Pakistani Kashmir', *Christian Science Monitor*, 2 July 2002. Online, available at: www.csmonitor.com/2002/0702/p01s02-wosc.html.

Spector, Leonard, Yuan, Jing-Dong and Saunders, Phillip, 'Hearing on China's Proliferation Policies and Practices', Prepared Statement before the U.S.-China Economic and Security Review Commission, Center for Nonproliferation Studies, Monterey Institute of International Studies, Monterey, California, 24 July 2003.

Srivastava, Siddharth, 'India Faces Terror from Another Front', *Asia Times*, 13 November 2008. Online, available at: www.atimes.com.

Stern, Jessica, 'Pakistan's Jihad Culture', *Foreign Affairs*, November/December 2000.

'Sunni Group Vows to Behead Iranians', *The Washington Times*, 16 January 2006.

Swami, Praveen, 'Flawed Justice', *Frontline*, Vol. 23, Issue 19, 23 September – 6 October 2006.

Swami, Praveen, 'Harnessing Hate', *Frontline*, Vol. 23, Issue 15, 29 July – 11 August 2006.

Swami, Praveen, 'Nairobi Arrest Points to Deepening Lashkar-Dawood Links', *The Hindu*, 22 July 2006. Online, available at: www.hindu.com/2006/07/22/stories/2006072225171800.htm.

Swami, Praveen, 'Quake Came as a Boon for Lashkar Leadership', *The Hindu*, 17 November 2005. Online, available at: www.thehindu.com/2005/11/17/stories/2005111705951200.htm.

Swami, Praveen and Shehzad, Mohammed, 'Lashkar Raising Islamist Brigades for Iraq', *The Hindu*, 13 June 2004. Online, available at: www.hindu.com/2004/06/13/stories/2004061306050100.htm.

Talbot, Ian, 'Pakistan in 2002: Democracy, Terrorism, and Brinkmanship', *Asian Survey*, Vol. 43, No. 1, A Survey of Asia in 2002, January–February 2003.

'Taliban, Qaida Trying to Take Over Pakistan', *Times of India*, 15 October 2008. Online, available at: http://timesofindia.indiatimes.com.

'Taliban Ready to Give Up Arms: TTP', *Daily Times*, 16 October 2008. Online, available at: www.dailytimes.com.pk.

Tandy, Karen, 'Afghanistan: Law Enforcement Interdiction Efforts in Transshipment Countries to Stem the Flow of Heroin', Testimony before the Subcommittee on Criminal Justice, Drug Policy and Human Resources, U.S. House of Representatives, Washington, DC, 26 February 2004. Online, available at: www.usdoj.gov/dea/pubs/cngrtest/ct022604.htm.

'Tehreek-e-Jafria Pakistan', South Asia Terror Portal, 2001. Online, available at: www.satp.org.

'The Secret War Against Iran', ABC News, 3 April 2007. Online, available at: www.abcnews.com.

'The State of Sectarianism in Pakistan', International Crisis Group, Asia Report No. 95, April 2005.

Walsh, Declan, 'Fear and Brutality Inside the Fiefdom of Islamist Shock Jock', Guardian Unlimited, 5 November 2007. Online, available at: www.guardian.co.uk

Watson, Paul and Barua, Siddhartha, 'Camps Thrive in Pakistan, India Charges', *Los Angeles Times*, 11 January 2002.

'Who are the Kashmir Militants?', BBC News, 19 February 2003. Online, available at: http://news.bbc.co.uk/1/low/world/south_asia/1719612.stm.

Yusufzai, Rahimullah, 'A Who's Who of the Insurgency in Pakistan's Northwest Frontier Province: Part One – North and South Waziristan', *Terrorism Monitor*, Vol. 6, No. 18, 22 September 2008.

Analytical

Ahmed, Mumtaz, 'Revivalism, Islamisation, Sectarianism and Violence in Pakistan', in *Pakistan 1997*, ed. Baxter, Craig and Kennedy, Charles, Westview Press, Boulder, 1998.

Ali, Mukhtar, 'Sectarian Conflict in Pakistan – A Case Study of Jhang', RCSS Policy Studies 9, Regional Centre for Strategic Studies, Colombo, 2000.

Andersen, Walter, 'A Selective War on Terrorism?', *Strategic Asia 2004–2005*, National Bureau of Asian Research, Seattle, Washington, 2004.

Andley, Priyashree, '"Zero Tolerance" for Fake Encounters: A Reality Check in J&K', Article 2210, 17 February 2007, Institute of Peace and Conflict Studies, New Delhi.

Bahadur, Kalim, 'Regional Implications of the Rise of Islamic Fundamentalism in Pakistan', *Strategic Analysis*, Vol. 30, No. 1, January–March 2006.

Bergen, Peter, 'Al-Qaeda's Media Strategy', in *Al-Qaeda Now – Understanding Today's Terrorists*, ed. Greenberg, Karen, Cambridge University Press, 2005, pp. 112–35.

Bergen, Peter, 'A Man, A Plan, Afghanistan', *The New Republic*, 24 September 2008.

Blanchard, Christopher, 'Al Qaeda: Statements and Evolving Ideology', Congressional Research Service, Washington, DC, 9 July 2007.

Brew, Nigel, 'Lashkar-e-Taiba (LeT) and the Threat to Australia', Research Note, No. 36, 16 February 2004. Information Analysis and Advice for the Parliament, Department of Parliamentary Services, Canberra.

Budania, Rajpal, 'The Emerging International Security System: Threats, Challenges, and Opportunities for India', *Strategic Analysis*, Vol. 27, No. 1, 2003.

Bukhari, Syed, 'Democracy Under Threat in Pakistan?', RSIS Commentaries, S. Rajaratnam School of International Studies, Singapore, 29 October 2007.

Burr, J. Millar and O'Collins, Robert, *Alms for Jihad: Charity and Terrorism in the Islamic World*, Cambridge University Press, 2006.

Byman, Daniel, *Deadly Connections: States that Sponsor Terrorism*, Cambridge University Press, 2005.

Byman, Daniel, 'Passive Support of Terrorism', MIT Security Studies Seminar, 6 October 2004.

Byman, Daniel, 'Proxy Power: Understanding Iran's Use of Terrorism', *Slate*, 26 July 2006. Online, available at: www.slate.com/id/2146532.

Byman, Daniel, 'The Changing Nature of State Sponsorship of Terrorism', Analysis Paper, No. 16, May 2008. Saban Center for Middle East Policy, Brookings Institute.

Byman, Daniel, Chalk, Peter, Hoffman, Bruce, Rosenau, William and Brannan, David, 'Trends in Outside Support for Insurgent Movements', RAND Corporation, 2001.

Chandran, Suba, 'Elections in Kashmir- XI: Real Threat Comes From the People', Article 841, 26 August 2002, Institute of Peace and Conflict Studies, New Delhi.

Chandran, Suba, 'People, State, Fear, and Counter-Militancy', Article 1989, 12 April 2006, Institute of Peace and Conflict Studies, New Delhi.

Chowdhury, Khaled Iqbal, 'BDR Mutiny and Its Security Implications', Bangladesh Institute of Peace and Security Studies (BIPSS) Special Report, Dhaka, March 2009.

Clarke, Ryan, 'The Pakistani Economy: A Much-Neglected Front in the Struggle Against Terrorism', News Brief, 19 December 2008, Royal United Services Institute, London.

Clarke, Ryan, 'D-Company: A Study of the Crime-Terror Nexus in South Asia', *International Journal of Business and Globalisation*, Vol. 4, No. 3, 2010.

Clarke, Ryan and Lee, Stewart, 'The PIRA, D-Company, and the Crime-Terror Nexus: A Comparative Analysis', *Terrorism and Political Violence*, Vol. 20, Issue 3, July 2008.

Curtis, Glenn and Karacan, Tara, 'The Nexus Among Terrorists, Narcotics Traffickers, Weapons Proliferators and Organized Crime Networks in Western Europe', Congressional Research Service, December 2002

El-Hokayem, Emile, 'Hizballah and Syria: Outgrowing the Proxy Relationship', *The Washington Quarterly*, Spring 2007.

Esser, Daniel, 'The City as Arena, Hub, and Prey – Patterns of Violence in Kabul and Karachi', *Environment and Urbanization*, Vol. 16, No. 2, 2004.

Fair, Christine, 'Militant Recruitment in Pakistan: A New Look at the Militancy-Madrasah Connection', *Asia Policy*, No. 4, July 2007, pp. 107–34.

Fair, Christine, 'The Educated Militants of Pakistan: Implications for Pakistan's Domestic Security', *Contemporary South Asia*, Vol. 16, No. 1, 1 March 2007, pp. 93–106.

Fair, Christine and Chalk, Peter, 'United States Internal Security Assistance to Pakistan', *Small Wars and Insurgencies*, Vol. 17, Issue 3, 2006.

Fallows, James, 'Al-Qaeda Then and Now', in *Al-Qaeda Now – Understanding Today's Terrorists*, ed. Greenberg, Karen, Cambridge University Press, 2005, pp. 3–27.

Fishman, Brian, 'Dysfunction and Decline – Lessons Learned from Inside Al Qa'ida in Iraq', The Combating Terrorism Center, West Point, 16 March 2009.

Ganguly, Sumit, 'Will Kashmir Stop India's Rise?', *Foreign Affairs Magazine*, Vol. 85, No. 4, July–August 2006.

Gilani, Tariq, 'US-Pakistan Relations: The Way Forward', *Parameters*, Winter 2006–7.

Gill, John, 'Pakistan – A State Under Stress', *Strategic Asia 2003–2004*, National Bureau of Asian Research, Seattle, Washington, 2003.

Gill, John, 'Regional Concerns, Global Ambitions', *Strategic Asia 2003–2004*, National Bureau of Asian Research, Seattle, 2004.

'Gulshan Kumar Killer Escapes after Temporary Release from Jail', *Express India*, 23 May 2009. Online, available at: www.expressindia.com.

Gupta, Shekar, 'The Memons: India's Most Wanted Family', *India Today*, Vol. XVIII, No. 12, 15 April 1993.

Harrison, Selig, 'Stop Building Up Pakistani Military Capacities Against India', *The International Herald Tribune*, 20 December 2001. Online, available at: www.iht.com/articles/2001/12/20/edsig_ed3_.php.

Haqqani, Husain, 'Pakistan's Endgame in Kashmir', *India Review*, Vol. 2, No. 3, July 2003.

Haqqani, Husain, 'Pakistan's Terrorism Dilemma', in *Religious Radicalism and Security in South Asia*, ed. Limaye, Satu, Malik, Mohan and Wirsing, Robert, Asia-Pacific Center for Security Studies, Honolulu, 2004, pp. 351–65.

Hasan, Parvez, 'Poverty and Social Justice: Some Challenges for Islamization', in *Islamization and the Pakistani Economy*, ed. Hathaway, Robert and Lee, Wilson, Woodrow Wilson International Center for Scholars, Washington, DC, 2004, pp. 57–65.

Hasnain, Ghulam, 'Inside Jihad', *Time Asia*, Vol. 157, No. 5, 5 February 2001.

Hoffman, Bruce, 'Al Qaeda, Trends in Terrorism and Future Potentialities: An Assessment', Rand Corporation, Santa Monica, 2003.

Hussain, Fawaz, 'Terror in Bombay', *India Today*, Vol. XVIII, No. 12, 31 March 1993.

International Crisis Group, 'Kashmir: The View From Islamabad', Asia Report No. 68, 4 December 2003.

International Crisis Group, 'Kashmir, The View From New Delhi', Asia Report No. 69, 4 December 2003.

Irfani, Suroosh, 'Pakistan's Sectarian Violence: Between the "Arabist Shift" and Indo-Persian Culture', in *Religious Radicalism and Security in South Asia*, ed. Limaye, Satu, Malik, Mohan and Wirsing, Robert, Asia-Pacific Center for Security Studies, Honolulu, 2004, pp. 147–71.

'ISI Agent Held in Hyderabad', *The Hindu*, 2 April 2007. Online, available at: www.thehindu.com/2007/04/02/stories/2007040217231100.htm.

'ISI Hand in 7/11 Mumbai Blasts, Say Police', *The Hindu*, 1 October 2006. Online, available at: www.hindu.com/2006/10/01/stories/2006100113440100.htm.

Ismail, Noor, 'The Role of Kinship in Indonesia's Jemmah Islamiya', *Terrorism Monitor*, Vol. 4, Issue 11, 2 June 2006.

Jamwal, N.S., 'Terrorists' Modus Operandi in Jammu and Kashmir', *Strategic Analysis*, Vol. 27, No. 3, 2003.

Jenkins, Brian, 'Terrorists Can Think Strategically – Lessons Learned from the Mumbai Attacks', Testimony presented before the Senate Homeland Security and Governmental Affairs Committee, 28 January 2009.

Jenkins, Michael, 'Countering al Qaeda', RAND Corporation, Santa Monica, 2002.

Jha, Sanjay, 'Delhi Blasts, Terror Networks and India's Internal Security', *Strategic Analysis*, Vol. 29, No. 4, October–December 2005.

John, Wilson, 'Lashkar-e-Toiba: New Threats Posed by an Old Organization', *Terrorism Monitor*, Vol. 3, Issue 4, 24 February 2005.

John, Wilson, 'Pakistan's Nuclear Underworld – An Investigation', Observer Research Foundation, New Delhi, 2005.

John, Wilson, 'The Jihadi Factor in India-Pakistan Peace Process', ORF Issue Brief 6, May 2006, Observer Research Foundation, New Delhi.

Jones, Seth, 'Counterinsurgency in Afghanistan', RAND Corporation, 2008.

Jones, Seth, Oliker, Olga, Chalk, Peter, Fair, Christine, Lal, Rollie and Dobbins, James, 'Securing Tyrants or Fostering Reform?', Prepared for the Open Society Institute by the RAND National Security Research Division, 2006.

Kartha, Tara, 'Countering Transnational Terrorism', *Strategic Analysis*, Vol. 23, No. 11, 2006.

Kartha, Tara, 'Tools of Terror: Light Weapons and India's Security', Knowledge World in association with the Institute for Defence Studies and Analyses, New Delhi, 1999.

Kumar, Neeraj, 'Organized Crime', *PoliceSpeak*, 1999. Online, available at: www.india-seminar.com/1999/483.htm.

Lal, Rollie, 'South Asian Organized Crime', *Orbis: A Journal of World Affairs*, Vol. 49, No. 2, Spring 2005, pp. 293–304.

Lalani, Arif, 'The Real Twin Towers – Al-Qaeda's Influence on Saudi Arabia and Pakistan', in *Al-Qaeda Now – Understanding Today's Terrorists*, ed. Greenberg, Karen, Cambridge University Press, 2005, pp. 135–59.

Lavroy, Peter, 'Pakistan's Kashmir Policy after the Bush Visit to South Asia', *Strategic Insights*, Vol. 4, Issue 4, April 2006.

Lele, Ajey, 'A Shift from Crime to Terrorism: Assessing D-Company', SSPC Paper, Society for the Study of Peace and Conflict, December 2005.

Malik, Iftikhar, 'Pakistan in 2001: The Afghanistan Crisis and the Rediscovery of the Frontline State', *Asian Survey*, Vol. 42, No. 1, A Survey of Asia in 2001, January–February 2002.

Malik, Mohan, 'The China Factor in the India-Pakistan Conflict', *Parameters*, Vol. 33, 2003.

Mandelbaum, Michael, 'Kashmir – the Perpetual Tinderbox', *Newsday*, 22 February 2002.

Mannan, Md. Abdul, 'China's Policy Toward South Asia – A Bangladesh Perspective', in *Asian Security and China 2000–2010*, ed. Santhanam, K. and Kondapalli, S., Institute for Defence Studies and Analyses, Shipra Publications, New Delhi, 2004, pp. 301–9.

Makarenko, Tamara, 'The Crime-Terror Continuum: Tracing the Interplay between Transnational Organised Crime and Terrorism', *Global Crime*, Vol. 6, No. 1, 2004, pp. 129–45.

Marwah, Ved, 'India's Internal Security Challenges', *Strategic Analysis*, Vol. 27, No. 4, 2003.

Mazari, Shireen, 'Current Situation & Trends of Terrorism in South Asia', *Strategic Studies*, Vol. XXIV, No. 2, Summer 2004.

Mazari, Shireen, 'Future of Terrorism: A Critical Appraisal', *Strategic Studies*, Issue XXVI, No. 1, Spring 2006.

Mickolus, Edward, 'What Constitutes State Support to Terrorists?', *Terrorism and Political Violence*, Vol. 1, Issue 3, 1989.

Nair, P.M., *Combating Organised Crime*, Konark Publishers, New Delhi 2002.

Nasr, Vali, 'Islamization, the State, and Development', in *Islamization and the Pakistani Economy*, ed. Hathaway, Robert and Lee, Wilson, Woodrow Wilson International Center for Scholars, Washington, DC, 2004, pp. 91–101.

Nasr, Vali, 'Regional Implications of Shi'a Revival in Iraq', *The Washington Quarterly*, Vol. 27, No. 3, Summer 2004, pp. 7–24.

Nasr, Vali, *The Shia Revival – How Conflicts within Islam Will Shape the Future*, W.W. Norton & Company, New York, 2006, pp. 81–119.

Nasir, Sohail, 'Al-Qaeda's Operational Corridor on the NFWP', *Terrorism Monitor*, Vol. 4, Issue 6, 23 March 2006.

'Pakistan: The Mullahs and the Military', International Crisis Group, Asia Report No. 49, March 2003.

'Pakistan: The Worsening Conflict in Balochistan', Asia Report No. 119, International Crisis Group, 14 September 2006.

'Pakistan's Tribal Areas: Appeasing the Militants', International Crisis Group, Asia Report No. 125, December 2006.

Palit, P.S., 'The 9/11 Report: Reaffirming Pakistan-Terror Nexus', *Strategic Analysis*, Vol. 28, No. 3, 2004.

Phillips, Andrew, 'How al Qaeda Lost Iraq', *Australian Journal of International Affairs*, Vol. 63, Issue 1, March 2009.

Pillsbury, Michael, 'China's Strategic Outlook – A Case Study of Japan and India', in *Asian Security and China 2000–2010*, ed. Santhanam, K. and Kondapalli, S., Institute for Defence Studies and Analyses, Shipra Publications, New Delhi, 2004, pp. 79–115.

Rabasa, Angel, Blackwill, Robert D., Chalk, Peter, Cragin, Kim, Fair, Christine, Jackson, Brian A., Jenkins, Brian Michael, Jones, Seth, Shestak, Nathaniel and Tellis, Ashley J., 'The Lessons of Mumbai', Occasional Paper, RAND Corporation, Washington, DC, 2009.

Racine, Jean Luc, 'The Uncertain Triangle: India, China, and Pakistan – The Regional and International Dimensions', Centre for the Study of India and South Asia, Paris, 2001.

Raman, B., 'Musharaff's Fate in bin Laden's Hands', International Terrorism Monitor, Paper No. 300, South Asia Analysis Group, 4 November 2007.

Rashid, Ahmed, 'How to Succeed and Fail in FATA', *Daily Times*, 5 February 2008. Online, available at: www.dailytimes.com.pk.

Riedel, Bruce, 'Terrorism in India and the Global Jihad', Brookings Institute, 30 November 2008.

Roughneen, Simon, 'The Simmering Conflict Over Kashmir: The Blame Game of the Subcontinent', Paper 493, 12 December 2002, South Asia Analysis Group, New Delhi.

Roul, Animesh, 'Lashkar-e-Jhangvi: Sectarian Violence in Pakistan and Ties to International Terrorism', *Terrorism Monitor*, Vol. 3, Issue 11, 2 June 2005.

Roul, Animesh, 'Sipah-e-Sahaba: Formenting Sectarian Violence in Pakistan', *Terrorism Monitor*, Vol. 3, Issue 2, 27 June 2005.

Samii, Cyrus, 'Seizing the Moment in Kashmir', *SAIS Review*, Vol. 26, No. 1, Winter–Spring 2006.

Scheuer, Michael, 'Islamabad Rides a Terror Tiger', *Asia Times*, 20 September 2008. Online, available at: www.atimes.com.

Shah, Mehtab, 'Sectarianism – a Threat to Human Security: A Case Study of Pakistan', *The Round Table*, Vol. 94, No. 382, October 2005.

Shazad, Syed Saleem, 'The Rise and Rise of the Neo-Taliban', *Asia Times*, 2 April 2009. Online, available at: www.atimes.com.

Shelley, Louise, Picarelli, John T., Irby, Allison, Hart, Douglas M., Craig-Hart, Patricia A., Williams, Phil, Simon, Steven, Abdullaev, Nabi, Stanislawski, Bartosz and Covill, Laura, 'Methods and Motives: Exploring Links Between Transnational Organized Crime & International Terrorism', National Institute of Justice, September 2005.

Subrahmanyam, K., 'Arms and Politics', *Strategic Analysis*, Vol. 29, No. 1, 2005.

Sulaiman, Sadia, 'Empowering "Soft" Taliban Over "Hard" Taliban: Pakistan's Counter Terrorism Strategy', *Terrorism Monitor*, Vol. 6, No. 15, 25 July 2008.

Swami, Praveen, 'India's Elections and the Islamist Terror Threat', *Asian Conflict Reports*, Issue 4, April 2009.

Tellis, Ashley, 'The Changing Political-Military Environment: South Asia', RAND Corporation, Santa Monica, California, 2001.

The 9/11 Commission Report. Final Report of the National Commission on Terrorist Attacks Upon the United States.

Treverton, Greg, Matthies, Carl, Cunningham, Karla J., Goulka, Jeremiah, Ridgeway, Greg and Wong, Anny, 'Film Piracy, Organized Crime, and Terrorism', RAND Corporation, 2009.

Verghese, B.G., 'A Jammu and Kashmir Primer – From Myth to Reality', CPR Occasional Paper 14, Centre for Policy Research, New Delhi, 2006.

Vohra, A.M., 'J&K: Demilitarization and Joint Management', Article 2057, 4 July 2006, Institute of Peace and Conflict Studies, New Delhi.

Warikoo, K., 'Islamist Extremism: Challenge to Security in South Asia', *Strategic Analysis*, Vol. 30, No. 1, 2006.

Wenmu, Zhang, 'The Issue of South Asia in Major Power Politics', *Hong Kong Ta Kung Pao*, 23 September 1998.

Yasmeen, Samina, 'Pakistan's Kashmir Policy: Voices of Moderation?', *Contemporary South Asia*, Vol. 12, No. 2, June 2003.

Yusufzai, Rahimullah 'The Impact of Pashtun Tribal Differences on the Pakistani Taliban', *Terrorism Monitor*, Vol. 6, No. 3, 7 February 2008.

Zahab, Mariam Abou, 'The Regional Dimension of Sectarian Conflicts in Pakistan', in *Pakistan: Nationalism Without a Nation*, ed. Jaffrelot, Christopher, Zed Books, London, 2002, pp. 115–31.

Index

69783714R00128

Made in the USA
Columbia, SC
17 August 2019